Foundations of Public Administration: A Comparative Approach

Other books by the same author:

Studies in African Politics, Hutchinson, London, 1970.

The Commonwealth: Political Realities, Longman, London, 1975.

Foundations of Political Science, Hutchinson, London, 1976. Second Edition 1986.

Hong Kong: A Study in Bureaucratic Politics, Heinemann Asia, Hong Kong, 1978.

Political China Observed, Croom Helm, London, 1980.

Reflections on Hong Kong: Life, Work and Politics, Heinemann Asia, Hong Kong, 1981.

Public Affairs and Public Administration in Hong Kong, Heinemann Asia, Hong Kong, 1983.

Hong Kong: A Study in Bureaucracy and Politics, Macmillan, 1988.

Foundations of Public Administration: A Comparative Approach

Peter Harris
Professor of Political Science Emeritus, University of Hong Kong

Hong Kong University Press

ISBN 962 209 243 8

Typeset in Linotronic 300 by
Bothwin Promotion Limited, Hong Kong
Printed in Hong Kong by Elite Printing Company Limited

Contents

Contents

THE PROFESSION OF GOVERNMENT

Chapter 5   The Administrative Profession

The 'value-free' idea of 'bureaucracy'. The 'ideal' and the 'real' and the 'conflict' between 'democracy' and 'bureaucracy'. Traditional hostility to officials, Western and non-Western. The public servant and his political master. Specialists and Generalists.

Chapter 6   Internal Problems of Administration

The balance between expansion and efficiency. The case of Parkinson's Law and the problem of the measurement of administrative time in organizations. The Peter principle and hierarchology. Administrative self-interest and the public good. Downs, Tulloch and Buchanan. Ethics in public administration, a brief analysis. Non-Western standards of administrative behaviour.

Chapter 7   The Problem of Bureaucratic Corruption

The temptations of discretionary power and the meaning of discretion. Specific cases of abuse of discretion. Cases in the Developing World. Africa, China, India, Indonesia. Schemes of control and anti-corruption agencies.

COMPARATIVE PUBLIC ADMINISTRATION

Chapter 8   Comparative Administration: Developed Countries — Some Approaches, Styles and Methods

The country-by-country approach. The difference of ideology approach. The different types of system approach. Administration: constant themes and variations. Structures based on various and varied styles and methods, recruitment, structure, central-local relations, party politics and the administrator.

Chapter 9   Comparative Administrative Systems: The Developing World

The role of the bureaucracy as a vehicle of development in selected countries in Africa, Latin America and South-East Asia. The African example. Natural disasters, drought, famine and administrative difficulties. Successes and failures. Military bureaucrats.

Chapter 10   Public Administration in Socialist States

Socialists and administration, historical antecedents. Democratic centralism. The idea of administrative levers and the economy. How socialist administrators behave. Socialism and corruption.

POLICY AND POLICY PROBLEMS

Foreword

This short book seeks to explore some of the foundations of the subject known as public administration, and to consider these from a comparative perspective. In particular, the analysis includes a number of new and developing countries in an attempt to see where the principles of public administration worked out in the West may be applicable.

The book follows in part the approach used by the author in *Foundations of Political Science*. A brief account of present Western knowledge in the field of public administration is given with examples drawn from Western, as well as non-Western, states. Some attempt will be made to see where countries can assist each other in public service organization. The approach is comparative with a bias towards new and developing countries.

A difficult and serious question asks how can non-Western states benefit from Western studies in public administration. There are perhaps a number of ways. Firstly, Western studies in public administration have unearthed several issues, if not pitfalls, which newer states would do well to consider. For example, administrators need training to avoid practising the art of administration according to a set of 'proverbs' or ill-considered rules-of-thumb. Though there is much debate as to how 'rational' or 'scientific' it is possible to be in public administration, there is at least some scope for improvement almost everywhere on more rational lines. A second possible benefit lies in the utilization of a comparative approach. To put this crudely, we have much to learn in seeing what other states do as a guide to action or inaction.

In all states too, both developed and developing, policy-making is a subject requiring constant thought and attention. Nowhere in the world do policy-makers find it an easy matter to make, sustain and then change a policy. Even so-called 'totalitarian' states face formidable difficulties with regard to public policy, its formulation and execution.

Many comments made about public sector administrators are hostile. Even the term 'civil service' is not without its detractors. The novelist Charles Dickens described a civil servant as a 'faceless mortal riding like a flea on the back of the dog — legislation'. A whole literature has grown up attacking the role of civil servants some of which will be considered in this book. Much of the criticism, though not all, is ill-informed.

This book is largely about the bureaucracy so-called, but there will be relatively little use of the term 'bureaucracy'. The word 'bureaucracy' is a very useful word, but it is unfortunately also a term of abuse. The term 'bureaucracy' — literally 'rule by officials' — was taken from the French word *bureau* referring to a writing-desk. Later the term came to mean 'office'. Even earlier the 'original meaning of *bureau* was the baize used to cover desks' (Williams, 1976: 40). The great social scientist, Max Weber, discussed the concept of 'bureaucracy', and he saw it in relation to the struggle between capitalism and socialism. Weber thought that the future would see the triumph of bureaucracy. Weber saw bureaucracy as value free; it was a term to be used without prejudices. Others vulgarized the term, and, in many cases, made it useless as a tool for scientific enquiry.

Speaking of the use of the idea of bureaucracy, one scholar, nevertheless, sees it as highly useful, even inevitable, in modern scholarship.

> We find appointed officials concentrated in the executive branch of government or in a hierarchy of offices, which may conveniently be called a 'bureaucracy'. The word has many unpleasant connotations, but I cannot think of a better term for any set of offices hierarchically arranged such that each position is filled by the authority of a superior, e.g., the head of state in a government. Other kinds of organizations such as corporations, churches and political parties also have bureaucracies under the authority of their heads whether called President, Pope or Chairman (Riggs, 1970: 571).
>
> Bureaucracies are in fact ancient phenomena, beginning very probably with ancient China and ancient Egypt. The Chinese are most usually associated with the development of the bureaucratic state and the rise of a mandarin class of scholars and rulers.

Two hundred years before Christ there existed a feudal system in China. Feudalism implied that persons worked for a ruler, lord or leader in return for protection. Out of feudalism bureaucracy developed, as China's rulers came to need support for personal services. Gradually a whole new class of officials emerged to supervise property, estates and workshops. When the state was at war the need for officials increased still further.

Gradually officials grew in number as they monopolized posts, created a regional administration and even developed 'ministries' under the emperor (Eberhard, 1977: 61, 74).

A very famous feature of Chinese bureaucracy was the emergence of a ruling scholar-gentry class, some two centuries before Christ. Bureaucratic power was, in due course, to be associated with learning, and knowledge of the Chinese classics became a test of recruitment, whose best side was the promotion of high ethical standards. From about 100 BC there arose on official examination system for posts in the official administration, which remained with numerous changes until 1904 (Eberhard, 1977: 77). The idea was to create generalists, that is officials who could analyse all types of problem, leaving other persons to carry out the 'policy'. The distinction between 'generalists' and 'specialists' was also found in the British civil service from the 19th century on. The separation possibly also resembles the modern Chinese communist distinction between those who are 'Red' and those who are 'Expert'.

Candidates for the competitive examinations, for example, during the Ming dynasty were able to take the examinations every third year. Candidates were required to write essays, poems and ultimately to answer questions on the art of government. The ancient Greeks as well as the British later (and possibly the Vatican) associated public service with learning and scholarship. British civil servants unlike Americans, later, were steeped in the classics, as were their European counterparts.

More often however, bureaucracies, particularly in the USA, have been much more specific and 'practical', and in the twentieth century officials are recruited with closely relevant skills. In China, where the bureaucracy has been particularly developed, officials are expected in the 1980's to favour 'modernization' rather than traditional values. Modern public administration everywhere however faces complex problems of change. Ancient administration was static; modern administration must be dynamic, and responsive to the immense technological changes of the twentieth century. Yet modern public administration is also supposed to provide stability and continuity, especially in those modern developing states which have serious internal political and ideological divisions. In Africa, Asia and Latin America there is need for an efficient, clean and incorrupt administration to allow for change and development. In Europe too, recent history has demonstrated the importance of neutral public administration as a counterweight to the more partisan approach of politicians and parties. And yet there is still considerable debate regarding the exact relation between the bureaucracy and the party politics of politicians, for example in Great Britain. The British historically developed a class of non-party officials capable of serving any government which the tides of electoral fortune might return to power (Parris, 1969: 36). Nevertheless there are everywhere complaints that civil servants are 'statesmen in disguise.' What we will show is that in some countries the civil service is relatively politics-free. In other countries it is less so.

This book also attempts to discuss the administrative problems of new and developing nations. The term 'Third World' is often used to describe these nations. However the term 'Third World' is itself believed to have become somewhat devalued. One writer thinks that the 'Third World' refers to a 'rough pattern of identity of Third World countries, which is formed by three main characteristics: being non-European, being non-Communist, and being poor' (Miller, 1966: xi). This definition is quite useful, but of course many new states are 'socialist' (if not 'communist'), and some new states are not poor even if they are not European or American.

If the capitalist West is the first, and the Communist group is the second, world, then the so-called 'Third World' is taken to refer to the rest. The Third World is usually taken to include 'most of the countries of Latin America and the recently independent states of Asia and Africa' (Bullock, 1977: 635).

The term 'Third World' (taken from the French *Tiers Monde*) is very imprecise, but is 'probably too deeply entrenched to be avoided' (Robertson,

1985: 317). Curiously enough however, many people react to the term 'Third World' in a somewhat emotional way. Thus if the Third World is not a rational grouping, it is nonetheless real to many people who see themselves as members of a common emotional grouping. The central feature of the Third World is its colonial experience. Third World states according to some scholars may exhibit certain properties. While they have modern forms of public administration, many of them still use traditional (i.e., non-Western style) rulers or modern rulers perhaps rule in a traditional way. The strongest aspect of many so-called Third World rulers believed to be 'patrimonialism', which dispassionately suggests 'the concept of authority which underlies it (i.e., patrimonialism) is that of a father over his children....' (Clapham, 1985: 47–48).

Public administration must necessarily relate to local conditions, social, economic and party political. At the same time we all require to live in a modern state, and modern public administration does try to follow the rules of reason and law as Weber pointed out. Even if reason and law remain vague and imperfect goals, they nevertheless are worth aiming at. *Per ardua ad astra* — through difficulties to the stars.

BIBLIOGRAPHY

Bullock Alan (Lord) and Oliver Stallybrass (eds) (1977), *The Fontana Dictionary of Modern Thought*, Fontana.

Clapham Christopher (1985), *Third World Politics, An Introduction*, Croom Helm, London.

Eberhard Wolfram Kent (1977), *A History of China*, Routledge & Kegan Paul, 4th edition, London.

Miller, J.D.B. (1966) *The Politics of the Third World* (Oxford)

Parris Henry (1969), *Constitutional Bureaucracy*, Allen & Unwin, London.

Riggs Fred W. (1970), *Administrative Reform and Political Responsiveness: A Theory of Dynamic Balancing*, Vol. I (Sage Professional Paper: Series 01-101).

Robertson David (1985), *A Dictionary of Modern Politics*, Europa, London.

Williams Raymond (1976), *Key Words, A Vocabulary of Culture and society*, Fontana, Croom Helm, London.

Part I
Fundamental Questions

1
The Scope and Characteristics of Public Administration

Public administration is easy to define by those satisfied with simple definitions, because it is apparently no more than the administration of public, as
opposed to private, bodies. In fact public administration is far more complicated than this. Public administration it has been said relates to 'all those
operations having for their purpose the fulfilment or enforcement of public
policy' (L.D. White, 1948: 3). We will mean by public administration all of
those organizationally centred directive activities pertaining to the implementation of public policies and/or the achievement of public goals (Palombara,
1974: 235).

Obviously we will be talking about government because it is the administration of public concerns which involves public administration most obviously. Burke defined government as a 'contrivance of human wisdom to
provide for human wants' (E. Burke, 1970). A modern writer, Richard Rose
held that government today should quite specifically be seen in the context of
public administration. According to Richard Rose, Government is 'A formal
administrative structure, established by the constitution, which is responsible
for the mobilization of laws, money and employees and the conversion of
these resources into programme outputs' (Rose, 1984: 13–14).

Public administration is now seen as a somewhat more mechanical matter
than it was in the eighteenth century. The public today requires the governmental machine to be effective and efficient — not merely moral. In the
developing states of the Third World it is the government, or at least the
public sector, which is often seen as the engine of development. There is little
possibility that the local private or business sector could provide for public
needs in most Third World countries. Moreover, in the developing world,
public administration has to be efficient, responsible, responsive to change in
order for the people of the developing areas to be rescued from poverty.
Indeed in the Third World the efficiency of public administration is often the
only force for development especially in conditions in which local politicians
maintain only a shaky hold over power.

Administration therefore is matter of universal need, though unfortunately
it is not universally understood. Dunsire (1973: 228–229) offers 15 definitions of the term 'administration', each of which is worth considering. For
the purposes of our enquiry however, we might perhaps begin with a useful
distinction between administration as *commanding* and administration as
serving the community involved.

This is an important distinction; it is important because those who are the state's administrators are normally called civil servants. They are indeed the servants of the public. Yet it would not be realistic to imagine that administrators do not actually deploy power — power which can have a great influence on the lives of many people. Civil servants make decisions which in effect order the lives of those whom they are supposed to serve. Civil servants are sometimes masters rather than servants, mainly because they have better knowledge of the whole system than those outside the 'corridors of power'.

In the West as in the developing world, public administrators have become more vulnerable. In the West as well as in the developing nations, people want more schools, hospitals, bigger pensions, better roads and services of all kinds. In the 1960's in the major industrial countries, less than 30 per cent of these states gross domestic products was spent on 'welfare' services. By the 1980's, 'public spending in the 24 industrial countries belonging to the Organization for Economic Co-operation and Development (OECD) is now (1985) about 43 per cent of their gross domestic products' (*Economist*, June 1 1985).

In the developing nations, government accounts for change but not enough and despite the hopes of many idealistic leaders it has been difficult to provide even the necessities of life. In Africa in particular, governments have as yet not acquired the resources to offer much welfare. Even in Western Europe and the USA, governments need to trim their activities for fear of becoming overloaded.

In all these developments, public administration has an important role to play. In times of expansion, administrators must be ready with workable plans to effect rapid development in many fields. In times of contraction, when schemes have to be postponed or even abandoned, administrators must learn to manage limited resources much more effectively. In the 1980's many governments have tried to curb public spending. But to reduce government spending, once established, is particularly difficult. Western countries have been unsuccessful in *reducing* public expenditure. They have merely prevented the rise from becoming even greater. In the USA and in Britain between a quarter and a third of workers are paid employees of government, local or central. Certain costs of public administration appear to be firmly entrenched.

PUBLIC AND PRIVATE ADMINISTRATION

There are some differences between public and private forms of administration, and these differences are, it would seem, much greater than the similarities. Essentially the purpose of public or state administration is to work for the public good, rather than any particular private benefit, group or special cause.

Now it is possible to argue that because human beings are the 'raw material' of organization, then all human beings experience the same needs whether public or private.

An old definition of public administration clarifies the special way in which government and public administration should be regarded. 'By public administration is meant, in common usage, the activities of the executive branches of national, state and local governments; independent boards and commissions set up by Congress and state legislatives; government corporations; and certain other agencies of a specialized character. Specifically excluded are judicial and legislative agencies within the government and non-governmental administration' (Simon, Smithburg and Thompson, 1950: pp. 6–12).

This definition makes it clear that the writers are referring to government departments for the most part. The simplest idea of public administration is that it concerns itself with the machinery of government, so called, and with the management of the civil service (Garrett, 1980).

Some writers refuse to see a distinction between public and private administration, arguing that 'whether one is studying the administration of a church, a labour union, a corporation, or a government agency, many of the basic problems will be the same' (Simon, *et al.*, op cit, loc cit). Administration on this analysis is naturally ultimately all-of-a-piece, it is in the last resort the same universal process, but only in the last resort. Of course administration is 'the art of getting things done' (Simon, 1957: 1).

Some observers point out that huge business corporations are often very similar to government departments. A large hospital with several thousand beds cannot be administered in the same way as a hospital with 50 beds. Again it is said that a publicly-owned airline and a privately-owned airline will fly the same aircraft in the same way, despite the differences in financial costing. A further example relates to the skills of specialists employed in private and public sector organizations. Some top administrators with experience of both the public and private sectors have sometimes commented that there is sometimes less 'freedom' in administering private companies than is the case in, say, nationalized industries. An example is President Eisenhower who moved from army to university to presidency. In short he headed quite divergent forms of administrative organization.

However the argument develops, it is clear that there will always be individuals who have successfully made the transition from the private to the public sector. Equally, there will always be those who argue that the differences between private and public administration are fundamental. Let us now consider some basic differences.

In the first place let us be aware that we may conveniently speak of the 'complex of Government Departments, local authorities, independent State corporations....' (Dunsire, 1973: 167). The idea of the public is very complicated but the *work* of government department is not. We are usually speaking, in public administration, of tasks performed by departments of state, national and local, according to law. Private administration is much less constrained than is its public administration counterpart.

5

PUBLIC AND PRIVATE ADMINISTRATION: DIFFERENCES

1. Openness

Public administration is ideally open administration. There should be relatively few secrets in public administration. Civil servants (including the military) are supposed to apply themselves to carry out policy laid down by their political supervisors. They are supposed to be able to explain their actions. In some countries, particularly the USA, the records of public policy-makers are open to the public (*Freedom of Information Act*). Of course in practice, public administrators often conceal what they might otherwise reveal.

In the private sector there may be some legal obligations for private administrators to reveal aspects of their businesses. Registration of businesses and publication of balance sheets may be necessary but all other actions may be *secret*, withheld from the public gaze. Indeed it is often essential in business management to *conceal* operations in order to protect business secrets.

2. Ethics

Public administration is required, as Self argues, to stay within the law, achieve fairness or equity, conduct its affairs with utter financial and moral probity, behave correctly at all times and in all circumstances (Self, 1971: Chapter 8). The public administration process seeks 'probity, impartiality, rectitude and fair and equitable treatment of individuals' (Brown and Steel, 1979: 199).

Such a high standard is of course daily infringed. It would be unreasonable to expect from the public official a level of conduct towards the public itself which was Utopian. However, there is a clear need for public officials to be seen to act properly in all ways at all times. There are many examples of ways in which public officials fail in their public duty, all too apparently, all the way from using general influence to adopting forms of bribery and corruption.

One problem is that in developing states the role of the public official is seen somewhat differently from the West (Riggs, 1964: 34).

The public official in new states is expected to use his office to reward members of his tribe, family or friends. The so-called extended family system is a case in point as some administrators see their duty as the need to give preferential treatment. In certain states in Asia, such as Malaysia and Indonesia, preference is given in many ways to Malays or Indonesians (called *bumiputras* and *pribumis*) respectively.

The neutral and impartial official is an urgent pre-requisite of all states, but especially those with large poor communities, rather than to other minority groups and races.

Ethics in public administration has long been a matter of concern both for philosophers from Plato onwards, as well as for practical administrators. Thus tax collectors, immigration officers, policemen, traffic administrators and even teachers daily face many complex ethical choices. To govern, it has often been said, is to choose.

In private administration, ethical choices nationally exist and must be confronted daily; however the structure of corporations ensures that managers are accountable largely to shareholders rather than to the public interest, so-called. The state administrator however is supposed to adhere to a high level of public morality.

A business allocates resources by *output*, public administration allocates these according to *outcome* (Self, 1971: 264). In short, private concerns produce for purposes of selling to a mass public whereas public concerns attempt to see the social implications of their actions at all times, without being satisfied with a mere profit or loss account.

3. The Test of Profit and Loss

At the purely financial level, the 'health' of a private concern can apparently be measured quite simply by its level of profit. A profitable venture is deemed to be successful, a loss-making venture is naturally unsuccessful. Socialist states usually reject measurements based on market performance.

In China, during the sixties and seventies the idea of profit was generally denounced as 'capitalist'. In the eighties however, the official view was to accept a distinction between acceptable and unacceptable profit. Enterprises were encouraged to make a profit and use profit as a method of calculating efficiency. China's leaders in the 1980's rejected the idea of supporting all productive enterprises, good and bad, irrespective of their profitability. It was seen to be wrong to encourage people to think that 'profit' was an improper test to use in public concerns. 'Capitalist profit' was to be shunned, but it felt some form of profit-or-loss test was to be tentatively applied even in a socialist state. Paradoxically in the West however some people feel differently. The profit/loss test has become less certain and less popular than it was. For the most part private organizations, including businesses seek to make a profit but not necessarily exclusively so. A newspaper seeks to make a profit in the capitalist world, but it also exists for its producers and readers who buy it as a means of conveying news and information.

4. The Operation of the Market

The purpose of business is to create new markets for its goods and services and to encourage customers to purchase its products. In practice, business administration attempts to expand the market, and the normal test of business success lies in its ability to expand the market. Governments on the other hand are faced with a wholly different dilemma. The public sector must try to reduce demands for its services. People however want schools, roads, hospitals and unpolluted air.

The contradiction is between private affluence, the push towards consumer goods and the low state of public services. As Galbraith put it: 'Alcohol, comic-books and mouth-wash all bask under the superior reputation of the market. Schools, judges and municipal swimming-pools lie under the evil reputation of bad kings' (Galbraith, 1958: 106). The difference between the private and public view of the market has been put very neatly as the difference between market *expansion* (characteristic of the private sector) and *market compression* (characteristic of the public sector) (Self, 1974: 266). Most developing states can afford neither consumer goods (seen as a 'right' in developed states) nor public goods. But even so there is often a conflict between consumer demands and public resources.

5. The Place of Values

Civil servants are in many ways the arbiters of values. Businessmen are mostly interested in the efficiency of their enterprise, and do not require to concern themselves with what might be called the public good. Other groups see the purpose of government from a purely selfish angle; government for them exists to grant concessions to particular groups. Civil servants are presumed to reach towards a higher standard, that of the qualitative assessment of social costs, seeing the outcome of their decisions in the round. There are costs and there are benefits at each stage. In an Islamic state the values are set by Islam and include a very harsh penal system and the subordination of women to the values of Islam. Civil servants but not businessmen perhaps are expected to ensure that Islamic values are maintained. In countries like Algeria, Egypt and especially Iran and Libya, the values are set by the religious often fundamentalist leadership, and administrators are not excluded from these values.

It would appear that the boundaries between private and public administration are generally capable of being drawn for good common-sense reasons. These include for example differences based on differing conceptions of openness, ethics, tests of efficiency and profit, the role of the market and the place values or ideologies in society. At the same time it is possible to perceive quite obvious similarities at the organizational level. There are, for example, certain problems common to all organizations, often of a technical nature. The 'chain' of command, the 'span' of control and the allocation of functions may have similarities whether one is speaking of public or private administration. Moreover theories or explanations of how organizations work may very well apply equally to private concerns. Office efficiency in the private sector may be equally applicable to the public sector. The defects of poor coordination, poor communication inadequate delegation, personality conflicts and low morale may be found in both private and public sector organizations, in the army and the church, in a chemical engineering firm as well as in private concerns generally.

In developing countries the public service is often inadequate to cope with the strains of modernization in a country with poor resources, say like Tanzania. Tanzania has remained poor and nothing that administrators could offer was of any real value.

We must conclude that the purpose of public administration is different from that of business administration. Public administration calls upon its participants to follow a high standard of ethics at all times, remembering that its public is the whole community and not merely a small group of profit-oriented shareholders.

ADMINISTRATION: THE FOUR ESTATES

Students of public administration have for long concerned themselves with the great categories of government — legislative, executive and judicial. The administrative part has been seen as an addition to the famous three legislative, executive and judicial, and one which does not fit well into the ancient trinity of governmental powers. The point is that administration covers all three and is common to all three. In practice however, administration is seen as an offshoot of the executive branch.

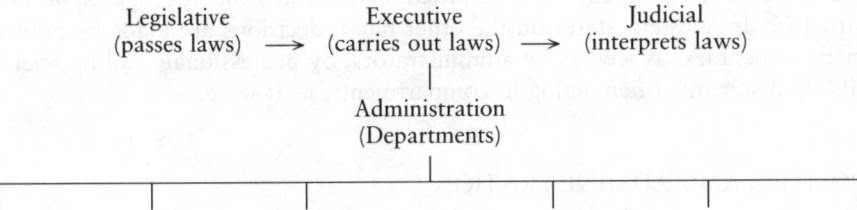

Legislative   Executive   Judicial
(passes laws) → (carries out laws) → (interprets laws)

Administration
(Departments)

Another interpretation which seeks to place administration in its proper context would consider four other elements, the political, administrative, technical and/or professional specialist and scientific. There are in fact the four areas of operation and may be represented diagrammatically as follows:

The Four Estates within the State Apparatus

Politicians	Administrators	Professionals	Scientists
by the electorate concerned with ends, values and goals	responsible for translating ends and values into practice	apply their specific knowledge to problems	fundamental research

Politicians and administrators enjoy a much greater degree of power than professionals and certainly scientists. Indeed the scientists are likely to be the most highly-trained of all, but are likely to enjoy the least power. On the other hand, power is greatest in the hands of politicians, whether state or party. Politicians however have little or no training for the work they have to do, despite the fact that they are charged with the task of ultimate decision-making.

These barriers as between the various categories are indicators only. People see themselves as members of one of these groupings, but they may just as well see themselves as members of any of these groupings. Thus in Japan for example, people move from the civil service into the ranks of the politicians. Indeed seven Japanese prime ministers since the end of World War II have moved from the ranks of the officials to become politicians. Mobility from the ranks of the professionals or scientists is always much lower than it is amongst the politicians and administrators. In the developing states of the world the differences between these four areas of operation are less well-developed than they are in the developed world. The four 'estates' are not well-separated because of the poverty and the often small size of a given territory.

The whole of the state apparatus in developed countries is well spelt-out. A politician is unlikely to be a research physicist while a doctor working routinely in the civil service is unlikely to know much about fundamental medical research. Public administration in the developing states may not have the specialization or expertise required to separate the four parts of the structure. In Western states on the other hand, decisions are made by politicians sometimes, as well as by administrators, by professionals and by scientific civil servants often acting in compartments, as it were.

POLITICS AND ADMINISTRATION

In the developing states of the developing world the distinction between politics and administration is not always clear. In some states membership of the (single) political party is a necessary prerequisite for senior civil servants (Clapham, 1985: 66). In the Soviet Union membership of, and support for, the Communist Party is essential for members of the state and military apparatus (Hill and Frank, 1981: 86). Many people argue that civil servants constantly make *political* decisions, and that it is not realistic to separate politics from administration. Of course civil servants are *in* the political world because elected politicians are in theory their masters. However civil servants are not *of* the political world because it is believed in many developed states that civil servants should be neutral and should not take sides. The fact remains however that most political scientists appear to deny any hard and fast separation between 'politics' and 'administration'.

Indeed, the neutrality of the civil service and the separation of administration from politics is not all that old. Indeed, it is only a century since British civil servants were chosen on the basis of their presumed merit.

SEPARATING POLITICS AND ADMINISTRATION
A: THE ACADEMIC APPROACH

Public administration was developed to explore how policy decisions are put into effect. 'It is about the machinery, processes and people through which or through whom public policy is made and carried out under political scrutiny' (R.G.S. Brown, 1975: 26). Public administration has seemed by some academics to be different from politics. Politics is concerned with the 'role of public opinion, the activities of political parties, the functions of legislative bodies ... the clash of opinion and the conflict of values' (D. Waldo, 1968: 145–155). Administration develops 'once a decision is authoritatively made and a law enacted....' 'For this, economy and efficiency are the central criteria, and science is the proper method for developing the criteria' (D. Waldo, 1968: 148).

Very briefly, one writer stated that 'administration (was) the neutral instrument of policy' (Bailey, 1955: 24). The classical notion that politics and administration can and should be separated was presented by Woodrow Wilson who argued a case for separating 'politics', in the sense of popular political activity, from administration. Proper and efficient procedures could and should carry out the popular will free from political interference (Woodrow Wilson, 1887: 197–222).

The point was also argued by Herman Finer who saw several factors operating to prevent British civil servants from an involvement in politics, namely that they were anonymous, neutral and impartial and part of a tradition which understood that the civil servant is on tap and not on top (H. Finer, 1949: 614–17, 882–83).

Such optimistic assessments were unsympathetically received by those who refused to see how *policy* could be separated from *politics*. It has often been pointed out that middle and upper-middle class persons often dominate the civil service and infuse their values into it. These persons bring with them a set of middle-class values, derived from their education and upbringing. Marxist scholars argue that it is false and wrong to separate politics and administration. It is also argued that senior civil servants do play and must play a political role and that they are in effect politicians or at least 'statesmen in disguise' (G.R. Fry, 1969).

Writers on the Third World developing countries point out that politics and administration are linked. Civil servants are frequently part of the local political process, 'identifiable with the class caste or regional groups from which they came, readily suspected of serving their own particularist interests on the one hand, while subject to influence and inducement on the other' (Clapham, 1985: 41). In China, which has a centuries' old administrative tradition, the Marxist-Leninist MaoZedong ideology supports the entire system. Ideology in modern China legitimizes the rule of the party, as in ancient times, the Confucian ideology legitimized the power of the mandarinate (Balazs, 1964).

SEPARATING POLITICS AND ADMINISTRATION
B: THE PROBLEM ON THE GROUND

Administrators are important actors (F.M.G. Willson, 1961) and they obviously can defeat or promote projects in many ways, some obvious and some less obvious.

The classical separation of politics and administration as set out in textbooks is difficult to sustain because administration is shot through with politics. Administrators find it difficult to arrange their lives so that they never make so-called 'political' decisions. There is always a tendency to politicize administration. After the arrival of the Thatcher government to power in Britain, it became increasingly obvious that Mrs. Thatcher believed that her economic policies could be trusted only to those civil servants who were in general sympathy with her 'monetarist' doctrines. It was no longer easy to see how civil servants could stand aside from large-scale radical political development, however undesirable in fact.

In the developing countries, it was clearly impractical to speak of the separation of politics from administration. The main reason for this is historical. Most of the developing countries are former colonial territories hitherto ruled by colonial administrators (Murray and Ballard, 1971). The size of colonial civil service was small in relation to the population served, and this was true whether the examples chosen are from Africa or India. Colonial development continued until the sixties, under colonial tutelage. The achievements were many, including rural development, forestry and animal health, veterinary and educational services amongst many others. Colonial administration was neutral administration, in the sense that it was not inspired by partisan or ideological politics. British, French and Belgian colonial civil servants were employees of the metropolitan government. They were unconnected with, and hostile to, 'politics'.

By contrast, politics was the strength of local, i.e., non-expatriate, 'politicians' whose cause was independence rather than the quiet routine of public officialdom. The colonial rulers therefore stressed the virtues of incorrupt efficient *administration* while the nationalists stressed the need to remove foreigners whether efficient or not. The position was neatly summarized by Manuel L. Quezon, the Filipino politician, who once said that he preferred a government run like hell by Filipinos to a government run like heaven by Americans. The Marcos Government in the 1980's offered an ironic twist to this comment.

Only with great difficulty anywhere in the world is it possible to conceive of a distinction between politics and administration. However, a neutral administration seeing men as citizens rather than as members of tribes or castes remains a ideal. The distinction between politics and administration however, is probably a Western notion not always applicable in developing states. The separation would be totally rejected in socialist countries where ideological politics as practised through the party dominate everything. However, there is much truth in the idea that, 'an administrative ability is the principal ability needed in politics' (Saint-Simon, 1819). The point is that political skills may not always be appropriate in administration.

PUBLIC ADMINISTRATION AND COMMUNICATION

Internal Developments

The state communicates with the citizen in many and varied ways. As an increase in size develops new aspects of state activity, so the state requires to speak to the citizen on a vast range of topics. Those would include for example the keeping of all sorts of records and files, such as income-tax returns, records of military service, identity cards, driving licences, the licensing of guns, animals, cars, television sets, applications for housing, passports, social service benefits in money and in kind, as well as birth, marriage and death certificates (Spiers, 1975: 229–40).

The keeping of records allows the state to communicate with the citizen, to make its demands upon his time, energy and resources. It was, of course, Max Weber who first remarked on the importance of records in understanding the modern state. To quote Weber's own words is instructive. 'The management of the modern office is based upon written documents ('the files'), which are preserved in their original or draft form. There is, therefore, a staff of subaltern officials and scribes of all sorts. The body of officials actively engaged in a 'public' office, along with the respective apparatus of material implements and the files, make up a 'bureau'. In private enterprise, 'the bureau' is often called 'the office' [Weber in Gerth and Mills, 1946: 196–8].

When Weber wrote in the first quarter of the twentieth century, the 'files' were still in a hand-written form or typewritten. Office organization was still relatively primitive, and the citizen could not expect much help from technology. Since the end of World War II however, and particularly since 1960, a vast number of technological advances have been introduced, of which the computer has been the most significant.

The computer is a management aid which has nevertheless important powers in the field of communication between the state and the citizen. It is a question of old wine in new bottles. The problem is old but the techniques are new. As far as the records of public administrators are concerned the computer has certain properties which have clearly taken communication into a new epoch. These properties may be summarized as follows:

1. Improved and enhanced powers of calculation.
2. Greatly increased speed of the operation or project in hand.
3. Capacity to control and classify complicated information.
4. Capacity to absorb, store and later recall or retrieve information.

To take but one simple example — that of the Inland Revenue — the state can call upon a computer's assistance to calculate quickly, to handle vast amounts of information and to retrieve data as and also when required. One of the problems of the computer age is unfortunately however, the growth of 'computerese' which is an impediment to sound communication.

Communications have, at an internal level, become significantly more sophisticated, and government itself has become transformed. Several techniques have proved to be particularly useful however. Network analysis is a technique of planning for example, but is also a valuable way of informing people of the intended operation of 'a complex project in a logical way by analysing the project into component parts and recording them on a network model or diagram which is then used for planning and controlling the inter-related activities in carrying the project to completion' (Stationery Office, London 1967). Other techniques include critical path analyses, informatics and systems analyses of a variety of types.

THE STATE ADDRESSES THE CITIZEN

The state addresses the citizen in a wide variety of ways. Given the advent of television in the post-war years and especially since about 1960, some commentators have spoken of television as government 'in the drawing room'. There have been many significant changes in the governmental process as a result of television. The most obvious example relates to those politicians who have succeeded in mastering the art of communication *via* the small screen. Two outstanding practitioners would appear to be Charles de Gaulle (1890–1970) and Ronald Reagan (b. 1912). De Gaulle used television in the late fifties as a means of conveying his intention to control crises. He saw the power of direct communication *via* television. On the basis of television de Gaulle sought to see a direct communion between himself and the public, without an intermediary.

Reagan has been called the 'Great Communicator', and he has grasped the potential of electronic communication, not to communicate the sense of drama and crisis 'a la de Gaulle', but rather to project an image of serenity calmness and well-being. As a former Hollywood film star he developed a facility for words and the presentation of his policies. He developed a sense of the central drift of the national mood, the mystique of communications.

Reagan's ability lay in his intuitive power to communicate at a level of common understanding together with an evident sincerity of purpose. This level of communication is not 'intellectual' or even 'political'. Reagan communicates American folklore or the mythology that Americans belong to a society which is direct, simple and pure. An example may be seen in the American novel *Coniston* which may assist in giving the flavour of American political life. In it are featured good, decent, God-fearing men, sensible and decent farmers who were good judges of cattle and also of men. Nostalgia and conservatism are allied by Reagan in an effective way (Harris, 1976: 217).

In recent times many of the most significant figures of the present century have been powerful communicators. Hitler, Mussolini, Roosevelt, Churchill are important Western examples, who in various ways all used radio or films very effectively (though they predated television). Without complex and sophisticated technology the scope of a 'message' may become rather restricted. There is considerable controversy regarding the role of the 'message' to be conveyed. Conventional wisdom after Marshal McLuhan would argue that the medium *is* the message, i.e., that the message is not readily separable from the message-giver. With television and films the message is often blurred. With radio the message becomes more important (McLuhan, 1964: 50).

Social scientists in the field of public administration now see the communications approach as an interaction between political actors and their environment. Research has attempted to identify the structures which send and receive messages. Moreover, they describe and discuss the channels which are used, as well as their capacities and rates of utilization. Such matters as information storage processes, feedback mechanisms and the codes and computer languages used are analysed. The actual content of the message in a sense becomes a secondary consideration — even if the object of the exercise is to communicate a 'message' to a public.

We have come to dig deep into many modern forms of communications technology including information theory, cybernetics, and the study of communications in relation to systems control. The intending investigator will find himself in sociology, social psychology, comparative government and economics in the social sciences as well as engineering. Indeed engineering has provided many sources of ideas for students of the social sciences and in this respect communications technology is but one of a number of borrowings from the world of engineering (K.W. Deutsch, 1963). Further, for Deutsch, the system of decision and enforcement (the political system) can be seen as a 'network of communication channels' (Deutsch, 1963: 150). No one has appreciated communication theory more comprehensively than Deutsch in the field of public administration. The organization and transmission of information is a very large part of the government process. More, Deutsch sees government as 'less than a problem of power and somewhat more as a problem of steering; and steering is decisively a matter of communication' (op. cit. pix: 182).

COMMUNICATIONS: THE CITIZEN ADDRESSES THE STATE

Communications between the citizen and the state present a number of particular difficulties. The classical approach was often to perceive of an identification of the interests of the ruler and the ruled. In short it was unnecessary for citizens to enter into a dialogue with their rulers. 'Those who labour with their brains rule' said the Chinese sage, thus implying that the vast mass of citizens, being uneducated did not have anything to communicate to their rulers. Information must however be transmitted from citizen to ruler.

The most important source of communication comes during an election campaign. Elections produce a mass of information for both sides, but above all they produce a hard decision in the election result. What has of course produced a profound change is the advent of public opinion polling which is seen as *the* effective means by which the public communicates with their leaders. Public opinion polling has been linked to computer technology for several decades and has attained a high degree of sophistication and accuracy (Butler, 1958: 59–75). Indeed it has become a 'science' in its own right with the label 'psephology' (Butler, 1956: 1, 2). Psephology was a term coined by R.B. McCallum, Master of Pembroke College, Oxford, to describe the application of statistical analysis to the study of elections. Once the state of the public political mind is revealed by sampling techniques, government may plan its policies accordingly (Harris, 1976: 162). Through a careful reading of public opinion polls, the public can be seen to *communicate* with government. The techniques of polling are of course very well developed, given their direct commercial application, though naturally the governmental aspects more properly concern this study (Sargent, Zant, 1970 and Thomas, 1975).

There are numerous examples of the impact of polling upon government. In Britain, France and the USA, polling results have often induced governments to modify or even change policies. The public has indicated its dissatisfaction with the broad methods of socialist planning, taxation and levelling-down policies. As a result a switch has taken place, for example, in the presumed left-wing socialist parties in Britain and France. In socialist states themselves, of course, polling is not allowed or encouraged. Communication in these states proceeds on the basis of democratic centralism, a term espoused by Lenin which argues that two 'values', viz., *opinions* from below and *authority* from above should mingle and merge in the middle.

In fact the Soviet Union, for example, sees no need to consult the citizen, neither will it allow polling, Lenin announced in 1920, 'We recognise nothing private' (Lenin, vol. 31, 291–2). Soviet people are 'socialized' into not communicating freely with the state or party (White, 1979: 75–83). The mass media is seen as 'a powerful instrument of the party'. Authoritarian regimes by definition reject the easy flow of communication from citizen to state, perhaps reaching their nadir in the case of North Korea and Albania where citizens are passive tools of directions and instruction from above.

Naturally the socialist states reject the view that there is any dissatisfaction with their various regimes, pointing to the power of organized capital over the communications media in Western states. In 1931 the then leader of the Conservative Party, Stanley Baldwin, denounced the proprietorship of various newspapers as holders of 'power without responsibility, the prerogative of the harlot throughout the ages' (Young, 1952: 162). With this comment

Soviet writers might agree, but for the wrong reason, namely that the media exerts a conspiratorial and pernicious control over men's minds. Western communications exist because of the impressive profits which are obtainable — or so socialists would argue. Socialist states, respond Western observers, exert a political stranglehold on the communications process. Socialist states ally ideology to the skills of the communicators. In the arts and literature, a clear purpose is spelt out — that of serving the state, and serving the state is a patriotic duty. The point was made succinctly by the Chinese spokesman on the subject, Hu Yaobang, who stated that: 'The most important political task of literary and artistic creation is to inspire patriotism' (*South China Morning Post*, 28 September, 1985).

COMTECH AND VALUES

The methods of communications technology are best seen as a means to an end. The computer for example is at bottom a tool, but for some it has become something of an end in itself. It is not hard to see why. Technology is properly equated with efficiency, and efficiency is a value (Simon H., 1957: 14). Efficiency may be the elimination of incompetence and the enhancement of an organization in terms of cost, time and effort. Efficiency may require the output of an organization to be seen in proportion to the sum of its inputs, in men and material. Above all efficiency is a matter of morale — the unmeasurable psychological dimension, summed up in the naval officers' cliche — 'an efficient ship is a happy ship'.

Efficiency aside, a particular problem relates to the usual claim that robotics is to be equated with to talitarianism and the sinister figure of Big Brother as expounded by Orwell in his classic *1984*. Comtech is in classical Orwellian terms a profound danger, and an enemy of the individual. Comtech can be seen as a weapon of control, surveillance, bugging and interference and essentially in any case a potential form of citizen abuse.

Orwell's anti-Utopia may not have been realized in quite the way which he envisaged (though North Korea has been cited as an exact copy of Orwell's version of the Brave New World). However we may give some examples where the state has used its power over modern technology to convey what Orwell, amongst many others, would see as a classical totalitarian message.

One example might be found in the notion of the 'state in the bedroom', or the notion that the state may make specific policies regarding the family. There are specific controls upon such matters as forced abortions (China), family separation (South Africa) and even a suggestion of eugenics (Singapore). In Eire, a presumed liberal Western state, the constitution prohibits birth control.

A further example might be found in the arts, education and language. Controls in these areas exist in the Soviet Union, China, North Korea, Singapore and South Africa. Communications in these areas are particularly sensitive for they are the raw materials of communication, asking the questions 'What may I say and how may I say it?'

A third example might refer to the activities of properly constituted interest groups, seeking to advance their own particular cause. Interest groups which can communicate with government do not exist or operate comfortably in totalitarian states. While there is much debate about the proper place of such groups, there is no denial that in the USA by way of contrast with the Soviet Union, there is a vast universe of interest groups (Wootton, 1985: chapter 7).

The two-way flow of communications from citizen to state as well as from state to citizen is seen in different terms in authoritarian/totalitarian states from those in the conventional Western liberal variety. The Chinese leadership asserts that there is an underlying harmony between the masses and the party. The masses provide a chemistry whereby 'the leadership can form its correct ideas only by adopting the method of "from the masses to the masses"'. People and policy are in harmony. The message from the leadership to the masses is communicated in mystical fashion without any need for *technology* as such.

A different line of argument might put the point that it is not a question of *abuse* but rather of *use* of comtech. The young bureaucrat or potential bureaucrat increasingly sees little or no conflict between efficiency (the values of comtech) and sees it rather as inevitable, a part of the furniture of the future. Network and critical path analyses are to be studied, appreciated and taught as a necessary element in the apparatus of the public administrator. As time goes by public administration is likely to absorb the most sophisticated possible technology. Government must become more precise in order to offset the overloading which threatens it.

PUBLIC CHOICE

Public administration has often been seen as a discipline quite different from political science. Public administration is often incorrectly seen as a somewhat institutional concern which asks how and by whom public services are provided. By contrast, political science is far wider in scope, concerned as it often is, with the science of power, and such concerns as the nature of the state, nation representation of the citizen and ultimately, the character of man. In fact, public administration has become progressively more rigorous, it has asked profound questions for example about the right form of the goods which the state provides, and especially whether it should supply them — the privatisation debate.

Public administration and political science have come somewhat closer together with the growth of a new subject area known as public choice theory. Thus public officials need to be concerned with what the consumer wants from public services rather than with the wishes of officials as producers. Obviously such an idea suggests the resources of the developed, rather than the developing, world. In particular, public choice theory suggests capitalism, particularly the US version, where the consumer is, at least in principle, sovereign. In developing countries, say like China, the notion of consumer choice and producer competition in public administration is quite novel. Thus China has only 15,000 private cars in a nation of over one thousand million people (*Economist*, June 18, 1988).

Public choice theory is very much the theory of group behaviour and is concerned with the provision of so-called public goods, clean air and water for example (Hardin, 1982). The subject of public choice stresses economic ideas (Mueller, 1979: 1), such as competition.

Western scholars believe that public goods are defined according to two criteria. In the first place they are indivisible. Fresh air, for example is for everybody. In the second place such goods cannot be charged for. Hence social scientists technically speak of free-riders. In poor countries, public goods may be impossible to provide. Any attempt to do so will only put the developing state into considerable debt. Nigeria, for example, has a total national debt of about US$25 billion. The ultimate public good however is political stability and sound incorrupt government. Unfortunately these things are scarce in many states in Latin America, Asia, and Africa. In a country like Vietnam, thousands of people leave in small boats and dangerous conditions to avoid the hardships of life in the Vietnam of the eighties.

Developing countries often lack suitable basic public resources, such as, water, roads, and a pollution-free environment. But developed countries also experience similar problems, and in the provision of public goods we might argue that it is a matter of degree whether public goods can ever be produced in such a way as to satisfy all peoples at all times. Experience shows that such demands are virtually without limit.

BIBLIOGRAPHY

Balazs Etienne (1964), *Chinese Civilisation and Bureaucracy* (translated by H.M. Wright, edited by Arthur F. Wright, Yale University Press), USA: New Haven.

Brown R.G.S. (1975), *The Management of Welfare*, Fontana, Collins, London.

Brown R.G.S. and Steel D.R. (1979), *The Administrative Process in Britain*, 2nd edition, Methuen, London.

Burke Edmund (1982), *Reflections on the French Revolution (1970)* ed., C.E. Vaughan, Percival.

Butler David (1966), *The Study of Political Behaviour*, Hutchinson, London.

Clapham Christopher (1985), *Third World Politics*, Croom & Helm, Kent.

Deutsch Karl W. (1966), *The Nerves of Government*, Free Press, New York.

Dunsire Andrew (1973), *Administration, the Word and the Science*, Martin Robertson, Oxford.

Finer Herman (1932), *The Theory and Practice of Modern Government*. Methuen, London and 2nd edition 2 vols 1946.

Fry G.F. (1981), *Statesmen in Disguise*, Macmillan, London.

Galbraith John Kenneth (1958), *The Affluent Society*, Hamish Hamilton, London.

Garrett John (1980), *Managing the Civil Service*, Heinemann, London.

Gerth H.H. and Mills C. Wright (1946), *From Max Weber: Essays in Sociology*, Routledge & Kegan Paul, London.

Harris Peter (1986), *Foundations of Political Science*, Hutchinson, 1976, 2nd edition, London.

Hill Ronald J. and Frank Peter (1981), *The Soviet Communist Party*, Allen & Unwin, London.

Jordan Robert S., ed. (1971), *International Administration* (David J. Murray and John Ballard, *The Legacy of British and French Colonial Rule*), Oxford University Press, Oxford.

Lenin V.I. (1966), *Collected Works* (trans J. Katzer), Moscow.

Macluhan M. (1964), *Understanding Media: The Extensions of Man*, Sphere Books, London.

Mueller D.C. (1979), *Public Choice*, Cambridge University Press, Cambridge.

Palombara Joseph (1974), *Politics within Nations*, Prentice Hall, New Jersey.

Riggs Fred (1964), *Administration Developing Countries: The Theory of Prismatic Society*, Houghton, Mifflin, London.

Rose Richard (1984), *Understanding Big Government*, Sage, London.

Sargent Lyman and Zant Thomas (1970), *Techniques of Political Analysis: An Introduction*, Wadsworth, California.

Self Peter (1971), *Administrative Theories and Politics*, Allen & Unwin, London.

Simon Herbert, Smithburg Donald and Thompson Victor (1950), *Public Administration*, Knopf.

Simon Herbert (1967), *Administrative Behaviour*, 2nd edition, Collier-Macmillan, London.

Spiers Maurice (1975), *Techniques and Public Administration*, Fontana/Collins, London.

Dwight Waldo (1968), *Public Administration*, Journal of Politics, 2, May 1968.

—— (1968), *International Encyclopedia of Social Sciences*, Vol. 13, Macmillan, London.

White L.D. (1948), *Introduction to the Study of Public Administration*, Macmillan, New York.

White Stephen (1979), *Politicial Culture and Soviet Politics*, Macmillan, London.

Willson F.M.G., ed. (1961), *Administrators in Action*, Vol. I, Allen & Unwin, London.

Wilson Woodrow (1887), *The Study of Administration*, Political Science, Quarterly 11, June 1887.

Wootton Graham (1985), *Interest Groups: Policy and Politics in America*, Prentice Hall, New Jersey.

Young S.M. (1952), *Baldwin*.

2
The Size and Scope of Government

Governments grow. The history of the West shows that the activities of officials have multiplied in virtually every state, community and nation on earth. The growth of government is the one factor which appears to be a constant, irrespective of ideology or structure. If we take certain European states over a period of time we can observe that they have demonstrated a very strong tendency to increase in size. This is the origin of Big Government. In a century from about 1850–1960, the population of Great Britain has not doubled; in this time however, the number of officials has increased forty times. The numbers of officials in British Central Government approximates 700,000 (*Britain, An Official Hand Book*, 1985). However to be added to this figure are the numbers of local government civil servants, military personnel, nationalized industries and other subvented bodies. All in all, the numbers of persons employed by the British Government even during the Thatcher administration was about 3 million. The British Government is that country's biggest employer.

In the case of France a similar story of growth can be recounted. Thus in French administrative history, the administrative power has so grown that we may indeed speak of France as an administrative state. In 1515, France had 19 million people, with some 4,000 royal officers, or one official for every 4,750 persons. By 1670 the ratio was one official for every 380 persons. By 1934, for a population of some 43 million persons, the number of royal officials had risen to give a ratio of one official for every sixty French men and women. By 1985, officials of one sort or another accounted for almost 20 per cent of the labour force.

In the USA we can observe a similar trend, with estimates that the US economy sees between 20–25 per cent of the labour force employed by the various governmental agencies in the USA. This would amount to about a million persons if the military were to be included. The USA is traditionally regarded as the home of private enterprise but the growth of government activity has been quite remarkable especially in the last thirty years and since the mid-fifties. In particular, the growth of the numbers of federal civil servants has been especially noteworthy. Of course, to be accurate, the USA has 51 governments which indicates the size of the government sector in a country which sees the private, rather than the public, sector as the rightful employer of labour.

Federal Civil Service: USA

1800—5,000
1860—100,000
1900—240,000
1965—2,500,000
1976—4,000,000
1986—5,000,000

In 1986, total persons in public employment of all kinds was 18.7 million, over the whole of the USA.

Non-Western states have experienced on even greater proportional growth in the numbers of their civil servants as a study of the International Monetary Fund demonstrates (*Economist*, December 17 1983). In developing countries almost half of jobs, excluding the agricultural sector, are in the public sector, compared with about 24 per cent in the developed world. In particular, non-Western states, the cost of maintaining the apparatus of officials is high, and higher in 'poor' than in 'rich' countries. In Japan, public officials share of the national income is only 2.5 per cent; in Jamaica, it is 15 per cent. Some cases, like India for example, are different, because there is severe competition in India for government positions and, in consequence, salaries are maintained at a relatively low level.

Industrialized countries in the West normally have much more extensive welfare states than those in the developing world, but the ratio of the average wages of civil servants in developing countries is about the same. The method of state activity is general in developing states necessarily differs from that in developed states. Developed states are able to finance large social service programmes, and indeed for electoral reasons, they will continue to do so. Welfare is, however, an expensive matter and poor countries cannot afford it. Paradoxically those which describe themselves as 'socialist' may well be unable to fund 'socialist' programmes. Often 'capitalist' states will be more 'socialist' in the provision of welfare than those poor states which describe themselves as 'socialist'.

The fact is that in many states of the world, government is the biggest employer of all with vast sums of money at stake. The determinants of public spending were first described as early as 1893 (Adolf Wagner 1893, and A. Robinson 1978, 4).

The reasons for growth of public spending were given in the 1890's and have been described as follows: (1) Public spending has increased on regulatory services far beyond its previous levels; (2) Public spending exists where private spending could not afford to take up the whole responsibility for development, such as railways; (3) Public spending on social services such as education and public health has greatly increased in response to social pressures. In Western states the particular growth areas are pensions, defence, health and education, in that order.

Since 1914, public expenditure in Europe and North America has greatly increased, in consequence largely because of war and the development of the welfare state.

HOW BUREAUCRACIES GROW

Organization have a definite propensity to grow, sometimes for necessary and understandably rational explanations and sometimes for less worthy reasons. If we consider how bureaucracies develop, we may do so most conveniently under four headings — horizontal, vertical, lateral and territorial. An analysis of each of these in turn is helpful to throw light on the general problem of bureaucratic growth.

HORIZONTAL

Organizations which grow horizontally do so when they combine with those already in existence. A simple explanation would refer to schools — primary schools lead on to secondary schools for example. Other examples would be deduced from hospitals as they take on more functions. In public administration proper, horizontal growth might suggest a series of departments dealing with environmental matters such as pollution, both in the air and at sea. The problem of pollution is such that it spreads over a wide range of administrative responsibilities from those concerned with engineering, environment and cleansing to those concerned with law enforcement and the policing of anti-pollution functions.

VERTICAL

When we speak of vertical growth we refer to processes rather than to institutions. A particular operation may be pushed 'backwards' to include the provision of supplies for a service already in existence. Thus it might be necessary for an organization to assure control over a printing firm in order to expedite its work. At the same time, it may be necessary for a department of health to improve its services by organizing blood supplies under its own control. The expansion of processes in further continuance of processes already performed is a vertical operation.

LATERAL

We may also discover further forms of growth. Lateral growth refers to the extension of 'outputs' into other fields. Thus a railway concern may take over or supply refreshment rooms in order to ensure that railway passengers can

23

have access to refreshment rooms. A railway station may contain many ancillary conveniences such as shops, kiosks or even banks. An airport may have an elaborate network of facilities, including post offices, money-changers, bus, taxi, underground transport services and even hotels. An airport may be a part of a government department in which case the department concerned may take on a whole range of new activities such as hotel management and ticketing.

TERRITORIAL

Territorial administrative growth refers to the setting up of new branches of the same operation in new areas. A government department will often have sub-offices or branch offices which are established to provide for some need in a new area. The idea of the branch office is to provide on a smaller scale than is found in the centre for the needs of a local community. A small local branch of a post office is a good case in point. A local post office will not provide all the services which are found at a main branch, but it will attempt as far as possible to offer its more limited services to the best of its ability.

THE PROBLEM OF BIG GOVERNMENT

Writers on public administration have frequently drawn attention to what they describe as big government, and we have already seen that the tendency to growth both numerically in size as well as in scope has been difficult to resist and control. Departments and ministries have under the stimulus of public demand, often increased in size. The public often asks simply: 'Why doesn't the government do this, or do that?' The expectations of individual citizens are, both in Western industrial states as well as in developing agricultural states, almost without limit. Government is all too often seen as the only agent which has a reasonable chance of meeting all these expectations. However, the costs of public policy have increased by 7.1 per cent, while national economies have grown at an average annual rate of 4.2 per cent.

Governments then are expected to provide and to have policy for, a huge variety of subjects, including education, transport, energy, inflation, crime, and especially in the West, for unemployment. Government has, it has been said, become 'overloaded' (Rose, 1979: 359). Government is becoming less able to satisfy public demand at the same time that it is growing rapidly. Interest groups and political parties, together with the media (especially television) generate many demands which eventually must either be met or rejected. To govern is to choose, in these circumstances. The choices however are limited. Pensions, defence, health and education cannot be reduced by much. Western states are expected to meet these claims.

Some commentators have seen elements of collapse in public institutions as

Great Britain Public Expenditure 1987 Pence in Every Pound			
Revenue		**Expenditure**	
Income Tax	(24)	Social Security	(26)
National Insurance	(16)	Defence	(11)
Value added Tax	(13)	DHSS Health and Personal	
Local authority rates	(10)	Benefit.	(11)
Road Fuel, Alcohol, Tobacco,	(10)	Education and Science	(9)
Corporation Tax	(6)	Other Departments	(19)
North Sea Revenues	(4)	Scotland, Wales and	
Interest and Dividends	(4)	Northern Ireland	(9)
Other Sources	(8)	Interest Payments	(11)
Borrowing	(5)	Other	(4)

more and more burdens are thrust upon them, and reference is sometimes made to 'ungovernability' (M. Crozier *et al* (eds.) 1975; Rose, 1979; Von Beyme, 1985). Essentially people see government and government departments as a means of providing a higher standard of living, but these people do not see that state activity has limits. Government is able to solve problems but it is just as likely to create problems. This was put very succinctly by US President Ronald Reagan in his 1981 inaugural address when he said 'Government is not the solution to the problem. Government is the problem'. In short, government is both '*conflict generating* and *conflict resolving*'.

President Reagan argued that 'there are no limits to growth and human progress when men and women are free to follow their dreams' (Second Inaugural Address). However, he saw growth as taking place outside the orbit of government. However, government *is* a problem, even in the USA, because even under Reagan it has proved impossible to reduce its size, but only to stop its increase. When Reagan took office in 1981 he promised to cut domestic spending from 23.5 per cent of gross national product (1981 fiscal year) to 19 per cent. However by 1985 the federal government's share of GNP had reached over 24 per cent. At the same time the national debt and federal budget deficit increased. The USA became a major debtor country.

'Government is big today because major programmes, education, health, pensions and military defence — make big claims upon society's resources' (Rose 1984). This statement may be made about Western states, especially Western European States, but Big Government is the norm in every part of the Western world from Australia to Finland. The solution to the ever-expanding world of modern government is a matter of great controversy. Some people believe that only modern government alone can solve social problems and that it is wrong to curtail the major programmes of social benefit. Government, they argue, should exist in part to help those who need help, the old, the sick, the unemployed and the handicapped. Government they suggest should be the agency which ensures a steady supply of funds to build hospitals, schools, roads and universities. Government, they believe, should maintain these things at a high and efficient level. Government finally, should finance research and development and keep the housing stock well-maintained.

Some people think that Government cannot undertake to maintain its present workload, let alone expand into new areas. For one thing the organs of public administration bodies cannot cope with the present work-load, let alone take on more duties. However, administrators almost invariably find the burden of work overwhelming but nevertheless work is often a form of drug. Indeed one writer speaks of 'the sheer intoxication of administrative responsibility' (Castle, 1984: 192).

BIG GOVERNMENT IN DEVELOPING COUNTRIES

Within developing counties, the state is indubitably a major element — often *the* major element — in development. The difference between developing and developed states in this regard is that there is usually no alternative to development apart from the state. During the 1980's, however, pressures upon all states produced a concern that development was too expensive in its present form, and some Third World states carried an enormous debt burden.

Large developing states like India, for example, may have several sorts, of government whose major purpose is to provide for and develop the second largest state in the world in population. Approximately one person out of every six persons in the world is an Indian, and India has a federal structure given its enomous size, consisting of 22 states and 9 union territories. There are three levels of powers in India depending upon whether these are on the Union List, the State List or the Concurrent List. The Union List contains functions like defence, currency and foreign affairs handled by the Centre, those on the State List refer to those handled by the state, while the Concurrent List is open to action by either party (subject to overriding control by the Centre).

Problems of government in very large states such as India, China or Indonesia in Asia or Nigeria, the Sudan or Zaire in Africa offer a different pattern from those of Western-style welfare states. Some of these states require extensive foreign aid and foreign investment, and in the case of the Sudan even require foreign aid to feed many of its people (*Economist*, November 30 1985), thousands of whom die daily from hunger.

Big Government in developing countries means something quite different from Big Government in developed Western states. Most writers on public administration in Western countries stress public demand for services, forcing government in its turn to decide on its priorities. Relatively wealthy countries have to make choices on what to spend their wealth. To govern is to choose. However in poorer developing states, government takes place in a context of resource poverty. In the absence of resources, government is impotent. When refugees from Vietnam arrived in Australia in the 1980's for example, they were amazed to encounter a wide range of social service benefits unknown in Vietnam. Vietnam has suffered from war and deprivation for decades. It maintains a large army and has no tradition of welfare state provisions. Vietnam is unlikely to have developed world worries about the provision of such welfare. Developing countries also frequently have to try to repay debts incurred in already completed, even if largely unsatisfactory, earlier developments. The following table indicates the problem of debt-servicing from the perspective of 1985.

STATE SPENDING

In most industrial countries, as well as in developing countries, government has progressively increased its share of the GNP (gross national product). A significant example would be Italy, where, in 1985, almost sixty per cent of the GNP consisted of government spending. In 1979, this figure (in Italy) was only about 45 per cent.

By contrast, in Japan government spending was only about 32 per cent. In the USA the government share of the GNP at all levels local state and federal, was a little higher, at thirty-five per cent. The Federal Republic of Germany remained constant at about 48 per cent.
(Source: OECD Annual National Accounts).

General government expenditure as % of GNP 1985

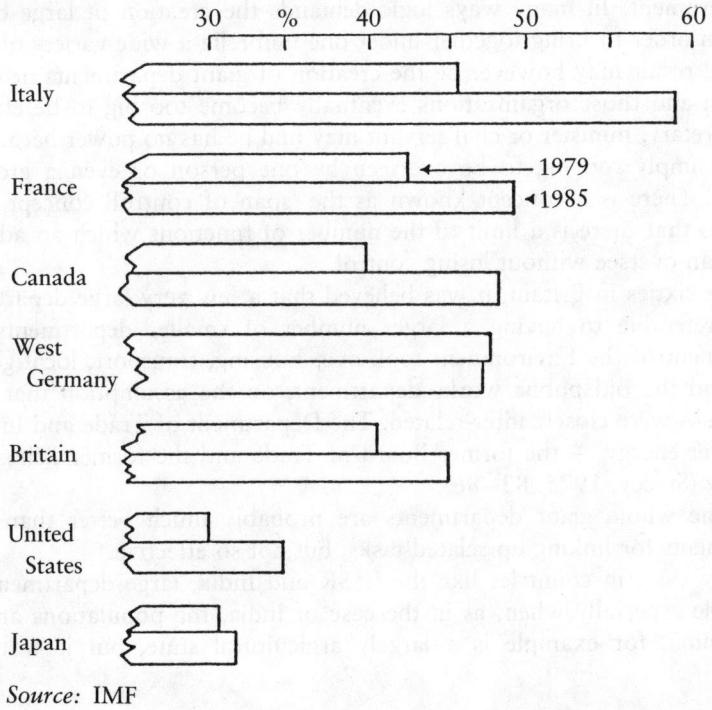

Source: IMF

SMALL IS BEAUTIFUL

Most rational administrators everywhere understand the need to limit growth, to avoid duplication and encourage coordination in the tasks of government. However, despite the wide differences to be considered as well as the scale and provision of resources required, there are many people who argue that administrative units should be broken down into small parts, more relevant and meaningful to the individual citizen. Ultimately it is the individual citizen who pays for and consumes resources.

An eloquent appeal came from Kurt Schumacher whose book *Small is Beautiful* expressed the central idea of his philosophy, a philosophy which has an ancient pedigree. We find it in Plato, Aristotle and Rousseau amongst others, the same yearnings for a face-to-face society which has been lost in modern life.

The modern administrator in the present century sees both costs and benefits, merits and demerits in large size. If we consider the environment itself, it may make much sense to link up particular environmental and urban problems, just as it makes much sense to link up trade and industry. Obviously, there is a close connection between environmental and urban factors. A decision made about towns is almost always a decision made about the environment. Similarly a decision made about industry naturally ties up with trade matters. The central government may find itself duplicating the tasks of local government and *vice versa*. One argument is that it is very sensible to collect together all these tasks and concentrate rather than dispense the tasks of government. In many ways logic demands the creation of large departments in order to bring together under one umbrella a wide variety of tasks. The end result may however be the creation of giant departments or organizations, and those organizations eventually become too big to be efficient. The secretary, minister or civil servant may find he has no power because the task is simply too big to be overseen by one person or even a group of persons. There is a concept known as the 'span of control' concept which indicates that there is a limit to the number of functions which an administrator can oversee without losing control.

In the sixties in Britain, it was believed that a few very large departments were preferable to having a larger number of smaller departments. The Department of the Environment took over housing, transport, local government and the old public works department, on the assumption that all of these tasks were closely inter-related. The Department of Trade and Industry took over energy — the former Board of Trade and the former Ministry of Industry (Stacey, 1975, 83–86).

On the whole giant departments are probably much better than small departments for linking up related tasks, but not so effective.

In any case, in countries like the USSR and India, large departments are inevitable especially when, as in the case of India, the populations are also huge. India, for example is a largely argicultural state, but it would be difficult to conceive of a ministry of agriculture for the whole state of federal India. In 1985 such a department, the Ministry of Agriculture and Rural Development, did exist, but its supervision could, of course, cover only very general matters. In India, in the towns, municipal corporations administered urban services while in the rural areas there were networks of *panchayati raj* (local traditional units of government).

In large socialist states such as China and the Soviet Union, state intervention means even larger units and more numerous officials and administrators. The very size of official administration at central provincial and state level is further complicated by ideological socialism which places control of the means of production in the hands of public administrators. In the Soviet Union for example, each significant industry is controlled by its own Ministry, thus reflecting socialism as much as public administration.

The argument that Big Government is *inefficient* government (or even bad government) is not always correct. It may however be true that government is *overloaded*, with large and expensive programmes (Rose, 1984). There are however about five aspects to the growth of the state, according to Von Beyme (1985: 15). These are summarized below as follows:

1. Growth of Government Agencies

Central government has grown in most parts of the world and, at the same time, large numbers of other bodies, ('state-owned, quasi-governmental, parastatal agencies'), have grown everywhere, not to mention a variety of advisory committees.

2. Growth of Public Employment

A country like Germany has long since experienced a growth in public employment. In developing countries, this growth has been associated with patronage and has led to an impressive growth in jobs in the public sector.

3. Growth of Taxation and the State's Share of the National Product

Wagner's 'law' has been quoted. When the national product grows, so does the state sector. Such an idea has largely been borne out in most countries.

4. Growth of Legislation and Programmes

Most parts of the world have seen the expansion in law-making. At the same time many policy programme have flourished.

5. Growth of Government Control over the Economy

Compared with the 1930's many Western countries allow large-scale control over their economies, but the unpopularity of nationalization has become universal (outside socialist states) in the 1980's. Complicated arguments have continued between Keynesians and monetarists about the extent of intervention (Bleaney, 1985: 202).

CAN BIG GOVERNMENT BE ROLLED BACK?

For political figures (in the capitalist world) like President Reagan and Mrs. Thatcher, as well as others, Big Government is undesirable because it is wrong for governments to do things which people should undertake themselves. Government should therefore be contracted as far as possible and thereafter kept in check, according to many people. There are several ways in which this contraction can take place. In the first place, government can be contracted by reducing the amounts of money available for governments to spend. Governments grow because governments believe that they should manage the economy and undertake many welfare programmes. Government expansion is sometimes seen as closely related to the economic theories of Lord Keynes but after the 1970's Keynesian economics become unpopular with policy-makers (M. Bleaney, 1985: 200).

In Britain, the home of Keynes, expenditure on the Welfare State reached £40,000 million per annum by 1985, when the Thatcher government tried to reform the dense complexities of public sector activities. Most of this sort of money is allocated in Western states without much scrutiny. In the USA, important elements of fraud were discovered in military spending, involving the 'padding' of expenses. Even low-cost items such as screwdrivers cost the taxpayer many times more than their anticipated commonsense cost.

It is indeed very difficult to reduce the level of expenditure on public services given the prevailing climate of opinion. One of the reasons relates to the large number of people who owe their livelihoods to government. Thus in the USA, almost 20 million people are employed by or through the activities of government. Local government in particular is a large employer. In Sweden almost 40 per cent of persons are employed in the public sector compared with under 20 per cent in the USA, with Britain's figure being about 32 per cent (Rose, 1984: 132). The following table illustrates the situation.

Another reason would appear to be the expectation that the benefits of the welfare state would continue to grow. When the welfare state was devised in Britain it was not envisaged that it would be such a large and unwieldy undertaking with such bureaucratic ramifications. In Holland we find a case of welfare support which has probably taken the matter to its logical conclusion. There artists can 'sell' their works to the state at attractively high prices. To meet this objective, government employs other artists as panel numbers and adjudicators. The works purchased are later stored. In Holland, the nation's 19 symphony orchestras are subsidized, irrespective of their number of performances. Foreign labourers are entitled to very high levels of welfare which, it is alleged, they often abuse.

	Growth of Public Employment		
Country	Civil Servants per 1000 of population	% of National Employment	Growth of Civil Servants % 1970–1980
Sweden	156	38.2	4.9
United Kingdom	96	31.7	1.8
USA	78	18.8	1.1
France	73	n.d.	1.4
West Germany	64	25.8	2.8
Japan	34	n.d.	2.2

Adapted from Table 2 in Klaus Von Beyme, *The Growth of Government*, International Political Science Review, Vol. 6, No. 1, 1985, p. 19.

PRIVATIZATION

The size of the apparatus of the state can be tackled by removing parts of the government machine from the public sector and handing it over to the private sector. This process is known as 'privatization' and has become a very common means of forcing the contraction of big government. In states all over the world, a tendency grew up in the eighties to end subsidies for industries which would decline without such subsidies. In effect, governments were using taxpayers' money to support enterprises which should, it was argued, not be so used. The belief gained ground that if a private firm, company factory or enterprise could provide a service efficiently then it should replace a public body.

The idea of privatization was part of the response to the dilemma of Big Government. Privatization was a world-wide tendency in the 1980's and appealed to a wide variety of different forms of political persuasion. The main reason for the appeal of privatization lay in the belief that the ability, powers and resources of government were limited. Those who asked for governments to do this or do that were no longer certain of finding that governments would act. The trend towards selling off state-owned businesses grew rapidly.

Privatization is not to be equated with selling off state industries — or denationalization as it was once popularly called. It covers deregulation, or taking away laws which restricted competition, the state contracting out of services and an opening up to market forces of public sector activities (Gray and Jenkins, *Parliamentary Affairs*, I, 1987).

Perhaps governments had lost their nerve. Certainly the economic 'philosophy' known as monetarism helped to create a climate of opinion which encouraged governments to consider privatization as a serious option.

Country	Form of Privatization
Bangladesh	Jute mills
Pakistan	Cotton mills
France	Renault
Hungary	Retail enterprises
Japan	Nippon Telegraph, Telephone
	Japan National Railways, Japan Airways
Turkey	State airline
Mexico	Group of 500 companies
Britain	British Aerospace
	British Telecom
	British Airways
China	Peasant holdings, selected enterprises
Singapore	Singapore Airlines
Brazil	100 companies

Source: *Economist*, 23 February 1985 and 21 December 1985

In Britain between 1979–1984, Mrs. Thatcher's conservative government 'sold' the larger part of 16 large, state-owned companies. Almost half a million workers were moved into the private sector. In 1979 nationalized industries (i.e., brought under state control in the 1940's and 1950's) were responsible for about ten per cent of Britain's GDP and 15 per cent of total investment in the economy. Those areas were transport, energy, communications, steel, ship building, defence engineering and even motor cars. In all, these industries employed a million and a half persons.

Privatization has been countenanced in China, albeit within strict limits. In a state in which previously the motion of private ownership was taboo, a greater degree of individual initiative has been permitted. Since the early 1980's, China has introduced a 'responsibility system' first in agriculture and then in industry which attempts to shift the responsibility for local management in some measure to the peasants and workers. Naturally some opponents of 'privatization' in China and other socialist countries such as Yugoslavia and Hungary have portrayed 'privatization' as a challenge to socialist principles.

The developing world may be largely based on agriculture which means that the complex debates about the levels of state involvement in the private sector do not have much meaning there. Nevertheless, revolutions have been brought about in a number of countries over land ownership. Peasants are generally seen as interested in land for purposes of *private* use; they are not enthusiastic, as the cases of Tanzania and China show, in working for bureaucrats.

Moreover, in the 1970's, state-owned enterprises in the Developing World effectively bankrupted national treasuries (*Economist*, 21 December 1985). In the Philippines privatization has not been successful given a lack of confidence in the structure of government. In Malaysia, privatization has meant that Chinese private enterprise has flourished at the expense of the

Malay locals (*bumiputra*). Privatization in Malaysia and in Thailand may be politically difficult. In poor countries generally, privatization may be complicated by the fact that unmodernized state concerns (even, for example, inefficient public bus authorities) will not easily find private buyers. In Africa, in particular in Zambia and Tanzania, public subsidies have become accepted by many public sector employees as a natural way-of-life. In Latin America, privatization is further complicated by the prevalence of military men in government. But everywhere governments appear to be very prepared to hive off tasks, in the expectation that the 'market' can take on eagerly what public administration increasingly sees as an unwelcome burden.

THE CONSEQUENCES OF THE GROWTH IN GOVERNMENT

Government activity can grow until it encompasses the whole of the activities of an entire community or state. The desirability or otherwise of the expansion of the state is of course a matter for keen ideological debate. On the whole the nature of this debate is changing. Governments are not always the most efficient managers of the resources of the state. On the other hand there are certain areas where government has an important even unique role to play in ensuring that those in greatest need of help do not suffer undue and unnecessary hardship. Between the one extreme of total intervention and the other of total non-intervention is a larger area for debate.

From about 1960 on governments have expanded in respect of their participation in a variety of activities and in the formulation of social and economic policies. These include increased expenditures on social services as well as subsidies for a range of activities, including the subsidizing of declining industries. Voters naturally approve of these activities where public expenditures operate to their personal benefit. Such activities (or 'programmes' as Rose terms them), involve increased taxation and produce a debate on the level of taxation in different states.

Tax Receipts as Percentage of GDP

	1965	1985
Sweden	36	51
Holland	34	45
France	35	45
Italy	27	41
Britain	33	39
W. Germany	34	38
Canada	26	34
Australia	24	31
USA	26	29
Japan	18	27

OECD, Paris 1987

N.B. *Variation in Composition of Tax Burden*
   e.g., France, income tax is 18% of total.
      Australia, income tax is 53% of total.

Leading Western politicians of the eighties believe that increased governmental expenditures destroyed the will of people to work, save and invest. If government can do it, then individuals will not. The argument was largely psychological and based on the 'common-sense' belief that human beings require incentives to work. If something can be provided 'for nothing', then it will be gratefully received.

From places as far off as China and Mexico, the notion of privatization has caught on (*Economist*, December 21, 1985). In the Soviet Union, it did not, although some discussion of the role of the 'market' has developed since the advert to power of Mikael Gorbachev. The interest in privatization in the eighties is extensive; perhaps the most significant example of an exchange of money and property between private individuals and their governments.

Big government is not significantly altered by privatization. In many countries, the public sector is still very large. In nearly all cases governments control posts, utilities such as electricity, gas, railways and, invarying degrees, airlines, oil and even steel, ship building. In less developed countries privatization is relatively slight, and Big Government is not successful in solving the pressing economic problems of poverty. In many cases privatization is popular on economic grounds, as is the case in some parts of Africa, as well as in some Latin American countries such as Brazil since the end of military rule. It should not of course be seen as a cure-all.

Big Government, however, does mean employment for millions who are absorbed into departments units and agencies of government. When privatization occurs there is often a problem especially for those lacking skills which are required in the (private) market place. Further, in theory where privatization takes place there should be a reduction in taxes (or at least no increase in taxes). In fact no simple lessons can be deduced from privatization. Each country defines, operates and interprets privatization differently. Some countries are satisfied to sell off a small portion of the state's assets, others try to sell most if not all. Above all, there are numerous political decisions which require attention. Privatization for example, may be very controversial, where a state monopoly protect(s) one group against another — Malaysia could be quoted here, in its desire to promote the interests of the Malays (the *bumiputra* element). On the whole, however, policies such as nationalization are, from the standpoint of the 1980's extremely unpopular, except of course in socialist states. Even in these, and most particularly in China, great interest at least is shown in developing private responsibility and initiative.

BIBLIOGRAPHY

Ascher Kate (1987), *The Politics of Privatization*, Macmillan Education Ltd., London.

Beyme Klaus Von (1985), *The Role of the State and the Growth of Government*, International Political Science Review, Vol. 6, No. 1, 1985.

Bleaney Michael (1985), *The Rise and Fall of Keynesian Economics*, Macmillan, London.

Castle Barbara (1984), *The Castle Diaries, 1964–1970*. Weidenfeld, London.

Crozier M.J. *et al* (eds) (1975), *The Crisis of Democracy: Report on the Governability of Democracies to the Triennial Commission*, New York University Press, New York.

Gray Andrew & William I. Jenkins, Public *Administration and Government in 1986*, Parliamentary Affairs, I, 1987.

Lane Jan-Erik (1985), *State and Market*, Sage, London.

Moe Ronald C., *Exploring the Limits of Privatization*, Public Administration Review, November 1987.

OECD, *Taxation in Developed Countries*, Paris, 1987.

Pirie M. (1985), *Privatization*, Adam Smith Institute, London.

Robinson Ann (1978), *Parliament and Public Spending*, Heinemann, London.

Rose (see Chapter One).

Schumacher E.F. (1973), *Small is Beautiful*, Abacus, Kent.

Stacey Frank (1975), *British Government, 1966–1975*, Oxford University Press, Oxford.

Wagner Adolf (1983), *Grundlegung der Politischen Oekonomie*, Leipzig.

3
Allocation of Functions

An old, but nevertheless important subject for students of public administration, is that of allocation of functions. This somewhat forbidding sounding title refers to a very important and complex topic which asks: on what basis should tasks be performed within the government machine? A typical example is the control of pollution. Some people see the control of pollution as an environmental matter, but of course the detection of polluters is the responsibility of the police, while an interest in the question of pollution is obviously a concern for the scientists in government as well as for a whole range of other possible departments such as public works, conservancy and finance, amongst others.

In many cases there is little difficulty, or so it would appear. Transport is transport and not education or health. But there is nonetheless overlap everywhere. If any senior figure in public administration were to be asked how the administrative tasks in any enterprise were to be explained, he might find it difficult to give a comprehensive answer. An examination of the actual composition and structure of any government organization would show many inconsistencies and anomalies. Governments see the nature of their problems in different ways; they see them in the light of topical issues or in the light of a given ideology or interest group. Furthermore, government work is, in most non-authoritarian states, heavily influenced by public opinion. There is no set of rules which can be applied at all times and in all places. 'There is no simple or single formula by whose application all the problems of administrative arrangement can be solved' (D.N. Chester and F.M.G. Willson, 1968: 390).

How, Aristotle asked, should the state organize the functions which it should discharge? The Greek sage put it as follows:

> We have also to consider whether to allocate duties on the basis of the subject to be handled, or on that of the class of persons concerned: e.g., should we have one officer for the whole subject of the maintenance of order, or a separate officer for the class of children and another for that of women (Aristotle, *Politics*, Book IV, Chap. XV).

Aristotle's perception was dramatic and basic and set out the basic dilemna as a choice between the task to be performed and the persons whose needs were to be catered for. Political philosophers however have rarely concerned themselves with the principles of organization except all too frequently to denounce these organizations themselves.

In the twentieth century, with the growth of government, the consideration, if not the solution, of these subjects has become pressing, both in developed and in developing states and the question of the organization of government has become a matter for continual discussion amongst those interested in macro-organization or the higher principles of distribution of functions between government departments and other public bodies. *The Haldane Committee on the Machinery of Government* (1918) considers these matters at length.

Aristotle's simple division of allocation of duties under two heads was taken further in the early part of the twentieth century. Such a long intervening period indicates how rare are the attempts to theorize about the question of the allocation of powers and duties in administrative history. Few practising administrators appear inclined to take a philosophical stand on administrative questions.

The Haldane Committee was set up in 1918 to consider the particular problems in the modern state which derived from the desire of Haldane to understand the machinery of government. Only infrequently does a government seek to ask fundamental questions about organization and in usually indirect ways. This was one of those rare occasions.

Aristotle's famous dual rules for allocation were restated. The alternatives were presented as 'distribution according to the persons or classes to be dealt with and distribution according to the services to be performed' (Haldane Report, Cd 9230/1918: 7–8). The Haldane Committee saw merits and demerits in both approaches. However as has been pointed out, both Aristotle and Haldane did not consider other possible approaches, such as the allocation of duties according to geography or the *area* principle, and the so-called *process* principle which refers to some very specialized operation like metereological observation.

In short we may locate at least *four* rather than *two* principles which might determine the various approaches to the ancient question of how to consider how the officers of the state discharge the duties. The four criteria for consideration are — allocation according to *persons* treated, according to the *task* or service involved, according to *area* covered, or according to *particular* and *specialized* process. Naturally no certainty exists as to whether this list of four criteria covers all the aspects of the allocation problem. We may at least however use the four criteria as useful stepping-stones in the argument, which is considered next.

THE QUESTION OF THE PERSONS INVOLVED

Apparently the question of allocating resources according to the persons, clients or classes involved appears to have great merit. People are seen as people. All tasks associated with children for example could be handled by a department for children. These would include education, health and welfare.

The central purpose of all tasks would be seen through the perceived need of children as children rather than as parts of some larger subject. The demand for special treatment for particular persons or clients continues to attract much attention. In the case of women for example, the movements associated with female rights have continued to stress the particular problems of women and from time to time, demands are made for the rights of women to be met by special treatment for women, and for women alone. At the same time demands are sometimes made for black people to receive special treatment as blacks on the grounds that they cannot receive proper treatment *unless* they are separately treated. The question of special treatment of persons has become more sensitive as it has become more topical.

In South Africa for example, there were separate departments and agencies for black people, for Indians and for Europeans. In some parts of South-East Asia, Chinese are separately administered and therefore given separate treatment from other ethnic groups. There are dangers as well as advantages in this approach. The main danger of administration according to the principle of the needs of the clients to be served is that it may create many mini-departments for each group. A Ministry of the Unemployed for example would need special services as well as ordinary services just for the unemployed.

In the USA there was a Bureau of Indian Affairs and a Children's Bureau. Indeed wherever there are pluralized societies a demand for separate treatment appears. The final stage is for whole societies to demand to break away or secede from the larger organization. The case of the Sikhs (India) and Tamils (Sri Lanka) in the 1980's is worth the mention. These groups want separate treatment on the client or class basis.

The desire for such separate treatment (even when separation implies equality) is not always easy to accommodate. As suggested: 'in its extreme form it would mean having separate police forces and fire brigades, and separate educational and health services, etc., for each category of persons' (Chester and Willson, 1968: 400). However it is difficult to see how a state which had a department for farmers would be anything other than a department to further the special interest of the farmers against every one else.

PURPOSE FUNCTION TASK OR SERVICE

The functional principle, as it is sometimes known, sees the proper task of government as the provision of services, and is the most common form of allocation. The purpose of government and its departments is to attend to a *function*, whether this is education, transport, defence, social welfare or whatever task is deemed appropriate for a government department. Usually the implication is that *departments* should be created to service and administer particular functions. People think of departments and functions simultaneously. Hence in the popular mind, the *department* and the *function* which it undertakes are linked up. The Haldane Report believed that the best results are obtained 'when the officers of a Department are continuously engaged in the study of questions which relate to a single service and when the efforts of the Department are definitely concentrated upon the development and improvement of the particular service which the Department exists to supervise' (Haldane, 1918: 7–8).

The organization of work according to function at purpose has a particular merit, which is to assist in making policy. The head of the department, when he is a political figure is clearly responsible for his undertaking. If policy is at fault the man-in-charge must assume responsibility for the policy for errors in its implementation. The problem arises however in defining 'functions'. A department set up to administer agriculture might also take in, for example, fisheries or trade, but not industry. Departments are sometimes added to other departments, sometimes they are taken away.

From time to time, moreover, the notion of functions change, particularly in a time of rapid technological change. Computerization, for example, has radically altered the workings of government departments. Indeed computerization might very well be a 'function' in itself. Nevertheless, when all the drawbacks are taken into account, the allocation of tasks according to function to be performed appears to be universally accepted and understood. For this reason, if not on the grounds of logic, it would appear that allocation according to service performed has remained the most commonly accepted method of allocation in general.

GEOGRAPHY OR AREA

We often discover that administration follows a geographical or regional framework of reference. Some authorities consider that 'it is useless to make a strictly logical distinction between those activities which are properly capable of being distributed according to the area in which they are administered and those which are not' (Chester and Willson, 1968, 404).

Federal states, i.e., those in which several units are related or associated in varying degrees differ in respect of administrative tasks of course from unitary states. People wish to be associated with the provision of services in their own locality as far as possible. They may resent control by some remote uncontrollable authority. In the United States (unlike the United Kingdom) the local state area is seen by many Americans to be as important as the entity (USA) itself, and people refer to the *federal* government as opposed to the state government. Powers may however be *devolved* from the centre to the localities by agreement. We have to remember to distinguish between legislative and administrative acts. Laws can be made in one of a number of states but the administrative process may extend over a number of states.

In Malaysia for example, the administration of finance covers a number of states. Compared with the states' budgets, the federal budget is quite considerable — about four times as great (Milne, 1967: 79). The federal nature of Malaysia is all important. Malaysia offers a very good example of the administrative problems which arise from geographical differences. Malaysia has altogether eleven states on the Malay peninsula, together with the federal territory of Kuala Lumpur, making up West Malaysia. However, East Malaysia consists of the states of Sabah and Sarawak on the island of Borneo. Borneo is, of course, geographically separated from West Malaysia, and Sabah and Sarawak 'enjoy some powers not available to the states of West Malaysia' (Dawson in De Lury, 1983: 653).

Hong Kong after 1997 will be administered separately from China, because of the application to Hong Kong of a notion of 'one country two systems'. The British have always administered the so-called New Territories differently from Hong Kong itself, and many services for the New Territories were differently administered from Hong Kong Island and Kowloon. The reason for this state of affairs was simply explicable in terms of geography.

However, it is not only the unitary state which demonstrates problems of administration in relation to geography. These difficulties are especially marked in Africa and may be seen to be in part the result of colonial rule. In huge tracts of Africa, the colonial powers brought together areas which were not natural administrative unities. A good example would be Uganda which was created from a number of different natural groupings into the state of Uganda in the 1890's (D.A. Low and R.C. Pratt, 1970).

British colonial policy was always sensitive to local rights so much so that they developed a practice known as 'indirect rule'. The British approach to colonial government is usually related to this general principle. Indirect rule was a means by which particular concern was paid to the localities by allowing traditional rulers in these localities to continue ruling according to local custom wherever possible. British colonial administration was somewhat different from that of French administrators in this regard. French colonial administration operated according to an idea of centralization. It follows therefore that British colonial administration was more aware of geographical i.e., local problems than were some other colonial powers for whom centralization was a desirable feature. There are benefit and costs in both approaches.

ALLOCATION BY PROCESS OR KIND OF WORK

In every organization there are very obvious tasks of a highly specialized nature which can be undertaken only by experts. These experts may be scarce and therefore have to be shared in common with other administrative units or departments. The example of a government printer is usually mentioned in this context as well as others like legal departments or providers of equipment (in old army parlance — quartermasters). Many departments have their own information or public relations divisions or units. It might well be argued that public relations could be a common service rather than spread out over a wide variety of different departments and units, allowing for a fragmented result.

In developing countries it makes good sense to have common services in order to share scarce resources. Experts who can readily be used over a variety of administrative agencies should be shared by those agencies wherever possible. For example, translation or drafting units can be shared to save scarce time energy and resources. For many years the military has had a tendency to require its own specialists. Doctors, for example, can be shared between different branches of the armed services. It does not seem to matter whether the medical man is in the army, navy or air force — at least to the administrator. Separate medical services appear to be an unnecessary expense and dispersion of scarce resources.

The question which arises is how far is it possible to see allocation of processes or kinds of work as a separate category, separate from allocation according to function alone. The answer is that allocation of functions according to the function task or job performed can be varied. Education may be grouped with related social services, police and defence matters can be separated or integrated according to a decision made at the highest level. As regards allocation by process, the task is so specific that it is regarded as quite naturally self-contained.

One point appears to be understood. There is no final best way of organizing the functions which a government department must discharge. For the most part it is true that the functional principle appears to be the most generally accepted form of organization. But from time to time there are many nagging doubts that there are better ways of organizing processes and services. In particular, the feminist movement has appeared to produce a whole new approach to the question of services for women. Many states do appear to pay attention to these special cases. Women's affairs are often given separate status in states where in particular, votes of and for women are a serious matter. At the same time there are often demands for separate administration on religious grounds, particularly by Muslims who demand separate schools for their children.

ALLOCATION OF FUNCTIONS: MERITS AND DEMERITS

On the whole it is worth asking how the administration of tasks should be carried out because despite the great age of the debate the problem of the allocation of functions still remains to be satisfactorily resolved. We have considered four ways in which functions might be allocated — according to the clients or persons to be served, according to function or purpose performed, according to geographical considerations and according to special process or expertise. All of these four approaches have merits and also points of criticism. We may now summarize these as follows:

	Merit	*Demerit*
1. Client	People are seen to be administered within meaningful groups of citizens. Services as appropriate to children, women.	'a tendency to Liliputian administration' (Haldane Report).
2. Function	Creation of ten or twelve basic departments dealing with basic needs, such as, Defence, Trade, Education, Medical.	Overlapping of areas of concern. Loss of contact with people served.
3. Geography	Takes care of strong regional interests. Associates people with the regions.	Logical outcome is devolution and may go against economic rationality.
4. Process	Highly specialized experts work for any department on call — e.g., printing, meterology, scientific research.	Departments lose control over a necessary resource. What suits all departments on average, may not suit particular needs.

On the whole governments only rarely re-think the whole administrative process. What was previously organized suits where it is seen to be functioning adequately. The administrative process is rarely disturbed frequently because other matters appear to be more pressing. The important survey of the allocation of functions principle undertaken during World War I under the chairmanship of Lord Haldane was a case in point. Haldane was a philosopher by inclination who sought to consider the machinery of government according to 'a clear-headed concern for basic principles' (Brown, 1972: 161). Haldane had previously attempted to reform the structure of the British army, according to his logical, philosophical abstract cast of mind or perhaps it would be fairer to say a clear-headed concern for basic principles. Haldane's Committee considered the general idea of the 'machinery of government', but concluded that there were 'two alternatives ... distribution according to persons or classes to be dealt with and distribution according to services to be performed'.

This is an oversimplification of the situation because it ignores other possible approaches, but also suggests that departments can be rearranged without reference to 'politics'. In each department and in each governmental unit there are vested interests, and these interests sometimes resist change. Moreover, in the real world of political parties and interest groups the question of departmental reorganization can sometimes be a highly controversial matter (as described in the diaries of R.H.S. Crossman).

In Britain both the Haldane Committee and the Fulton Report of 1966 suggest that it is possible to be over-rational in the study of public administration. The Haldane view (and the Fulton view later) suggested an Olympian approach to administrative reform, while ignoring the close interaction of party politics and the machinery of government, in the actual day-to-day business of government.

It is not completely possible to separate administrative from political, questions Politicians are often vitally interested in the civil service and often seek to politicize it. Policy decisions can determine administrative structures. Indeed the policy needs of government at any particular time may themselves shape the forms of government. One example is that of defence. In wartime those departments associated with the war effort expand, but in peacetime they must necessarily contract. Another example is the welfare state in which the administration and provision of welfare is a central concern. In many ways, the motto should be 'structure follows function'.

The Haldane Report is still fundamental because the questions which it asked are still constantly asked. A particular example comes from the USA, and concerns the rights of 'minority' groups such as blacks, women, North American Indians and others. These groups demand that services should be administered according to group interest in order to provide for the *clients* rather than for the function performed.

In the developing countries there is often an agreed ratio of groups, communities and even ethnic units to particular posts. In some states, for example, in Malaysia and India it may be laid down in the constitution that certain posts in the administrative service are reserved for particular groups. Hence the principle of allocation according to client rather than according to function or any other feature is still a lively issue.

THE 'HIVING-OFF' OF GOVERNMENT DEPARTMENTS

'Hiving-off' is a term much used in public administration to describe the splitting off of tasks performed within one department, unit or organizaion. The term 'hiving-off' is of course borrowed from the world of the bees. Bees make beehives but at the point at which the hives become too big clumsy or unwieldy it is time for the main hive to cast off its overgrown parts to form separate 'colonies'. In public administration 'hiving-off' is a useful figure of speech to describe the process whereby government organizations or functions are removed from a parent administrative unit to continue an independent existence. A common aspect of 'hiving-off' is the setting up of small agencies or subordinate bodies to carry out specialized services, for example, the administration of an airport, a railway or industry.

'Hiving-off' is not quite the same idea or process as privatization, although the two concepts may be related. An administrative arrangement can be made to hive-off a body either retaining the service provided within government control or by offering it to private companies. Hiving-off is of course an administrative act. Indeed government may operate a broadcasting station, for example, and it may allow private stations to operate broadcasting services too. 'Hiving-off' allows an administrative body the right and power

43

to enjoy special privileges associated with autonomy. Indeed 'hiving-off' may permit a central body the right of making its own decisions regarding its operation, formulating its own plans and, most important of all, administering its own budget.

'Hiving-off' envisages handing over certain defined tasks to other bodies. Often these tasks may be taken from established departments of government and handed over to private concerns (privatization). Alternatively these tasks may be alloted to special agencies with varying degrees of control. We will see benefits as well as disadvantages in the concept of 'hiving-off'.

ARGUMENTS IN FAVOUR OF HIVING-OFF

1. When the number of tasks or functions which government undertakes is reduced, it may have beneficial results both for government itself, as well as for the service or function hived-off. Government itself should be improved when bottlenecks are eliminated at the top levels of administration. At the same time the hived-off body or agency can concentrate on its major purpose. For example, there are likely to be bad effects if a government department were to interfere in a highly specialized agency. A department of transport might create administrative obstacles to the smooth running of a transport network in a state, nation or other territory.

   Regular government departments may be wholly inappropriate to the discharge of some semi-commercial undertaking. We might mention in this connection, a post office (especially telecommunications), banks, transport services either generally or separately, and even many local government activities such as the collection of refuse. The economic benefits from hiving-off these undertakings have been considerable.

2. The administrative benefits from hiving-off are paralleled by other benefits in public administration. The whole operation may save money where subsidies are reduced if not eliminated. A 'hived-off' agency may be able to borrow money, enter into contracts and acquire property. These are important considerations. Where there is less unnecessary administrative involvement in the process of decision-making there is likely to be a better relation with the public. Hiving-off should mean that services can relate directly to public needs and demands.

3. A civil service government department normally has formal, even complicated, rules by which its employees are administered. Personnel management in a hived-off body is usually more flexible in terms of departmental structure than is the case in a formal government department. This flexibility should make the smaller hived-off body much better able to compete in the market place for staff.

4. A hived-off body is visibly producing goods and services. Often it is a single-purpose agency, conscious of its work, and with an incentive to be

productive. By contrast, accountability may be lacking where a particular good or service has to wait decisions from the top-levels of some particular organization.

'Hiving-off' is not however carried out in a vacuum. People may have strong views which are not always grounded in reason, for the discussion of 'hiving-off' often takes place in a context of political argument, controversy and even bitterness. In short, political factors may interfere with the cold logic of, rationally, formulated reforms. Those who wish to 'hive-off' may be regarded as 'empire-builders' who merely want power for themselves in disguise. It is sometimes the case that the setting up of a new secondary agency creates as many problems as it solves. Within the new agency there is likely to be a demand for many of the same resources or facilities which are found in the parent body — personnel officers, accountants, public relations officers, information officers and specialist personnel of all conceivable kinds. In short, the separated unit may become as large as the original parent body, and it could even be the case that the whole problem is no closer to resolution after the hiving-off process has taken place.

One of the few attempts to make out a reasoned case for 'hiving-off' was contained in the Fulton Report (1968) which argued strongly that 'hiving-off' was a useful and constructive approach to the question of accountability. The report said: 'To function efficiently, large organizations, including government departments, need a structure in which units and individual members have authority that is clearly defined and responsibilities for which they can be held accountable. There should be recognized methods of assessing their success in achieving specified objectives' (Fulton, Cmnd 3638: para 145).

Commercial, revenue-earning enterprises are particularly suitable for hiving-off, Fulton argued, and the examples of the Post Office and Atomic Energy Authority were quoted. A wide variety of activities could however be hived-off, ranging from coin and note-producing agencies (the Royal Mint) to air traffic control, and some parts of the social services.

The country in the West in which hiving-off is most fully developed is Sweden. In Sweden, it was pointed out the arrangement is to create central departments which are relatively small and which mainly deal with policy-making. These policy-makers need not necessarily be very experienced. However the autonomous agencies to which management have been hived-off are frequently very experienced administrators.

Policy-making is in Sweden seen as a separate operation from its execution. The former is centralized, but the latter is not necessarily. Of course any rigid separation of policy-making from its execution is wrongfully-conceived but the Swedes appear to have discovered a good balance in their public administration (C.H. Sisson, 1959: 102–3). This experience is sometimes copied but in the United States, the so-called independent regulatory commissions have not been so successful outside the normal departmental structure. There are, of course, many of them, but the American political culture sees special merits in the 'constitutional' approach. The U.S. constitution is always paramount in the thinking of the American public.

In developing countries the benefits of hiving off are possibly financial as much as anything else. It follows that the smaller the government, the less the expense of administration. It also follows that governments will be generally reluctant to pass on any savings in the form of tax reductions. Hiving-off may indeed be the *administrative* equivalent to privatization, the latter having more strictly financial implications.

Developing states can sometimes benefit in their administrative organizations from key ideas or relevant experiences from developed states. The example of hiving-off is helpful in showing that the usual departmental structure is not always the best form of organization. The Fulton Report argued that it was possible to distinguish between departments which provide for services now as opposed to those which have to make extensive plans for the future. In both types hiving-off may have some use, but more particularly the former. But in all cases the object of hiving-off is to make management accountable for their responsibilities and try to find ways to measure, as objectively as possible, the performances of all units of government.

DIFFICULTIES FACING HIVING-OFF OPERATIONS

1. Claims Made for Hiving-off may be Extravagant

If the departmental structure is working well there might be no need to hive-off on 'ideological' grounds. Where bodies are hived-off they still need to be co-ordinated with the machinery of central administration. For example, a post office may be separated from a larger department but the result may not be particularly significant after all. Units should not be unnecessarily multiplied because the new problem which extensive hiving-off creates is that of a need for coordination.

2. Hiving-off may not be Financially Beneficial

Separation of, say, a railway network from a ports administration may be a costly exercise if higher freight rates are charged in consequence. The benefits of large scale enterprise may be lost where are large numbers of small concerns which compete wastefully with each other. This is quite likely to be expressed in terms of cost.

3. Hiving-off may Produce a Fragmented Administration

Hiving-off inevitably creates a number of smaller units, and services may as a result, become fragmented. Hospital services may be centralized in one medical department but where they are not, smaller separate offices may be set up which make for a sense of fragmentation.

46

4. *Hiving-off may Confuse the Public*

People *understand* the meaning of transport, immigration, defence, education and health. A well-established functional office is firmly fixed in the public mind. Social security benefits are seen as a whole by the public. To separate unemployment benefits from supplementary benefits, including the payment of pensions, may make good administrative sense but may be highly inconvenient, if not confusing to the public.

We are faced with the question on a continual daily basis: what are the proper functions of government and how may it best discharge them? In a socialist state the question is unlikely to be asked as readily as in non-socialist states. For example, in the Soviet Union, resources are allocated according to policies and procedures determined by central authorities. General guidelines for all forms of development are determined by the directives and decisions of the Communist Party of the Soviet Union. Ideally, the vast administrative structure within the USSR should mesh together. But as elsewhere, exactly what the administrative structure does is often unclear as Party General Secretary Gorbachev has often indicated.

In the Third World as a whole, the state and its apparatus remains the driving force, largely because there is no other. To ask what are the proper functions of government is less relevant than in the developed capitalist world.

There is no alternative to the state apparatus other than foreign multinational companies firms and organizations. The proper functions of government and the allocation of such functions is harder to answer than is the case in the developed world. In Islamic states it may be impossible to ask questions about the allocation of powers where such matters are determined either by mullahs or family connections. Theocracies may not be amenable to rational public administration (Clapham, 1985: 48–49).

Nevertheless, the ideal of a rational organization of government still remains. To ask questions about the best allocations of services functions and departments may be worthwhile in the interests of 'efficiency'. However it must be realized that the enemies of this 'efficiency' are likely to be patrimonial governments, personal and 'feudal' forms of public administration, well summed up in the Chinese word *guanxi* (connections).

BIBLIOGRAPHY

Brown R.G.S. and Steel, D.R. (1979), *The Administrative Process in Britain*, Methuen 1970, 2nd edition, 1979, London.

Chester D.N. and Willson F.M.G. (1969), *The Organisation of British Central Government*, Allen and Unwin, London.

Clapham, see Chapter One.

Low D. Anthony and Pratt R. Cranford (1970), *Buganda and British Overrule, 1900–1955*, Oxford University Press.

Milne R.S. (1967), *Government and Politics in Malaysia*, Houghton Mifflin, Boston.
Sisson C.H. (1959), *The Spirit of British Administration*, Faber and Faber, London.
Report of the Machinery of Government Committee. (Lord Haldane) 1918, Cmnd. 9230, London.
Report of the Committee on the Civil Service 1966–68. Cmnd. 3638 London.
Lury De, G.E. (1983), *World Encyclopedia of Political Systems*, Longman, London.

4
Administration and Culture

People are different. Cultures vary. However, we may often wonder whether there is a core knowledge known as public administration, which can be utilized; irrespective of cultural differences. We may hope to discover a body of knowledge, in this case public administration, of universal application. We may moreover hope to utilize at least a technical method of administration. For example, it may be that the principles of such matters as delegation, decentralization, span of control, allocation of functions and, of course, computer studies may have great value in all public organizations.

However, technical matters are not the whole of the story. Most administrative matters need to take careful account of social habits and customs. One of the earliest observers to have noticed this point was the eighteenth-century French writer, Montesquieu. He discussed the social habits of many different peoples, and concluded that a form of government is influenced by a variety factors — customs, psychology and climate.

In the final analysis, however, Montesquieu thought that 'a society is essentially defined by its political regime' (Aron, 1965: 56).

More recently, writers have studied both state and plural societies (Smith, 1974; Banton, 1983; Rex, 1986). The term 'plural society' was used by J.S. Furnivall to describe communities which contained several races. A 'plural society' refers to one which tends to 'comprise two or more elements or social orders which live side by side within the same political unit yet without mingling' (Furnivall, 1939: 446 and 1968: 304).

Few writers have seen that the *state* is normally expressed in administrative terms. In fact, the first front-line official to meet the public is most likely to be the policeman. This encounter is likely to be a street encounter. Thus in Britain, in the 1980's the Scarman Report drew attention to the difficulties implicit in the police-community relationship where the so-called ethnic minorities were concerned. But other difficulties are also apparent. A whole system of public administration may be tilted against a particular part of the community. We will consider a number of examples at a later stage in this chapter.

Cultural differences may in the end have to be subordinated to the overall sovereign authority of the state. We would not expect that cultural differences should dictate the wider interests of the community. However, it is true that for centuries, serious conflicts have arisen in the clash of cultures. We may see a conflict between culture and administration in numerous parts of the world. When we use the word 'culture' in the context of the conflict between administrative convenience and cultural values, we need a careful definition. 'Culture is one of the two or three most complicated words in the English language' (Williams, 1976: 76). Williams suggests that the term 'culture' is almost equivalent to society itself.

There are a number of related elements in the modern usage of the term 'culture', including tools used, works of art produced, abstract ideas and values. Indeed, it is much easier to describe cultures, than to define them (Gould and Kolb (eds), 1964: 152–4). Moreover, culture may also well include types of organization and forms of government (Bullock and Stallybrass (eds), 1977: 150).

POLITICAL CULTURE AND ADMINISTRATION

The term political culture has been defined as 'the totality of ideas and attitudes towards authority, discipline, governmental responsibilities and entitlements and associated patterns of cultural transmission, like the education system and even family life' (Robertson, 1985: 263). History, culture and personality are very broad terms which cannot be quantified. Clearly, all administrative acts take place in a cultural context, for there is a obviously Chinese, Japanese, Nigerian, Mexican and Australian way of doing things. If we study Chinese public administration for example, we have to be careful that we do not approach it through Western eyes, if we are Western, and we must be prepared to be criticized for our inability to understand because we are not Chinese. It is of course true that the basic concepts of administration, such as 'participation', 'decentralization', 'ministry' and 'official' are all open to varying interpretations in different cultures. They mean different things to a Canadian compared with a Malaysian.

Even the question of time is cultural. The official who fails to keep an appointment or the citizen who fails to attend on time for interview will have a disturbing effect upon the world of the administrator. In the USA, some American courts have overruled administrative procedures on grounds of unnecessary delay (*McNabb* v. *U.S.* 318 U.S. 332: March 1 1943). Procrastination is not necessarily a vice in a country where life is regulated, not by clocks, but by the sun, rain or seasons. It may however, be something of an excuse to say that cultural differences make a universal study of public administration impossible, that because of cultural differences, systems have nothing to teach each other. Western administrators have greatly developed (even if they have not invented) the necessary paraphernalia of the administrative aspects of the state, including for example, drivers' licences, passports, social benefits, tax systems, computers and traffic engineering. Developing systems must come to terms with these things.

Chinese cultural traditions generally remained resistant to foreign influences. But China itself greatly influenced administrative thought in the past particularly with regard to the education of public administrators/mandarins. The term 'mandarin' itself has proved to be exportable as a concept denoting aloof officialdom. Chinese political culture has always been partly in favour of and partly hostile to bureaucratism (Seymour, 1985). It has been elitist, hierarchical and compliant except perhaps during such upheavals as the Cultural Revolution.

The Chinese government subsequently repudiated the so-called 'Cultural Revolution'. After Mao's death, administrative skills once again become acceptable, and large-scale reforms were instituted in state, party and army, which became an integral part of Deng Xiaoping's approach to development in China. Chinese administrative traditions have stressed such things as the rectification of names, proper language, and ritual. Chinese understand the notion of *guanxi* or personal connections — a concept which sees people in relation to each other rather than through impersonal laws.

The Confucian tradition has had an incalculable impact upon many East Asian cultures including Korea and Japan as well as China itself. As a result, it has not been easy to apply indiscriminately apparently 'scientific' principles of administration and management to non-Western states. Westerners assume that Asians will behave in a given way, that in every Asian 'there is a Westerner trying to get out'. Many mistakes have been made by numbers of Westerners in their dealings with developing states, but the central mistake may lie in the Western view that administration is a neutral concern and that public office is a trust.

China has a long history of administrative control. Indeed, it might be said that China has a bureaucratic culture. It has been said that whatever happens to the Chinese state, 'the long-fingernailed mandarins keep coming back'. The classical mandarinate was a conservative force, the present-day mandarinate (the Chinese Communist Party) is a vehicle, so we are told, of modernization.

In some states, such as Iran, culture is hostile to the modern official; rulers in the Iran of Ayatollah Khomeni; and his successors are controllers of a theocracy (*vilayat-i-fagih*). Officials such as judges must rule according to the precepts of the Koran, the Holy Book of Islam. This implies a severe penal code, for example — cutting off the hands of thieves, the stoning of adulterers and the flogging of those who consume alcohol. Against this background the administration of a complex modern state is made a very difficult proposition.

Government in a strict and fundamentalist state is frequently a matter of not making mistakes. Religious leaders are not necessarily equipped to undertake the responsibility of ruling, especially in the routine administrative sense. However, they are prepared to intervene in the operations of the state if they believe that the actions of the state run counter to the precepts of religion. The case of Iran again, is instructive on this point. The population is obliged to follow a code of proper behaviour or suffer the consequences.

Many people, particularly those living in new states, argue that the colonial legacy was negative in form and content. Post-colonial states often deplore Western institutions as well as Western political ideas. Unfortunately merely

51

calling this process 'imperialism' does not help. The West exports *all* of its ideas along with its technology (Robinson (ed.) 1971: 103–6). However, public administration is a set of ideas and practices largely borrowed from the West. The public sector is dominant in developing countries. Sometimes traditional views on public administration are appropriate, but not often for modernization. Modernizing governments must work with traditional cultures; they must nevertheless subject operational government to critical appraisal seeking to limit or extend power to officials when and as appropriate. Culture should not necessarily be the excuse for rejecting the benefits of modern public administration. Arguments based upon tradition or religious beliefs often predominate in the developing world. However, these arguments sometimes run counter to modernity, to efficiency and equality before the law.

Yet, only limited attention has been given to the problems of public administration which have been seen too much in general and abstract terms. But, public administration is a practical art, which takes place in offices and work places. Police officers, for example, may as suggested have to face conflicts between persons of different cultures. They may also have to enforce laws which fail to satisfy certain groups at least. Where groups complain about discrimination, they may often do so justifiably on cultural grounds. But administrators may often reply that their decisions are frequently criticized as being biased against a minority cultural group when such a decision has been fairly reached. Such a situation may be serious as it indicates a lack of trust most probably on both sides.

ADMINISTRATION AND THE COLONIAL EXPERIENCE

Most former colonies have had to live with the form of administration devised for them by the former metropolitan power. Colonies were conquered settled or otherwise acquired. Many errors were clearly made by the colonizing powers in their trying to enforce their rule, especially when Western and non-Western values came into conflict.

A very well known example comes from India. British rule in India lasted for about four hundred years and the British were forced to come to terms with traditional Indian culture. They were frequently unsuccessful. The East India Company received power to lay down laws for the good government of the affairs of the Company, provided those laws were not contrary to the greater laws of England. However it was assumed that what was good for the Company was good for India. The Company could coin money and punish offenders and in the eighteenth century could also tax the inhabitants of the areas which they ruled. Gradually, especially after 1784 (Pitt's India Act), British control was consolidated and British concepts of local administration became established after the three India Acts of the 1850's (1853, 1854 and 1858). British administrative concepts were gradually grafted on to Indian practice and have been retained in some measure even today.

However considerable cultural difficulties remained. India's two major religions groupings based on Hinduism and Islam presented major challenges to Western administrative modes. These were revealed early on. The Indian 'Mutiny' of 1857 against British rule, revealed the intense complications of attempting to administer a territory where cultural bases were completely at variance with the niceties of administrative convenience. Muslim soldiers refused to comply with an order to grease their rifle cartridges with grease from the flesh of an 'unclean' animal — the pig. The Indian practices of *sati* (wife burning) and *thagi* (ritual murder) were seen as wholly repugnant to Western culture and were suppressed by British administrators, who counted only some 500 administrators and about 65,000 troops.

The problem did not disappear with the end of the colonial period. During the 1980's, a total breakdown appeared in India in the conflict between the Sikh community and the Indian government. Within independent India incompatible cultural attitudes made the administration of common services difficult. The recruitment for the national administration was an especially sensitive issue. In its recruitment for central or national services, the Indian government reserved places for scheduled castes (*harijans*), within a system of competitive examination. These arrangements resulted in riots especially in 1985 when the *harijans* came under attack from Indians who rejected government policy.

In India, today as in many other plural communities, it is necessary to develop a rational administration even when there is political disagreement. Services need to be provided on an equitable basis for divergent communities. In India, communities and groups were catered for separately as communities demanding separate treatment.

India however developed an administrative cadre known as the Indian Civil Service which was an elite body of generalist administrators which inspired the British administrative civil service. The notion of an administrative *class* (which was later criticized in the Fulton Report, 1968) was also taken to Malaya, Pakistan, Britain's African colonies and Hong Kong. As in Britain, examinations and interviews are used to select future senior officials. In India, administrative class officers are the 'steel-frame' of the whole civil service, but these officers constitute a mere two thousand people out of India's ten million civil servants. However, this 'steel-frame' is a foreign importation (although it has been Indianized) and suggests a foreign, not a home-grown culture.

Another example was Nigeria. The British made a colony in Nigeria out of a number of disparate groups: a second task was to turn it into a nation. Nigeria hoped to developed 'the creation of a sense of territorial nationality transcending parochial loyalties of race, ethnicity, religion, language and region' (Rosberg, 1971). Nigeria has had to weld together very disparate groups, in a country where, as Schwartz has said, Mr. Hyde can easily turn into Dr. Jekyll, so a Nigerian can turn into a Yoruba, Ibo or Hausa.

There are, in Nigeria, certain fundamental facts — religion, ethnicity and administrative convenience. Given religious and tribal differences, how can there be developed and appropriate administrative structure? In colonial times, Nigeria was divided into twenty-four provinces, and these administrative divisions could still be useful. However, religious and ethnic questions have continued to tax Nigeria's rulers.

ADMINISTRATIVE DECOLONIZATION: CONTINUITY

To a large extent much of the machinery of central public administration both in Africa and Asia follows the colonial example. Former British colonies naturally and normally resemble each other far more than they do former French colonial dependencies. Anglophone systems show marked differences from Francophone types. For example in the English-speaking states the ministers with their senior permanent officials dominate the scene (even when the ministers are military men). In case of former French territories the administrative structure shows strong French influence. After two or three decades of independence much of the civil service structures and procedures remain similar. Former British colonies recommend and write minutes upwards to senior civil servants, and matters of lesser importance are settled at lower levels. By contrast, French administrative tendencies, which still persist in Francophone states, include an appreciation of the virtues of centralized authority and logical problem-solving (Blondel & Ridley, 1969: 371).

We must of course remember that administration is carried on in a variety of ways in different times and places, consequently many approaches are relative. The colonial legacy was both negative and positive but 'administrative' as distinct from 'political' processes have been seen as more positive than negative. And otherwise, we may ask why the former colonial power's approach to administration has been retained after independence. (Murray and Ballard in Jordan, 1971: 86–7)

Colonial administrators may have made many mistakes but it is remarkable how often administrative procedures and practices continue with only minor alterations long after the removal of the former colonial power. Some institutions like the military, have gone from strength to strength. In many other areas, however, such as educational qualifications and the use of the English or French languages, the influence of the old colonial rulers may often continue virtually unabated. It may be true in general however, that 'colonialism' was above all public administration introduced from afar, and its key symbol was the poll-tax.

In newly-independent states good administration has proved an urgent and important matter, especially as the main agent for change has been the new state itself. New states have proved to be developing states, and they have embarked on extensive programmes of development in education, health planning and public works. In particular many more posts were created at the lower levels. British notions of indirect rule, based for example on Lugard's classic book *The Dual Mandate in Tropical Africa*, had encouraged a two-tier approach — a British expatriate administration over a local indigeneous administration (Lugard, 1922). By contrast, the French colonial administrators were more interested in centralization and assimilation, characteristic French attributes. Local government mattered less to French colonial theorists than the notion of the absorption of colonial peoples into French civilization. In practice French colonial administration was *élitist* (Brogan, 1945: chap 6). Africans and Asians were judged on their 'French-ness' but only a few living in towns modelled on Paris were likely to be absorbed into French culture. After the French Revolution of 1789 the spread of liberal ideas was not welcomed in French overseas territories. Liberty, equality and fraternity were a trilogy of virtues not for export, although the superiority of French administration was.

In both cases there was only a thin colonial veneer in evidence. In British-ruled Nigeria in the 1930's there was a very thin administrative superstructure which overlay one for every 15,000 inhabitants, while in French West Africa, the figures were one for every 4,000. In other places, the former colonists attempted to create a modern administration and policies which both reflected the *ethos* of the colonial power as well as ensure the due authority of the local government. The Dutch model followed that of the United Kingdom in some respects, except that the Dutch tended to envisage a kind of federal relationship between the Crown and overseas territories. The Belgians, especially in the Congo, set up a network of councils in the various provinces of the dependent territory on which Africans served only in an advisory capacity. The Portuguese and Spanish sought to assimilate and integrate their colonial possessions into the mainland — *assimilado* — even the USA has had its colonies — including the Philippines, Hawaii and Puerto Rico.

All of these colonial powers were aware of the overall need for central administration, but not all took many pains about local institutions. British dependent territories saw the development of vigorous local government forms. Ambitious politicans set their minds upon the capture of the central government, both executive and legislative forms. However in colonial times the paramount administrative figure was usually the District Commissioner. The D.C. was looked upon as 'scaffolding' erected while the building of a self-governing state was in progress. Ultimately the 'white scaffolding' would be replaced by 'black' scaffolding. The term D.C. is still employed in many areas, and local government is of critical importance in developing states.

RACE, CULTURE AND ADMINISTRATION

At this point we need to probe the complex question of the impact of race and ethnicity on administration. Where ethnic problems intrude we will find that the process of administration undergoes complex and difficult changes.

One of the most difficult ideas in modern societies is the idea of race. Cultures often, but not always, take their cue from race. Race however, implies government and government implies administration. Demands for separate government according to racial groups presumably implies separate government. Indeed the demand for separate treatment according to race almost always involves separate government.

The problem of defining 'race' is highly contentious, and there are many ways of approaching the problem. One method is to speak of a 'race relations situation' (Rex, 1986: 20). We cannot say what is a 'race' in fact, because Basques in Spain and Tamils in Sri Lanka, for example, are hard to categorize as race groupings distinct from, say, Spaniards and Sri Lankans. However, there is often a considerable degree of conflict between many sub-groups inside a given community. This conflict makes a 'race relations situation'. Sometimes racial conflicts also include class conflicts. Marxists often argue that class conflicts are more 'fundamental' than those based on race.

How does the bureaucrat cope with ethnic and cultural diversity? We may suggest two answers. Firstly, as a civil servant he must follow the policy of the state. Philosophical matters fall outside the province of the administrator for the most part. The civil servant is supposed to carry out the orders of those who may have been chosen in electoral competition for certain value choices. Thus, if the state either protects or promotes the interests of particular ethnic groups, the administrator's task is clear. He is a servant of the state. Normally, state policy will stress harmony or minimize differences, rather than exaggerate them.

The second answer to the question of how administrators cope with ethnic variety is that they use their discretion. This second level is the face-to-face level. Police officers, immigration officers, social workers and even post office officials among many others, meet the public direct. They could take a particularly unsympathetic approach to different community interests. As a result they may lay themselves open to attack when they have dealings with minority ethnic groups. Public service officials, in an ideal world, will be strictly neutral as regards those persons with whom they come into contact. Yet, very often there are many examples of discrimination, some real, and some imagined.

Normally, state policy will stress harmony or minimize differences. Administrators are expected to behave with probity, according to high ethical standards. Nevertheless, ethnic minorities may find themselves at the bottom of the heap. Institutions may be structured in such a way that discrimination becomes literally 'institutionalized'. Some critics will complain of race discrimination, of 'racism' or 'racialism' and public administrators may frequently find themselves at the receiving end of hostile comment as they carry out their duties. At this point we must consider the meaning of certain commonly used terms such as race, racism, racialism and ethnicity.

The term 'race' is supposed to refer to no more than a descriptive category (Bullock and Stallybrass, 1977: 520). However, 'race' and 'race relations' are highly emotional ideas, suggesting difference and, by implication, conflict, over such a difference. The term 'racism' appears to refer to theory or even ideology. Thus some social scientists have actually supported an interpretation of society in terms of race difference. For example, A.S. de Gobineau wrote an Essay on the *Inequality of the Human Races* (1853–55). He was later followed by H.S. Chamberlain with his *Foundations of the Nineteenth Century* (1899). Some of the racist ideas contained in these and other books found their way into the ideology of Nazi Germany. Hitler's rule in Nazi Germany (1933–1945) was at least partly based upon a dogmatic espousal of anti-Jew and anti-black doctrines. A study of the administrative policies of Nazi Germany indicate how Nazi public administration was utilized. Thus, in an attempt to preserve racial purity, all marriages were prohibited when they involved Germans and persons of one-quarter (or more) Jewish race. Jews were not allowed to belong to the professions or engage in business. In short, public administration was closed to Jews in Nazi Germany, except in the context of control and punishment.

Perhaps we may summarize the position as follows: we can speak legitimately of certain concepts relevant to race differences. This we might term *race-ism* or the scientific study of race. However, where people, discriminate against particular (race) groups then we could speak of 'racialism' (Horowitz, 1985). It is difficult to avoid either state or public discrimination (or private discrimination) in many countries in the world today. Such is the sad reality.

ADMINISTRATION AND DISCRIMINATION

Although it is not always generally admitted, racial differences often lead to, or are at least associated with, discrimination (Barzun, 1965: 16). There are many examples of discrimination on racial grounds, of which South Africa could be the most notorious. South Africa's public administration is largely structured on its internal ethnic patterns. Different criteria are applied according to race classification. Four major groups are officially recognized in South Africa (1990) — white, black, coloured and Indian.

Public administration in South Africa saw departments created according to these race categories. Education, for example, is separately administered according to race. At one time there was a Department of 'Bantu' Education, now university education has an increasing degree of integration in some universities. In 1982–3, the expenditure on education upon white pupils was 1.5 times that for Indians, 2.75 times that for coloured (or mixed race) persons and 7 times that for blacks.

The Ministry of Home Affairs in South Africa had powers to decide where married couples of mixed race may live. However since April 1985, persons of different race may now live together, the decision regarding where they may live is an administrative decision. At the same time segregation in housing has led to the creation of so-called black townships. Many public facilities are separately administered. In some cities bus services are segregated. Cinemas were segregated. Theatres are not segregated as a rule. All of these matters are inevitably matters of public administration.

Public administration in South Africa is also fully absorbed in labour matters. Blacks are not permitted to work in 'white areas', unless the need for their labour is established. In 1985 the South African Government announced certain restrictions on the right of blacks to own property in areas outside the designated 'homelands' areas. In 1990 sweeping changes were announced.

However, controls on black movement are unlikely to be fully lifted. All blacks formerly had to possess 'pass books' — a form of internal passport. In 1983, there were 262,904 arrests for pass law offences. According to the 'Grand Design' of South African politics, African tribes belong to African 'homelands'. These are Transkei (1976) (for the Xhosa), Bophutswana (1977), Venda (1979) and Ciskei (1981). The administration of South Africa is based upon an assumption that there exist four provinces (Cape, Natal, Free State and Transvaal) with the six non-independent homelands, but excluding the four 'independent' homelands.

The case of South Africa however illustrates the administrative 'costs' of *apartheid* or separate development. These costs can be illustrated by reference to the administrative expense of creating the so-called Black Homelands for separate tribal/racial groups. There are also administrative costs to be met for other internal policies. Thus there are separate education systems, schools and universities for whites, coloureds, Indians and blacks. A single Ministry of Education for all races has not been accepted, despite a demand for this from black teachers and parents and recommended by the Human Sciences Research Commission in 1981.

The lesson would appear to be that racial differences within one sovereign state almost-invariably carry administrative costs. Public administration in plural societies is complex. Muslims want Muslim schools, colleges and all other relevant amenities whether or not they live in 'Christian' communities. Indeed all social differences suggest more public administration. In many 'Protestant' states, Catholics call upon the authorities to allow, even pay for, 'Catholic' schools. A separate public administration appears to be tolerated where the demand for more bureaucracy comes 'from below'. Where a separate public administration is *imposed*, (even on the 'separate' but 'equal' principle) 'from above', then it may be resented, if not actively rejected.

Racialism or racial discrimination contains a further idea that accepts separate governmental or administrative organization on the basis of race. In general, people who are 'different' are not allowed to compete for employment, or other social rewards. Government is so structured, in a racist culture, so that certain persons of different ethnic background are not permitted to take up positions or status reserved for members of the indigenous culture.

The example of Japan may further illustrate the point. All non-Japanese are *gaijin* (literally 'outsiders'). Koreans resident in Japan for generations find it difficult to compete with Japanese. There is deliberate bias against most Koreans, 750,000 in all, in Japan. Even when a *gaijin* acquires Japanese citizenship, he is disadvantaged. The Japanese prize racial homogeneity, and well understood the comments made by the Prime Minister in 1986 that the average American intellectual standard is lower than that of the average Japanese because of America's blacks and Hispanics.

By any standards, Japanese racialism is *official*. Foreigners (*gaijin*), not Japanese, are fingerprinted. The low-caste *burakumin* are victims of hostile discrimination. In other places government seeks to play down the racial tensions in society. A particularly illuminating example is to be found in Israel. Israel was set up as a home for Jews everywhere, hence its original intention was racial homogeneity. The government of Israel sees itself as the political expression of a Jewish state, although Israel has many Arabs. However, there is clear evidence of the existence of tension, sometimes violently expressed, between Jews who have emigrated from various parts of Europe and Middle Eastern Jews. Racial homogeneity has been difficult to achieve in Israel, but the tension between different forms of Jewry, not to mention between Jews and Arabs, has been considerable.

Discrimination, it must be stressed, exists in a large number of states outside South Africa. In Asia currents of discrimination run deep. Chinese living in various parts of East Asia (and South-East Asia) are often the recipients of adverse treatment. Chinese are not administered as part of the state in many cases but are the object of discrimination. The use of the Chinese language is banned in Indonesia for example. Moreover, ethnic Chinese are refused basic rights, particularly voting rights in several South-East Asian countries. Fear of mainland China has exerted a powerful effect upon the states of South-East Asia. Chinese were seen as subversives or communists even when they were not.

In Malaysia, the position of the Chinese who constitute more than a third of the entire population, is distinctly uncomfortable. Chinese in Malaysia carry identity cards which describe them as Chinese. The state uses its apparatus to ensure that Malays may enjoy preferential treatment. The root of the matter is, of course, economic, given the record of economic success enjoyed by the Chinese as contrasted with Malays. In consequence, Malay politicians use the state apparatus to redress the economic imbalance. Their difficulties are compounded by the growth of Islamic fundamentalism in the region, but there are also other forces which present the central government with particular difficulties.

In Sabah which is part of Malaysia in Borneo, an election held in 1985 actually removed the Muslim-led state government. This election came about partly as a result of the disaffection of groups, (in particular Christians and local Chinese), who demonstrated that ethnic conflicts have serious political implications.

In Sri Lanka, ethnic conflict has been particularly difficult and in the 1980's relations between the Sri Lankans and the Tamil communities in Sri Lanka deteriorated. The Sri Lankan government saw Tamils as 'terrorists'; the Tamils complained of genocide. A *de facto* separation exists between the two racial groups with continual military activity in the north of the country.

In Thailand, second-generation ethnic Vietnamese suffer numerous disadvantages and the state apparatus operates to their disadvantage also. In Thailand ethnic groups such as the Chinese as well as the Vietnamese, may lose their voting rights or educational opportunities. A similar situation exists in Japan where 65,000 ethnic Chinese are excluded from civic life.

Similar problems do however occur in different parts of Asia. In Indonesia, thousands of Chinese were killed after the 1965 communist coup attempt as a matter of deliberate state policy. Other race groups have also experienced problems in Indonesia. In 1975, after a fierce compaign, Indonesia began the process of assimilating East Timor and Irian Jaya. The conflict was in part seen by the Melanesian population and local aboriginals as an attempt to overwhelm their distinctive culture by Muslims from Java.

China too, has been traditionally xenophobic, or anti-foreigner. Blacks living in China, including students, have found many barriers against their involvement in Chinese society. In 1986 and 1989, riots occurred in Beijing which involved black African students. Perhaps unconsciously, the Chinese have discriminated against others on grounds of cultural superiority. Oppression of minorities was commonplace, and until 1949 they were effectively feudal serfs, and minorities were also persecuted in the Cultural Revolution (1966–69). Tibet and Xinjiang were particular areas of resentment at Han domination. Serious rioting took place in Tibet in 1988 and 1989.

In Chinese the words which correspond to the notion of equality under the law was unknown. Confucian law was based on hierarchy. 'The rules of polite behaviour (*li*) do not reach down to the common people; the punishments (*hsing*) do not reach up to the great dignitaries' (Steinberg, 1971: p. 224). Non-Chinese were often described as 'barbarians' in an un-self-conscious way.

The Chinese tended to stress social relationships as part of an intrinsic perceived code without reference to legal obligation. Chinese administration has a long and ancient history and saw stability as the most precious value. Instead of concerning itself with 'liberty', 'citizenship' or abstract justice, Chinese thinkers on the administrative process spoke of the correct 'modes' to be adopted, including the rectification of names.

In Hong Kong, Chinese views on who are to be counted as 'Chinese nationals' after 1997, when China's sovereignty over the former colony is established, has led to certain difficulties for non-Chinese born and brought up in Hong Kong. In particular, the Indian community has expressed fears for the future.

The Middle East is obviously of prime concern for students of ethnicity and administration. A particular and sad case is that of Lebanon where a paramount example of 'religious ethnicity' is tragically evident (Kassis, *International Political Science Review*, 1985: 216–229). Ethnicity in an Arab culture has particular connotations involving folk affinity as well as a specific 'Muslim community of faith'. In administrative terms, Lebanon has shown the dimensions of ethnic non-integration. Christians came to live in the north and Druze in the south, with the Damascus — Beirut highway as the dividing line between two. The other Muslims were also divided as Sunnis and Shiites. For practical purposes, Lebanon become divided according to race or ethnic grouping. Unnecessary contact was reduced to an absolute minimum. 'Thus a road from a Christian town to the coast would be constructed so as to pass a Druze village that lay naturally on the route.... Each group attempted to manage its own affairs without reference to the others' (Kassis, 1985: 225).

Beirut could not be administered as a city, because it was 'an agglomeration of ethnicities' (Kassis, 1985: 227). Middle Eastern conflicts are often the product of a complex of factors, but especially ethnic elements. India has many distinctly different peoples races and linguistic differences. The British entered India in the seventeenth century and found Bengalis, Rajputs, Punjabis, Gujuratis, Sikhs, Muslims, Christians and many other people, but not a nation, recognizably India (Rushbrook William, 1938, repr. 1985). Ethnic diversity in India is a matter of extreme sensitivity, but all public administrators in India must confront the difficulties. Outside the main groupings there are smaller groups actually described as hill tribes whose condition calls for administrative development. A separate administrative set of practices exists for these tribal groups, in particular the Himalayan peoples.

Above all, however, is India's problem of caste, for the divisions of Hindu society whose basic features are hierarchy and tradition. The groups are Brahmin–Kshatriya–Vaisya–Sudra (priests–warriors–merchants–servants). Additionally there exist scheduled castes which have traditionally been given separate treatment.

According to the Indian Constitution, untouchability is abolished and its practice in any form is punishable. But it is a fact that certain castes in India do enjoy a certain status (Rex, 1986: 14, 81). Caste is socially and politically strong in India, and its organization is a formidable exercise in public administration.

Indian public administration is, of course, of gigantic proportions. Apart from the central government itself, and the states, there are many hundreds of state agencies and public undertakings. Competition amongst India's many groups and racial entities extends to competition for employment in the public administration. It is almost universally true that ethnic differences are at their most complex when job competition exists between ethnic groups. Competition for jobs has always been accentuated when such competition has an ethnic aspect. Public service employment is particularly difficult and poses severe political strains. There will in inevitably be charges made of unfair discrimination, sometimes justified, sometimes not.

THE CONCEPT OF ETHNICITY

Almost everywhere, administrators must face up to the massive importance of race, culture and ethnicity, to use a popular term. The word 'ethnic' has tended to be used as a substitute for 'racial'. The term 'racial' has an increasingly derogatory implication, and some other term would be very helpful. What confuses the situation still further is that 'ethnic' refers to a simple statement of fact—namely that people are different. Thus Japanese are different from Chinese. Moreover they *want* to be different. The Japanese in particular 'will instinctively avoid close contact with foreigners, an attitude which isn't so much racism as a fear of the unknown' (George Fields, 'Japan's Race Problem', *Asian Wall Street Journal*, 30 October 1986).

In 1985, Koreans long resident in Japan protested about the 'Alien Registration Law'. (*Keesings Contemporary Archives*, Vol. XXXII, Col. 34556, August 1986). This law required 'aliens' so-defined to be finger-printed, and some 261 persons were involved in difficulties with the police because of their refusal to be finger-printed. It appeared to outsiders to be a matter of race, but the Japanese saw it differently, given their sense of national exclusivity (Weeramantry, 1986).

Culture in Africa if not elsewhere suggests the tribe in one form or other. Despite much disagreement regarding the notion of the 'tribe' it has clear relevance to the calling of public administration (Apthorpe, ed. Scott, 1970: 92). *Tribes* in so far as they exist, are in a sense *nations*. *Tribes* characteristically have a strong sense of language and culture, much stronger perhaps than is the case with nations. For with the tribe as with the nation, there exist sentiments of kinship which continually force themselves upon politics and administration (Lewis, 1965: 25).

One of the strongest sentiments is for tribes to be self-governing-self-administering or both (Zolberg, 1966: 46–47). If we assume that there are such things as tribes, then it is important to ask how tribes are constituted for the purpose of organization in the modern world. Tribes aspire to become nations and nations may see themselves in due course as states. The problems of modernity are then forced upon them.

Some observers reject the notion of tribalism as unacceptable, because 'tribalism' was invented by Westerners to explain, so they argue, certain social facts. There is a somewhat grudging acceptance of the concept of ethnicity. The term *ethnic* in fact comes from the Greek *ethnos* which actually means tribe or even race. The point is that ethnicity is applicable to Western as well as non-Western states (Robertson, 1985: 111–2). In the Third World so-called ethnic *divisions* are usually the raw materials with which scholars have to work.

So we are brought back to the question of asking questions about tribes and ultimately, races. Let us consider the following: 'A member of a Nuer age-set can recognize a fellow member anywhere by the scars imprinted on his face at the time of circumcision. This perhaps sums up the matter; there is recognition, communication and shared experience common to all members of the tribe, and to no others' (W.J. Mackenzie, 1967: 204).

Many post-colonial territories agonize over ethnic questions. In spite of hopes for ethnic unity rather than division after independence, many conflicts between tribes and other ethnic groups persist. There exists in many states a condition of 'internal discord predicated upon ethnic diversity' (Connor, 1973: 2). Even old states like the United Kingdom find new problems with would-be secessionist groups and sub-groups. The process was summed up by the English historian Maine: 'England was once the country in which Englishmen lived: Englishmen are now the people who inhabit England' (cited in Jones, 1966: 56).

In its most extreme form, ethnic differences lead to a demand for secession, a desire to be separately administered in a separate territory. The wish is to have a 'space to which identity is attached by a distinctive group who hold or covet that territory and who desire to have full control over it for the group's benefit' (Knight, 1982: 526 and 1985: 251). Such an idea has important political and constitutional implications. Above all, it has implications for public administration, as seen in the Soviet Union in 1990, with its secessionist difficulties.

Self-determination then, has important implications for public administration. People almost universally wish to be administered separately. Between 1804 and 1930, 18 Central and South American states were recognized as independent states. From 1848 the idea of self-determination grew rapidly. Independence in the 19th century in various forms was achieved by Italy, Romania, Luxembourg, Serbia, Montenegro, Germany, Bulgaria, Norway, Albania, Canada, Cuba, Panama, Australia, New Zealand and South Africa. This process was intensified during the present century. The ethnic factor has important political and administrative implications.

CONCLUSION

It is important at all times for the student of public administration to be aware of the cultural values which lie behind the administrative process. Indeed, it is not possible to describe the task of the administrator without reference to the *values* both of the administrator as well as of the administered. It is futile for the observer to proceed if he forgets for one moment that people are the raw material of the art and science of public administration. It therefore follows that if there are cultural differences between one community and another then administration of needs and services must always be arranged accordingly (Self, 1972: 13).

Patterns of administration which suit, for example, Islamic peoples, might not necessarily suit Japanese or Latin Americans. Indeed the difficulty is further compounded for public administrators because they are aware that the major academic writings on the subject were compiled largely in the

West. What suits Western peoples does not always suit peoples living outside Western states.

Nevertheless, if we are to make some progress, we must assume that the knowledge of public administration has something to offer everybody, especially in understanding something about the process of government as well as making it more rational and more modern at the same time. There is no real difficulty about the technical aspects of administrative practice, such as budgeting, some aspects of planning and even the provision of special services. Western administrative skills are useful, if not necessary, to development. However, it is always most important, to take account of what might be called the 'cultural' aspects of administrative practice. Recruitment of civil servants for example, may be made on merit tested in examinations or by patronage. In Malaysia, for example, recruitment to the public service appears to favour Malays as against other races. In South Africa, Afrikaners have tended to fill the higher ranks of the civil service. Public administration is a cultural phenomenon in many parts of the world.

We may imagine that cultural differences can be minimized by modern trends and developments, including the extensive use of word-processors and sophisticated methods of training. At the same time the procedures of modernity make little impact when it comes to basic matters of culture. In Japan and in Mexico for example there is a strong sense of the relationship between patrons and clients (oyabun-kobun in Japan, and patronal — obrero in Mexico). Government officers may be patrons, handing out jobs, services and even cash, though they should be seen as servants of the public at large rather than servants of particular groups and interests.

Many years ago the British Prime Minister Disraeli said: 'What words truly mean few men can say, but with words we govern men.' Western language has attempted to find concepts and the words which give effect to these concepts. In their European context these terms make sense for two reasons. Firstly, the terms were derived from Western experience and examples might be 'legislative', 'executive', 'judiciary' and even 'administration'. Secondly, the terms usually have Latin or perhaps Greek, origins, which relate to Western European culture. Nevertheless, Western students of public administration persist in applying Western modes of thought to non-Western environments. Westerners have devised certain procedures which are applied mechanically to problems. Abstract law and procedure is however sometimes difficult or inappropriate in some contexts.

When we come to consider non-Western states and nations we often discover a totally contrasting approach to government and administration. In many cases the best illustration of this proposition is found in language itself. Some languages in some states for example, have no direct words to explain the idea of a separate judiciary or 'law' itself. In the Sino-Korean tradition of East Asia, the term 'law' has had the meaning of punishment rather than an abstract set of rights.

We have stressed that the state and its policy-makers face highly delicate problems when confronted with questions relating to culture, race and ethnicity. In many cases administrators are able to contain or conciliate racial differences. On other occasions they fail to satisfy the demands of some of the constituent parts of the state. On some rarer occasions in some states, administrators may even exaggerate and inflame racial differences. However in the end there can be no substitute for the consistent use of objective formal rules applied as fairly as possible.

The most certain fact about race and ethnicity lies in the growth of special forms of administration to implement governmental policy where ethnic groups demand separate treatment there must inevitably be a bureaucratic cost to be paid. To demand rule by one's own racial or ethnic grouping will necessarily increase the administrative costs. A new level or tier of government for culturally different groups is an expensive undertaking.

BIBLIOGRAPHY

Adu A.L. (1969), *The Civil Service in Commonwealth Africa*, Allen & Unwin, London.

Aron Raymond (1965), *Main Currents in Sociological Thought*, Penguin.

Banton Michael (1988), *Racial and Ethnic Competition*, Cambridge University Press, Cambridge.

Barghoorn Frederick C. (1972), *Politics in the USSR*, 2nd edition, Little, Brown & Company, Boston.

Barzun Jacques (1965), *Race: A Study in Superstition*, Harper & Row, London.

Blondel Jean and Ridley Fred R. (1964), *Public Administration in France*, Routledge, Kegan Paul, London.

Brogan Denis (1945), *The Development of Modern France*, Hamish Hamilton, London.

Bullock and Stallybrass (eds), see Forewords.

J. Connor (1973), *The Politics of Ethnonationalism*, Journal International Affairs, 27.

Furnivall John S. (1939), *Netherlands India — A Study of a Plural Economy*, Cambridge University Press, Cambridge.

Furnivall John S. (1968), *Colonial Policy and Practice*, Cambridge University Press, Cambridge.

Gould Julius and Kolb, eds., 1964 *A Dictionary of the Social Sciences*, Tavistock, London.

Gutteridge William (1968), *The Military in Africa*, Methuen, London.

Hough Jerry (1969), *The Soviet Prefects*, Harvard U. Press, Cambridge, MA.

Horowitz D.L. (1985), *Ethnic Groups in Conflict*, Berkeley, U.S.A.

Jones E. (1966), *Human Geography*, Praeger, New York.

Kassis Hanna E. (1985), *Religious Ethnicity in the World of Islam*, International Political Science Review, Vol. 6, No. 2.

Knight David B. (1985), *Territory and People or People and Territory*, International Political Science Review, Vol. 6, No. 2.

Jordan (1971), see Chapter 1.

Lewis W.A. (1965), *Politics in West Africa*, Allen & Unwin, London.

Lugard Sir F.D. (Baron Lugard), (1922), *The Dual Mandate in Tropical Africa*, Blackwood, Cameron 1939.

Mao Zedong, in Stuart R. Schram (1971), *Mao Tse-Tung and the Theory of the Permanent Revolution*, The China Quarterly, April–June 1971, No. 46.

McKenzie W.J. (1967), *Politics and Social Science,* Pelican, London.

Rex John (1986), *Race and Ethnicity,* Open University Press, Milton Keynes.

Robinson R. (ed). (1971) *Development in New States* (Cambridge).

Scott Roger (ed.) (1970), *Politics of New States,* Allen and Unwin.

Seymour, James D. (1985), *The Government of China,* in Curtis Michael, *Introduction to Comparative Government,* Harper.

Simis, Konstantin (1982), *USSR: The Corrupt Society,* Simon and Schuster.

Steinberg (1971), *Law, Development and Korean Society,* Journal of Comparative Administration, Vol. 3, No. 2, 1971, p. 224.

Weeramantry G.C.W. (1986), *Human Rights in Japan,* Fontana.

Zollberg A. (1966), *Creating Political Order: The Party States of West Africa,* Rand McNally, Chicago.

Part II
The Profession of Government

5
The Administrative Profession

Many hundreds of thousands of people are professional administrators in the public sector. Some are 'born' administrators in that they have the gift of, or feel for organization; some are 'made' administrators, almost as it were by accident; some have administration 'thrust on them' when they do not wish it. In Sweden approximately 40 per cent of the population are employed in the public sector; in Great Britain the figure is 32 per cent, in the USA about 20 per cent, but in Japan probably no more than 10 per cent.

There is a profession of administration though there is no real agreement regarding the correct training for administrators and, unlike medicine or law, there are no generally acceptable qualifications. Administrators are found within these and other professions, and they are professionals within a profession. In fact as administration is an all-pervasive activity it is difficult to draw hard and fast lines around something which might be called a profession of administration. We are largely concerned with public administration and its ramifications in the broad area of the public sector.

The ideal public servant is of course one who operates automatically — which explains perhaps the prevalent use of computers in government. In short, the ideal *public* servant would be one who requires nothing except to be plugged in. Let us consider some examples. A parking meter is a machine which performs a public service that of allocating space for money. The parking meter *is* a public servant. Moreover 'he' collects the money to pay for 'his' performance.

A second example would be a traffic light. A traffic light performs a public service of high sophistication. By producing colours with well-understood meanings, traffic lights convey messages of great sophistication. The traffic light fits traffic to traffic, traffic to people, people to people in a matching exercise of impressive skill. *At bottom, administration is often really a process of matching laws, things, money and people.* The machine can do these things as well as human administrators. But there are limits to the role of the machine as an administrator.

The task of the professional administrator is to serve the public within fixed rules, but which rules are not always clear. Paradoxically, the administrator attempts to follow 'fixed' rules which are very frequently not fixed. The professional administrator does not always know where he is free to act and where he is constrained. A good example is to be seen in the operations of the European Economic Community, where administrators attempt to apply the common rules of the community irrespective of political differences between the twelve participant states.

Administration may not be as volatile as politics but it is essentially a *human* undertaking. Administrators may of course exercise political powers, but everyone expects these to be exercised in a non-partisan spirit. However pressures upon civil servants have everywhere increased, for example in Britain, as a series of articles in the The Times in 1986 argued. (*The Times*, March 24, 25, 26, 1986).

Many people have recognized that the use of administration confers powers but that these powers must be exercised responsibly in all cases. The difference between the flashing traffic light and the passionless meter and the public servant is to be found in a idea — that is *discretion*. Discretion is however a complex concept, one which cannot always be defined in simple terms. Perhaps it refers to the 'necessary exercise of human judgment'. Saint-Simon argued that administrative ability is the primary requirement of a good statesman, and he distinguished between the administration of things and the politics of men. The administrator has important work to do, beyond the level of the machine. Matthew Arnold saw the interconnection between art of discretion and the science of government. 'He who administers governs, because he infixes his own mark and stamps his own character on all public affairs as they pass through his hands'.

Administrators have a much larger area of discretion than for example judges. Judges follow either the Common Law (in Anglo-Saxon systems) or they attempt to apply the laws in particular made by Parliament. Lawyers are professionals who may use their knowledge of the law to advise the public. Administrators have the complicated task of applying the rules laid down by parliament through particular cases.

Some writers have despaired of 'politics' and 'politicians' and have concluded that the administrator is the saviour of the state. Perhaps the most famous quotation on the subject comes from Alexander Pope. 'For forms of government let fools contest; whate'er is best administered is best!' By contrast, early communist writers also concluded that administration was a simple matter which could be undertaken by anyone. This idea is prevalent in Marx, Lenin and the authors of the *A.B.C. of Communism (1922)* Bukharin and Preobazhensky (See also Carr, 1966, 1917–1923 (1): Chap 9, Note A). The 'government of men' (i.e., politics) would in the ideal socialist order, give way to the *'administration* of things'. Socialist states have discovered that expert administrators have an important role to play. The case of China is highly illustrative of this point. Experts who were reviled, degraded and punished, have, since 1976, been gradually reinstated.

However, after the events of June 1989 when over an estimated 1000 people were killed by the army, China saw a return to hard-line ideological communism.

THE ADMINISTRATIVE FUNCTION IN A 'LIBERAL STATE'

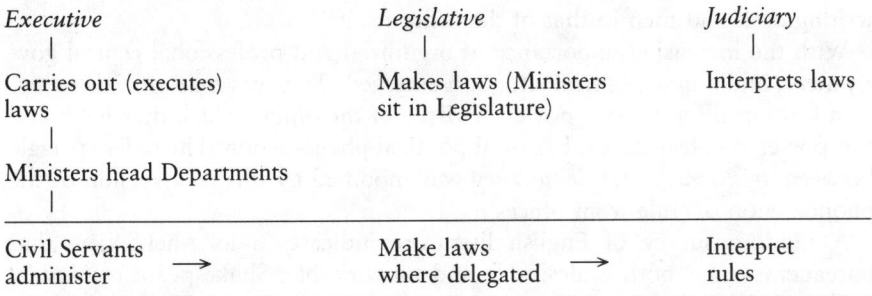

Executive	*Legislative*	*Judiciary*
|	|	|
Carries out (executes) laws	Makes laws (Ministers sit in Legislature)	Interprets laws
|		
Ministers head Departments		
|		
Civil Servants administer $\rightarrow$	Make laws where delegated $\rightarrow$	Interpret rules

PUBLIC SERVANTS MAY MAKE, CARRY OUT/INTERPRET RULES, REGULATIONS

Administrators in liberal states have increasingly moved into areas in the public sector where they were previously not expected to be, into law-making for example. The extensive activities of administrators is not of course new as we shall discuss later but what is new is the combination of administration and the making of laws, and indeed of *adjudicating* on laws also. Of course it might be properly argued that there have been in history many administrative states, and that officials have traditionally been 'generalists'. However in modern times, communications technology has made a vast difference to 'bureaucratic' states.

The twentieth century is distinguished by the large number of bureaucrats in a modern social service state but also by the fact that they have at their disposal modern weapons of communication and modern records as shown by Max Weber. Since Weber wrote, the need to understand the power of bureaucratic communications has been allied much more intensively to modern technology, including such devices as computer records, word processors and telecommunications. These developments lend a greater weight to the analysis of Weber which saw the growth of bureaucratic government as a most significant development.

BUREAUCRACY AND UNPOPULARITY

The term 'bureaucracy' must be used with great caution, largely because it is a term of abuse for most people. To describe a person or process as 'bureaucratic' is to denounce it harshly. In fact bureaucracy should be a mere description of a form of government — one in which officials exercise a good deal of power. Bureaucracy is both a word and a concept. As a word it was borrowed into English from the French *bureaucratie*, but soon absorbed a

71

derogatory implication. The original meaning of the term 'bureau' referred to the baize used to cover desks. The word was transferred to the idea of a writing-desk and then to that of the office itself.

With the increasing importance of organized and professional central government, and a new political situation emerged. This was that officials enjoyed a form of discretionary power in virtue of the *offices* which they held, and this power was seen as a substantial political phenomenon. The older struggle between *aristocracy* and *democracy* was modified by this new version of the phonomenon of 'rule from offices'.

A random survey of English literature indicates a long-held view that bureaucracy was both undesirable and unworkable. Shakespeare in *Hamlet* spoke of the 'insolence of office' to indicate the often held image of the remote and surly official. John Stuart Mill (1848) argued against the concentration of all the power of organized action in a dominant bureaucracy. The French writer, Honoré de Balzac (1836), said that bureaucracy was 'the great power wielded by pigmies ... a government as fussy and meddlesome ... as a small shopkeeper's wife'. In *Little Dorritt* (1857), Charles Dickens described the whole science of Government as the Circumlocution Office. Thomas Carlyle in *Latter-day Pamphlets* (1850) wrote of the 'continental' nuisance called 'Bureaucracy'. The term 'red tape' became popular to refer to the tape which was used to wrap around files and led the *Daily News* (1871) to bemoan the 'routine of tape, wax, seals and bureau-ism'.

The scientific and analytical study of bureaucracy began with the German political theorist, Max Weber. For him, bureaucracy is the formal codification of the idea of rational organization. A bureaucracy is characterized by legal rules, a salaried administrative staff, a well-developed specialization of function, the authority of the (non-hereditary) office, and the keeping of written records and documents.

To take it even further, the whole world was depicted as drifting towards a greater spread of officialdom. The idea of bureaucracy helped to make the world a more rational place. All the great ideas of the world meet certain social facts and forces. Socialism for example, was incomplete without the information and organization of the files. Inspired leaders eventually must come to terms with the need for humdrum organization and routine (called the bureaucratization of charisma). Even capitalism and socialism may be overtaken by the victory of bureaucracy (Rizzi, 1939/1985: 88).

Weber's own words are themselves worth quoting. In the course of giving a talk, he said: 'But horrible as the thought is that the world may one day be peopled by professors (laughter) — we would retire on a desert island if such a thing were to happen (laughter) — it is still more horrible to think that the world could one day be filled with nothing but those little cogs, little men clinging to little jobs and striving towards bigger ones — a state of affairs which is to be seen once more. This passion for bureaucracy as we have heard it expressed here, is enough to drive one to despair'.

Weber was familiar with the European continental tradition. Originally public servants were the king's servants. The citizen gave them obedience, not expecting to question his authority. The civil servant was almost by definition an authoritarian, somewhat fearsome, figure. The notion of the civil servant as accountable to the 'public' was quite foreign to the traditional European royal official. He was not a public *servant* except of the king. Only in the twentieth century have demands been made for controls to be developed over the operations of officialdom (F.J. Goodnow, 1905: 368).

One argument against Weber is that, like many other opponents of the presumed evils of bureaucracy, he is somewhat romantic. In a mass collectivist age, bureaucracy is perhaps inevitable. Each individual is of course entitled to fair and equitable treatment by public officials. However the hard facts of social organization call for officials to implement social policies. A complicated social service cannot exist without records, but Weber particularly noted the use of *files* which in fact provide in part an objective record of the lives of citizens. It is true that the insidious build-up of information on files has worried many people, and has led to the feeling that nothing is private any longer. The growth of licensing and the extensive use of credit cards is something which Weber could not have forseen.

In our own days attempts have been made to reduce the amount of such secrecy and to open files to public view. The Freedom of Information Act was first passed in the USA in 1966, and amended in 1974. Under this Act, any individual citizen, non-citizen or company may request to see, by right, any documents in which he is interested which have been produced from any agency of the federal government. No reason is required for wanting the information. Certain exceptions are made — defence and foreign policy, trade secrets, and medical files amongst others. If a refusal is forthcoming from the agency questioned, the onus is on the department or agency concerned to explain the reasons for non-compliance.

By contrast, the Official Secrets Act in Britain prohibits the unauthorized disclosure by any public servant of any information which he has acquired in the course of his duties. Even more tenacious is the control exerted over state and party officials in socialist countries: communications between authority and the public are largely if not wholly a one-way traffic — a case naturally very true in the USSR (White, 1979, 75–83).

POLITICAL MASTERS AND PUBLIC SERVANTS

A distinction may be drawn for convenience between *politics* and *administration*. It is a convenient distinction through not necessarily a hard-and-fast one. Perhaps the simplest approach would be to see administration (like government) as regular, procedural and predictable, while politics is irregular, spontaneous and unpredictable. In the Westminster model, the conventional wisdom presumes that ministers, or political actors will be charged with implementing the policy platform of the victorious party at election time. Civil Servants will on the other hand, attempt to make a workable policy out of an ideology. It has been frequently pointed out that civil servants are not always servants and that politicians are not always the masters (Crossman, 1977; Aberbach, Putnam and Rockman, 1981: Chapter 3).

The conventional distinction between *politics* and *administration* is that politics dominates, sets the goals or objectives, while *administration* is the servant to translate policy objectives into action. Politics is spontaneous, controversial and partisan, on this analysis, while administration is routine, without passion and indifferent as to whichever political party is in power. The classical view is that politics and administration are two different ways of looking at the world and that they represent different careers. They interact only where they touch but in general inhabit a related world.

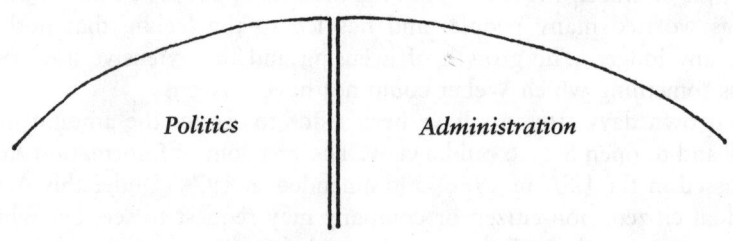

Politics   *Administration*

A contrary view is that the distinction between *politics* and *administration* is artificial and unreal (Campbell and Peters, 1988: 79–87). Power in the hands of some senior civil servants may in fact exceed that of some politicians. Politicians have a vested interest in politicising the senior ranks of the civil service and civil servants are often tempted to manipulate politicians. Politics is not necessarily an activity suitable for persons designated as politicians. Political skills, in the sense of having a capacity to bargain or to persuade or to reach acceptable compromises, are not the monopoly of particular individuals, not even professional politicians. Moreover, in lower levels of government, in local government for example, politics and administration are frequently extremely close.

Perhaps the most important fact about politics lies in its spontaneity. It is not possible to know when an issue is likely to arise, or when it is likely to become a significant, important or even critical element in the life of a community. Administration, it is true, sees an untroubled regularity. The key idea is represented in the word 'procedure'. An official seeks to discover and follow 'procedures'.

For the administrator, he needs to pour all his efforts into achieving the maximum degree of regularity and, consistency into the system — which is what his notion of efficiency often amounts to. The secret of the successful bureaucrat is that he has his major interest in the *how* not the *why* of policies. Politics addresses itself to the content of policies rather than to the means of policies. Administrators invest their emotions not in the substance of policies or arguments about the desirability of policies, but rather in procedural questions.

However there are frequent occasions when these stereotypes break down, as issues arise which are not easily processed by the administration. One writer put the matter as follows: 'Political activity is like lightning, in that it may suddenly strike into any corner of the administrative system, but only rarely does so. The great bulk of administrative operations continues in political obscurity, and the main interactions between politics and administration, occur at the top levels of government' (Self, 1972: 151).

The classical picture of a separate administration outside the struggles of party politicians has been recently challenged in Britain — the home of the idea. According to the classical notion, politics was for politicians, administration for administrators. However several developments have created in Britain like elsewhere a new atmosphere (Plowden, 1985: 393–414).

The political neutrality of civil servants is no longer taken for granted. Civil servants respond to policy and politics as well as to administration. A noted case concerned the senior civil servant Clive Ponting. Ponting was faced with being made party to what he saw as a deliberate deception of Parliament by a government minister. In consequence, Ponting broke the *convention* of bureaucratic neutrality (as well as the *law* in the form of the Official Secrets Act 1911), in leaking official documents to a member of Parliament. Ponting was prosecuted under section 2 of the Act, and was found guilty. The judge argued that the government of the day had the right to plead 'public interest', and to protect its policy secrets.

The distinction between politics and administration still appeared in 1985 to the British judiciary to be worth sustaining (Drewry, 1985: 203–12). In 1986 the government (of Margaret Thatcher) still supported the idea that ministers should assume responsibility for 'politics', and the related political neutrality of officials (Cmnd 9916, 1978). Of course, the idea of separate politics and separate administration has suffered a severe blow as a result of the case of Clive Ponting (as well as a similar case in 1986 involving Sarah Tisdall who also leaked certain documents to the press).

The *idea* of the political neutrality of officials nevertheless is fundamental to the present understanding of the British constitution (Thomas, 1986, *The Times Higher Educational Supplement*, 17 October 1986: 14; Parris, 1969: 147). Such an idea is however constantly under attack, because politics cannot be separated from administration on every occasion. The separation of politics from administration is a relative, not an absolute idea. In the USA, for example, the federal civil service is much more 'political' than is the case in Great Britain. In France, ministers are assisted by officials who advise on 'political' matters in a special policy-making unit called a *cabinet* (Fortin, 1988).

In most developing countries, administration and politics are generally much closer than is the case in Westminister. A good example would be the case of Africa's most populous country, Nigeria. There have been several changes of regime, including military and civilian types in Nigeria since 1960. Many civil servants were dismissed in the 1970's in a purge of administrators. Nigeria's military rulers turned the Nigerian civil service into an instrument of military rule. However in a country prone to military take-over like Nigeria, both political institutions and public administration are weak (Ademolekun, 1986: 169). In Nigeria, as in a number of other 'Third World' countries, there is not sufficient agreement about the very bases of government, its purpose, organization and workings. Hence public administration suffers, not only in Nigeria, but throughout Africa generally, where 'there is no country where the civil service norms of anonymity and political neutrality are respected'. Moreover, 'Efforts to enforce accountable behaviour of civil servants have been largely unsuccessful' (Ademolekun, 1986: 170). The solution would appear to call for a *career* civil service characterized by 'permanence, impartiality, meritocracy and professionalism' (Ademolekun, 1986: 184).

By contrast, the territory of Hong Kong offers an example of a career public administration in a non-political (in the sense of party-political) context. In the past, Hong Kong has been an almost 'pure bureaucracy', i.e., an administrative state, in which all decisions could be taken on grounds of administrative convenience — a benevolent colonial model.

In consequence, political argument was kept to a minimum, and it was possible to make and execute policy with a minimum of fuss and delay. For example, an underground railway network was exceptionally quickly constructed in the seventies. Hong Kong's bureaucrats took decisions on a bureaucratic justification alone (Harris, 1980: 113 and 1988).

The future of such a system may be questionable. Even before 1997, when the 'colony' is to be transferred to Chinese sovereignty, broadly 'political' changes may be anticipated. These are liken to threaten 'many organizational traditions and assumptions on which the Hong Kong civil service has been based' (Scott and Burns, 1984: 291). Hong Kong is no longer an 'administrative state' though it is a state in which the administration is dominant. In cultural terms, Hong Kong is more comfortable with 'bureaucracy' than it is with 'democracy', or 'politics'. Both the British and Chinese aspects of Hong Kong's development have been 'bureaucratic', with a marked distaste for 'politics'. Many observers have been inclined, in this regard, to contrast the economic success of Hong Kong with the economic tardiness of China. They have further attributed Hong Kong's success to its emphasis on good administration and its rejection of strident ideology, so marked in Maoist China. Even in the 1990's, China appears to stress the need for officials to meet political tests and applicants for government offices must pass such tests which are applied both to himself and to his family.

The question of the reality of the distinction between politics and administration — or between the politician and administrator has often been raised in this book. While in the real world bureaucrats and politicians do similar work, there are many variations. In Japan for example, of 14 Prime Ministers since 1947, 7 have been former bureaucrats usually in the Ministry of Finance or Foreign Affairs. The bureaucracy in Japan is correctly seen as the senior partner in the relationship with politicians. The most senior administrators in Japan (the supreme first-graders) consist of only about 1,000 persons. In the developing world generally, administration is not seen in abstract terms. Jobs are often related to tribe, ideology or political persuasion. Administrators may be chosen in the first place to reflect certain social facts such as a need to preserve racial or ethnic balance, rather than their administrative capacity.

SPECIALISTS AND GENERALISTS

At the top-levels of government there are a number of people whose main expertise is nothing except administration. Of course political figures are not really expected to know anything very much about their various departments. They might not stay long. Civil servants at the summit of the profession of government are invariably 'generalists'. Often these people were trained in the humanities and were able to take an abstract view of administration. They were often put into a special 'generalist' category. They exemplified a particular view of administration which saw administration as an art, not a science, which was intuitively grasped, in the bones, as it were.

There is a view that at the highest level of administration, at the mountain-top level, the view is everywhere the same. Such a notion was enunciated by Walter Bagehot, who, writing in 1867 said: 'The summits of the various kinds of business are, like the tops of the mountains, much more alike than the parts below but it needs travelling to know that the summits are the same' (Bagehot, ed. Crossman; 199). Put in this graphic way the argument was that administrators must move from post to post at the highest level — the principle of rotation — bringing as they move a *general* appreciation of the needs of administration.

The qualities of a good general administrator were summed up by Lord Bridges, one-time head of the British civil service as follows:

1. Power of rapid analysis
2. A capacity to recognize the essential points in a situation
3. A sense of timing
4. The capacity to think of likely developments a year ahead

The administrator on this analysis is akin to the artist or the don. The administrator is possibly a higher order of beings (different from a mere manager). He must have style, vision, a sense of history, and an almost religious devotion to public service.

The Chinese classical tradition seems to suggest a distinction between intellectual and manual capacities. Mencius said that those who use their minds should rule and should rule those who labour with their muscles. In modern China this distinction has largely disappeared. During the Mao régime China's rulers were expected to be ideologically rather than professionally, sound, i.e., 'red' rather than 'expert'. Generalists were preferred to specialists, provided of course that they were ideologically sound. It is however, easier to state the problem than to solve it; the generalist is at the end of the day, a specialist too — in being a generalist.

SPECIALISTS

In 1853, the famous Northcote-Trevelyan report on the structure of the British civil service enunciated the famous distinction between administration as 'intellectual' and administration as 'mechanical' work. Administration seen as 'intellectual' clearly involved 'policy', whereas 'mechanical' work referred to the routine tasks of day-to-day departmental work. Sir Ivor Jennings in his classic *Cabinet Government* showed how, at the top levels of British Government, there were a number of people who were expert in nothing except generalist administration.

A contrast, of course, is made between generalists, and professionals, such as engineers, medical personnel, and lawyers who actually are members of professional skill bodies. The term professional or specialist was first used to depict the person whose skills were not necessarily or primarily in administration but were technical, special and supportive. The professional might be seen as the tool of the amateur. The generalist had no professional skills. Nevertheless at the very top, he had a role to play. The result may well be to establish a very British approach to administration — that of government by amateurs advised by experts.

The 'laws' of organizations however appeared to suggest that those who could do everything but, paradoxically, nothing in particular, occupied a strategic role in any organization. Moreover, the man who had skills became downgraded by those who had none except a somewhat nebulous capacity to generalize. It was an apparent inversion of priorities. Some of it may have had something to do with the fact that *special* techniques and knowledge may become outdated in a matter of years. What was actually learned in a professional capacity may in fact well be out-of-date a mere decade or so afterwards. What the professional actually retains may be no more than a diminishing body of knowledge.

The humanist was often a snob, believing that technology is a sort of barbarism, and that the man who mends the machine is a philistine. To this end the humanist could quote Plato and Aristotle (because they were normally the beneficiaries of a classical education). Aristotle sneered at people who (like the artisans) had to ask why we did certain things. To be always asking 'what is the use of' is a question beneath the dignity of a cultured gentleman. After all, we may ask, what is the use of a baby?

THE FUTURE OF THE DEBATE

In some countries like the USA, the public servant is seen as an expert with some particular tasks to perform. The task of operating the economy it is argued, is best left to private capitalist enterprise. Public servants are charged with certain tasks, narrowly defined, but which are seen as the province of the 'state'. The US case differs somewhat from the European, particularly British, example. In eighteenth-century Britain, the state was seen not as a benefactor but as 'pain'. Where the state at that time touched the citizen, a *painful* operation ensued. Judges, soldiers and executioners were the typical public servants, and they were practitioners of the 'painful' aspects of the state. They were professionals of pain.

In the twentieth century, professionals serve the welfare state not as practitioners of pain but practitioners of benefits. In the USA perhaps public servants are still rather closer to the eighteenth-century model. In the developing states the problem of the generalist and the specialist still remains largely because the problems of policy-making invariably call into question the roles of both the generalist and the expert. Tensions on this score appear to be universal.

BIBLIOGRAPHY

Auerbach Joel D., Putnam R.A. & Rockman B.A. (1981), *Bureaucrats and Politicians in Western Democracies*, Harvard.
Ademolekun Ladipo (1986), *Politics and Administration in Nigeria*, Hutchinson.
Bagehot Walter (1965), (edited, with an Introduction by R.H.S. Crossman) *The English Constitution*, Fontana.
Bukharin Nikolai Ivanovich and Evgenii Alekseevich Preobrazhensky (1969), *The ABC of Communism*, Penguin (Introduction by E.H. Carr).
Campbell Colin and B. Guy Peters (1988), *The Politics/Administration Dichotomy: Death or Merely Change?* Governance, Vol. 1, No. 1.
Crossman R.H.S. (1978), *The Diaries of a Cabinet Minister*, Hamish Hamilton.
Drewry Gavin (1985), *The Ponting Case — Leaking in the Public Interest*, Public Law, Summer, 1985, 63(3).
Fortin Yvonne (1988), *Reflections on Public Administration in France, 1986–1987*, in Governance, Vol. 1, No. 1.
Goodnow F. (1905), *Politics and Administration*, Macmillan.
Harris Peter (1988), *Hong Kong: A Study in Bureaucracy and Politics*, Macmillan.
Jennings Sir Ivor (1936), *Cabinet Government*, Cambridge.
Parris Henry (1969), *Constitutional Bureaucracy*, Allen and Unwin.
Plowden William (1985), *What Prospects for the UK Civil Service?*, Public Administration, 63(4) Winter, 1985.
Ponting Clive (1986), *Whitehall, Tragedy and Parce*, Sphere Books.
Rawls John (1972), *A Theory of Justice*, Oxford University Press.
Rizzi Bruno (1985), *The Bureaucratization of the World*, Tavistock.
Schonfield Andrew (1965), *Modern Capitalism*, Oxford University Press.
Scott Ian and John P. Burns (1984), *The Hong Kong Civil Service*, Oxford.
Self, See Chapter 1.
White Stephen (1979), *Political Culture and Soviet Politics*, Macmillan.

6
Internal Problems of Administration

THE BALANCE BETWEEN EXPANSION AND EFFICIENCY

The expansion of the administrative profession appears to be one of the great features of the present century. We saw in Chapter 2 how governmental growth has characterized modern states and how according to some critics, productivity and 'efficiency' may be difficult to achieve. The question of efficiency is extremely complex when speaking of administration and is not readily defined. Very often the question of what is 'efficient' is a matter of opinion, is a value-judgment. In organizations, efficiency appears to be an ideal but many people become aware, on the vaguest grounds that the organization should be, even if it is not, efficient. Efficiency can mean an efficiency in *cost* (or value for money). It can also mean an efficiency in *time* (or productivity or effort). It can also refer to a *psychological* malaise — a question of *morale* in an organization. Indeed all these elements, cost, time and morale are related though it is hard to say where the problem begins. The question of 'efficiency', as well as its close partner 'effectiveness', is a central value in public administration (Christopher Hodgkinson, 1978: 182–185; Self, 1972: 264). The worst organizational evil is inefficiency, or so it would appear.

People perceive this in different ways. In the USA, disillusioned administrators point out that incompetence is actually preferred by some heads: 'the pressure toward mediocrity is simply too enormous to resist' (Time, *The Making of a Bureaucrat*, 1979: 5.3.79, p. 25). In Britain similar disillusioned administrators ask economic questions ... 'how much does it cost to borrow a library book, deal with a planning application, empty my dustbin, educate my child for a year ...? If you were to let me know, then I should have a clearer idea of whether I am getting value for money. After all the price is clear if I buy a book, engage a consultant, employ a contractor, educate my child in a private school ...'

Efficient organizations can be usually recognized rather than defined, because morale is as much a part of the problem as the more publicized notion of value for money. The cynic may argue that: 'To refer to the activities of the departments of government as 'public services' bestows on them a sense of honour and dignity which they do not deserve'. This however is to argue that some form of moral, if not financial, 'corruption' has set in.

A discussion of the notion of efficiency is to be found in the work of Herbert Simon. Briefly, Simon casts some doubt on the concept of efficiency, believing it to be a concept of doubtful validity where organizations are concerned. On a broader scale, it could be pointed out that the efficiency expert may mistakenly believe that there is only one best way to do a job (Henry, 1975: 130). Simon sees the difficulties in knowing what efficiency is both in theory and practice, and he refers to 'administrative man' as comparable in administration to 'economic man' in economics (Simon, 1957: 39). Efficiency refers to an understanding of the choice by the administrator of the various alternatives which face him (Simon, 1957: 179). Efficiency for Simon can almost be conceived in engineering terms; it is simply the ratio of input to output. For some people efficiency is not merely a value; it is a metavalue. A metavalue 'is a concept of the desirable so vested and entrenched that it seems to be beyond dispute or contention' (Hodgkinson, 1978: 184), such as, clean water, clean air and honest, incorrupt administration.

PARKINSON'S 'LAW': THE MEASUREMENT OF TIME

Parkinson's 'Law' simply states that 'work expands in order to fill the time available for its completion' (Parkinson, 1958: 9). There is some doubt as to whether Professor Parkinson's 'proposition' (rather than 'Law') is meant as a joke or as a statement of a serious relationship between work and time. It is a mixture of the serious and the flippant but underneath there is a critical point about the measurement of time in organizations. As an historian, Parkinson applied himself to the analysis of administrative growth in several widely contrasting areas, in the case of an apparent *decrease* in services provided or enterprise undertaken, concomitantly with an apparent *increase* in the size of the administrative function. The 'data' provided by Parkinson is instructive at least to pose the problem. There is a serious point however which is the 'unaskable' question and 'a fundamental part of the administrator's value bias': 'Should my organization exist?' (Hodgkinson, 1978: 181).

COLONIAL OFFICE STATISTICS

To show *administrative* expansion

Colonial Office Statistics: To show Administrative Expansion

Year	1935	1939	1943	1947	1954
Staff in Colonial Office	372	450	817	1139	1661

N.B. 1935–1939 — No increase in colonies
     1939–1943 — Contraction in numbers
     1947 — India becomes independent
     1956 — Ghana becomes independent

Note that the numbers of administrators employed at the Colonial Office increased as the number of colonies declined.

(Source: Parkinson, 1958)

It may well be that Parkinson's theory (rather than 'Law') is essentially a static view of administrative behaviour. The administrators whom he attacks and who are located in the Colonial Office in London contained, in say 1960, very different sorts of persons, that is, both general administrative officers as well as highly specialized persons, e.g., veterinarians, hydrologists, forestry officers. But the older-style colonial bureaucrat was a generalist.

Admiralty Statistics			
Classification	Year		% Increase or Decrease
	1914	1928	
Capital ships	62	20	−67.74
Officers and Men in Royal Navy	146,000	100,000	−31.5
Dockyard Workers	57,000	62,439	+ 9.54
Dockyard officials/ clerks	3,249	4,558	+40.28
Admiralty officials	2,000	3,569	+78.45

Parkinson, concludes 'For every new foreman or electrical engineer at Portsmouth, there had to be two more clerks at Charing Cross' (p. 7) and 'The officials would have multiplied at the same rate had there been no actual seamen at all' (p. 18).

An actual example of the growth of the administrative sector was provided for the London borough of Camden as follows:

Year	Population		Staff
1965	220,000	:	4,260
1977	191,000	:	7,000

Another example comes from the British National Health Service. Between 1965 and 1973, bed occupancy declined by 11 per cent. During this time hospital staff increased by 28 per cent, and administrative/clerical staff increased by 51 per cent (*Report on Public Provision for Medical Care in Great Britain*, Max Gammon, 1976). An examination of the problems of relating productivity to staff numbers has led to many value-for-money exercises in a number of countries. In Britain, in 1979 Mrs Thatcher appointed Lord Rayner (from Marks and Spencer the well-known department store) to enquire about spending in government departments. Several reports were produced, and several examples of administrative and financial waste were discovered. Thus to check upon unlicensed cars costs far more than it saves. A woodland scheme cost £91 in administrative costs to give away £100. The Inland Revenue kept two totally separate registers of the same information. The cost of keeping a man overnight in a prison cell was apparently £176.

There are many other examples. In Britain it was suggested that only 'half the planned savings had been achieved' within a time frame of twice as long (Ponting, 1986).

Government subsidies in the USA are often extremely impressive. The cost of subsidizing farmers in the USA in money terms is estimated to be of the order of $35 billion. In relative terms this figure exceeds the amount spent on medicare and on food stamp allowances. Defence costs consistently increased during the Reagan years, and suppliers of equipment have created a vast military-industrial complex held together with an administrative superstructure.

Parkinson does not conclude (as he begins) his appraisal of the 'bureaucracy' in a light-hearted way, rather concluding with a cynical assessment of the whole administrative function.

'For the final objection to bureaucracy is that it destroys the bureaucrat as an individual. The man condemned to spend his life with files and minute sheets has, broadly two alternatives: Realizing the futility of his work he can cynically decide to make the most of it, striving ... or else he can convince himself that his work is of national importance'. Speaking of administrative routine Parkinson states that: 'It is a work that undermines character, a work that destroys the soul' (Parkinson, 1960: 143).

Parkinson's point of bureaucratic expansion is of course quite serious. He perceives a bureaucratic growth of some 6 per cent per annum. This is roughly true whether one speaks of colonial civil servants or admirals. As a statement of fact however it is probably exaggerated to see a pattern of universal growth or of a necessary connection between bureaucratic growth and inefficiency.

Efficiency in any case may be related to informal structures or social processes. Islamic administrators are Muslims before they are administrators. Western-educated administrators may clash with their more traditional colleagues in the public administration sector. Sometimes a Western-style administration may be no more than a screen through which traditional rulers operate, as in the Middle East. Finally, socialist states may be prepared to sacrifice 'efficiency' before 'ideology'. Experts are suspect on ideological grounds and socialist states themselves may be a new form of élite which spawns administrative inefficiency.

AUTHORITY AND HIERARCHY

One of the most important notions in organization theory is the concept of authority. All organizations naturally embody the notion of authority, in an intensely practical way. Each organization has objectives which are laid down in its title–library services, engineering services, and educational services, to mention but a few. These services have to be directed by a person who is charged with the task of giving purpose, point and direction to the enterprise.

The Prime Minister in a government is so called because he or she is the first minister, exercises overall authority with the right to 'hire and fire' other ministers. But it is a central feature of all organizations, especially *political* organizations, that they imply subordinates, advisers and technical staff to support the supreme policy-matter. Each of these will probably be responsible for a broad functional area. Even in a socialist state, the talk is of 'democratic centralism' and the attempt is to explain, or perhaps justify 'authority', the centralism part, with so-called 'democracy'.

Organizations tend to reveal certain characteristics, including the principle of hierarchy and of staff-line relationships, the span of control theory, as well as problems of delegation. We will consider each of these in turn.

HIERARCHY

That there are levels of authority, and superior and inferior parts of organization is a fact well appreciated by everybody from a very early age. One's position in the organization depends only partly on the level of difficulty of the work performed. The term 'hierarchy' covers a large universally well-understood concept. Some attempts have been made, again partly serious and partly frivolous, to study the question of hierarchies.

'Man orders his affairs in hierarchies. His schools are ordered in grades from kindergarten through graduate school. His businesses are operated with employees arranged in order of rank. His government is organized with the taxpayers forming the base of the pyramid and the national leader as the apex. Similarily, the military, fraternal orders social welfare, sports and the Mafia are all structued in hierarchies' (Peter, 1972: 4).

There are very few organizations which entertain the notion of equality within the institution. Peter's view is that there is a direct relationship between inefficiency (or incompetence) and membership of any organizational hierarchy. He believed that ultimately 'every post in a hierarchy tends to be occupied by an employee who is incompetent to carry out its duties' (Peter, 1972: 24).

Peter's 'laws' are of course based upon an extremely pessimistic view both of human nature and of the potential efficiency of organizations. Serious problems arise within every chain of control or demand. For all the failures, there may well be a set of impressive statistics. Ultimately we must face, if not solve, the problem of administrative incompetence within organizations.

SPAN OF CONTROL

The problem of the span of control is very old and can be stated very simply. Nobody can oversee more than a limited number of enterprises or exercises. The actual number is open to debate. One of the most famous (or notorious) examples is from the French management theorist Graicunas who believed that there were possibly five tasks which could be supervised by one person (Baker 1972: 33–49).

Other writers argue that the span of control theory can be related to a variety of other numbers of function, perhaps six. There must however be a limit to the tasks that can be meaningfully supervised before some form of delegation is necessary in most organizations. Delegation is not however a precise science and depends in large measure upon the personality of the administrator concerned. Those who delegate too much are possibly incompetent but those who do not delegate enough are possibly dangerous. Administrative theory does not appear to have produced satisfactory answers to the question of delegation, possibly because it is so much a question of style.

Delegation may also be a question of culture. Some cultures see delegation as undesirable and even a form of weakness. Obviously delegation cannot succeed where, as in the Chinese case, it is perceived as unacceptable.

ADMINISTRATIVE SELF-INTEREST AND THE PUBLIC GOOD

While public officials generally accept their special concern with a 'higher' conception of the public good, it would be wrong to ignore the fact that officials often fall short of this high ideal for the most part. We should perhaps best consider that officials are no more selfless (or selfish) than any other group in society. Once all illusions about administrators have been dispersed we may the more effectively learn about their performance. Officials are no more idealistic (and possibly less so) than anybody else. They see themselves as the operators of a machine rather than as idealist philosopher-kings. Several basic propositions about administrative self-interest appear, at least on the superficial level, to be true.

1. Each official will tend to mix his private or personal advantage with the success (or otherwise) of the particular department to which he belongs at a given moment. This proposition has been put, in a very striking way as 'Miles Law', viz., where you stand depends upon where you sit! Miles noticed that when he belonged to a particular unit or organization, he naturally tended to give loyalty to that body. However when he was transferred or posted to another department he found that his former loyalties disappeared and were transferred to the new body. If an official identifies his loyalties with his department (including material benefits, promotion prospects and salary), he will very possibly be eager to further its policies. Where he *stands* on an issue or policy therefore, depends upon where he *sits*, or is located at that moment, as is suggested in 'Miles Law'.
2. Policies to be followed will depend not upon their goodness or even appropriateness, but rather upon a consideration of a balance of advantages and advantage of these factors as he sees them. Where administra-

tors do act they appear as cautious actors. They will ask themselves questions about the benefits and costs of the strategies which they are (or have) to follow. They must not necessarily expect to perform altruistically. They will not exercise discretion, for example, to the benefit of the applicant unless it is convenient. Thus a police officer may or may not accept an apology for a traffic offence, even if this is trivial and committed innocently. He may apply the rules rigidly in every case unless it is inconvenient to him, say, to cope with the paperwork involved.

3. All organizations are strongly influenced in their structure by the purposes which they are supposed to follow. Thus the army, a church or university will always be their own special organizations. Such a remark may appear obvious, but if it were not true then it is possible that all administration would be always the same everywhere, irrespective of the purpose of the undertaking. While the management of enterprises eveywhere is a matter of *techniques* which could be identical, administration should serve the fundemental goals envisaged and not vice versa.

Administrators obviously behave like any other human beings, despite the fact that they are public servants. Of course classical studies from Plato onwards have constantly sought to discover the ideal ruler. There is little doubt that in many cases officials have a strong sense of public duty. However as a general rule self-interest dominates the behaviour of officials. If this is the case, self-interest can be detected at every point. No organization can expect its civil servants to aspire to higher levels or ideals.

Some of these very realistic ideas are present in the writings of Anthony Downs and in particular in *Inside Bureaucracy* (1967). Downs often uses the language of economics to see how a delicate balancing act takes place between goals, jobs, money and the bureaucracy both at the *political* as well as at the *organizational* levels. Politics is therefore often about the struggle for *votes*; organization is often a struggle for resources. Downs offers a highly realistic birds-eye view of bureaucracy at work as the title of his work shows.

Administrators like to have easily attainable objectives placed in front of them. Where the objectives become more difficult they will demand more resources. When even a goal is relatively easy to achieve, administrators may still not succeed.

Many complex issues, Downs believes must be recognized and if necessary, disentangled. Officials prize power, income, promotion, prestige, security, convenience loyalty to the organization, pride in their past achievements and a wish to advance the perceived interests of the public. All of these goals are well exemplified in the bureaucracy of the army for example, but could apply to any hierarchical administrative structure (Downs, A., 1967: 2).

There are many people who try to stipulate 'laws' of social behaviour and we have already referred to Parkinson and Peter in this regard. However, Downs offers serious and 'scientific' propositions which could be seen as 'laws' of administrative behaviour. Within any bureaucracy, it appears

Downs believes, there are certain imperatives. Thus a selection of these might be

1. The conservatism of organizations with age.
2. The prevalence of a hierarchy in organizations where free markets do not exist.
3. The desire to conserve.
4. The near-impossibility of anyone being able to exercise control over a large-scale organization.
5. The problem of controlling growing organizations.
6. The problem of coordination of operations in growing organizations.
7. In the case of conflict, solutions are sought from the top.
8. The attempt to monitor one large organization will involve the creation of a new monitoring organization.
9. The demand for information will always increase, irrespective of the nature of the enterprise.
10. Subordinates will attempt to avoid control over their behaviour.
11. An agency cannot produce enough 'free goods'.
12. Loyalty depends to a large extent upon the level of job security and promotion provided by the organization.
13. Organizations will tend to be in conflict with other related organizations.
14. Organizations which seek to reform themselves suffer strains if the pre-scribed goals are not clear. Organizations which enforce discipline suffer strains in harnessing people (Downs, 1967: 262–3).

The behaviour of administrative officials is therefore not to be taken for granted. If they do not wish to implement an order they may refuse to give their full cooperation to the project. In other words, the official will work best when he identifies the relevant programme with the goals which he has set himself. These are general rules and do not necessarily apply at all times. Officials do not everywhere come from the same social background. It makes a difference, for example, whether an official is a Catholic, Muslim or Buddhist. Culturally different environments will produce different results. But irrespective of these cultural differences, we do meet certain universal bureau-cratic traits: 'Red tape strangled the civilisations of Byzantium and Mandarin China. Bureaucracy thrives on delays and complications. We need to make our procedures quicker and simpler' (Hill in Adedji, 1908: 78).

PROBLEMS OF EFFICIENCY IN DEVELOPING COUNTRIES

The term 'bureaucracy' in many developing countries has a particularly unfortunate connotation. In Latin America, for example, the problems of bureaucratic mismanagement are particularly complicated. In many Latin American states the growth of administrative organizations has been rapid, extensive and even excessive.

In Mexico, for example, the size of the federal administration exceeded that of the USA. Despite its huge size, the Mexican administration has not performed adequately nor has it shown any tendency to reduce itself. Similar stories may be told about other Latin American states such as Venezuela, where the public sector 'accounts for 60 per cent of the Gross Domestic Product, and directs over 200 agencies and companies' (Sloan, 1982: 309). In Chile, between 1940 and 1970 when the population increased 30 per cent, the public service increased 400 per cent, while in Brazil, the public sector almost encompassed everything. In Columbia, much attention is paid to the creation of a large multipicity of agencies. Nevertheless, decisions were pushed upwards to ministers whose desks were clogged with demands for simple decisions so much so that the Treasury Minister in Colombia was compelled to sign 200 to 300 documents daily. Similar problems are in evidence in Guatemala, Argentina, Bolivia and Brazil.

If we turn to Africa, administrative efficiency is a necessity for development, but administrative efficiency is often scarce. The case of Nigeria, Africa's most populous state, is instructive. After independence from Britain in 1960, Nigeria naturally sought development as fast and far as possible. The need was for a committed, effective force for social change and sustained, mass-based economic development.

The civil service grew in quantity if not in quality. The following figures illustrate the trend:

1914: 1,100 (colonial service)
1952: 39,100 (pre-independence administration)
1960: 71,693 (federal and regional)
1974: 632,000 (federal, state, police and other levels)
(*Public Service Review Commission Nigeria*, 1974).

Nigeria's problems are three in number. Firstly, the British inheritance left certain assumptions about how a civil service should be run. For example, a generalist class was placed in a pre-eminent position in the administrative hierarchy, but below politicians (and soldiers). As in Britain, much feeling has been created about generalists. Nigeria, too, has its administrative class which is the advisory body to ministers. Of course, professional officers tend to condemn 'the bureaucracy'. The classical conflict appears to be repeated in many places (Aluko in Adedeji, 1968: 69).

Secondly, conflicts developed between regions and the centre and between regions and regions over the size, shape and structure of the Nigerian civil service. Northerner and Mid-Westerner amongst others saw the needs of individual regions as paramount as against other regions. Regionalization has been vigorously pursued and many people believe the federal civil service should contain a balance of regions on a representative basis. After Nigeria's several coups (1966, 1975, 1983 and 1985), the civil service has had to work closely with the military. Some writer even argued that under pressure from the military, 'a unitary state had been set up in federal disguise'.

Even after twenty years of independence it is interesting to see that in Nigeria, 'the administrative pattern is such that a British civil servant or local government officer would fit in quite snugly' (F.M.G. Willson in D.J. Murray (ed.), 1969: viii). In contrast with the French pattern in adjacent francophone states, Nigeria has tended, to have permanent secretaries with the practice of 'minuting up' to the permanent secretary and minister or military ruler (Murray D.J. and Ballard J., 1971: 86).

Later developments have been interpreted as a departure from the British classical tradition of political neutrality. Permanent secretaries have been rotated very quickly. Politicization has proceeded swiftly, but essentially because of the nature of politics in independent Nigeria. Nigeria's civil servants have had to serve many masters, federal, local, regional and tribal.

As a result political neutrality has been placed under severe strain. In Africa as a whole governments are subjected to enomous pressures (Lancaster 1985, 146–8). Population continues to increase, production of crops is inadequate, and debt repayments are heavy. Armies often mutiny, initiating coups, and single-party states under ambitious politicians made the quest for administrative efficiency very uncertain.

ETHICS IN PUBLIC ADMINISTRATION

If the Downs, analysis is correct there is only a limited opportunity to see public administration as a matter of morality. Officials tend to perform a 'moral minimum'. However there is a keen debate on the question of ethics. It may be true that administrators generally behave in a proper way with regard to their duties. Even if it is accepted that officials are not enthusiastic about their duties, we would not expect them to do the opposite, and behave negligently to the detriment of the public they are committed to serve. We would not expect positive neglect, or avoidance of direct instructions or of 'malpractice'. But naturally, it is not enough to avoid malpractice. Civil servants should not accept bribes and certainly not openly solicit them (Cap. 7 below).

Finally we must note that the use of the term 'ethics' as applied to public administration is essentially narrow and restricted to the behaviour of officials. It is not concerned with morality in the widest sense.

THE CONCEPT OF THE PUBLIC OFFICE

Public offices are those established by, or in furtherance of law. The duties of the office are public and are seen to attach to the office so created. Public offices are made through election or appointment even in the civil service. State governments in the USA sometimes elect persons to what are *administrative*, rather than *political*, offices. Doubt may be cast upon the moral worth of elected officials, particularly if they have to canvass support for their election.

In developing countries, public offices are often allocated on the basis of race, tribe, creed or political persuasion. Examples may be found in many areas of Africa as well as in Asia and Latin America. Where ethnic factors predominate, public officials face particularly difficult choices.

THE QUESTION OF ACCOUNTABILITY

People who hold public office must eventually answer for their actions, or 'render an account of their stewardship'. This is of course clear in the case of elected officials. Unsatisfactory performance will be 'punished' when and if the person involved is rejected by the electorate. Paid officers are less easy to control. Their performance can be measured by annual reports or by reference to tasks satisfactorily performed. If necessary, paid officials can be dismissed. They will not be dismissed without due cause nor until after exhaustive investigation of the case.

In a government department, the head is made the answer for his junior officials and the politician answers to a parliament for any 'mistakes' made on his part, if the parliamentary system is efficient. Accountability, or answering for a programme or policy, is unfortunately a very imprecise notion. Those who disagree with the policies themselves will naturally speak in disparaging and derogatory terms about the persons responsible for the policies. Every person sees accountability as a good; few people, however, know how to promote it.

In some developing societies the strongest loyalty is to the family or clan, and the office-holder must be seen to use his office to the benefit of his relations. Under such conditions accountability may not to the abstract notion of public administration ethics, but rather to loyalties of the family or clan. The office-holder may be expected actually to use his office to the benefit of his relations. Nepotism, or the promotion of one's own family to positions of power authority or influence, may indeed be seen as a virtue, particularly in developing states of the Third World.

A Chinese example taken from the *Analects* of Confucius may illustrate the point. Confucius was once approached by the Duke of She, who said to him: 'In my part of the country, there is a man so honest that when his father appropriated a sheep, he bore witness of it'. Confucius replied: 'The honest in my part of the country are different from that, for a father will protect his son, and a son his father. That is honesty indeed'.

Quite clearly where the notion of abstract justice, as implied in the notion of modern public administration, is missing, what happens is that old loyalties prevail. These are obviously loyalties of the family or tribe. The Chinese notion is *guanxi*, or connections. Public administration in the modern sense is presumed to apply an impartial standard throughout. It is secular, non-partison, rational and established in the state rather than in the partison group, tribe or extended family. Public sector ethics are abstract because the concept of public office accountability must relate to a set of formal rules which stand apart from bonds of personal loyalties. In the last resort, modern public administrators are presumed to distinguish private from public acts.

THE QUESTION OF RESPONSIBILITY

The question of responsibility is perhaps more precise than the question of administrative accountability. 'Responsibility' presupposes a set of *procedures* by which officials can be made 'responsible' for their actions. Procedures include departmental controls, personnel controls and legal remedies to make officials perform in a certain way. Responsibility is therefore quite specific, and differs in this respect from *accountability* which is a much vaguer idea, though perhaps more important. At bottom the hope is that public officials will properly carry out their specified duties without constant direction. They must ultimately be controlled yet free to act without impossible constraints. They must also expect to be judged according to a higher level of morality than are people in trade or commerce.

Government is a trust and cannot operate if there is too much or too little control. The community entrusts the governors with powers in the hope that the trust is not misplaced. However the age-old classical dilemna exists. We ask: who will control those who control us? This is perhaps the central moral issue of government: 'In framing a government which is to be administered by men over men, the great difficulty lies in this: you must first enable the government to control the governed: and in the next place, oblige it to control itself' (*The Federalist*, 1787–8; No. 51).

There is a subtle difference between being 'answerable to' and 'answerable for'. The idea of responsibility covers the former notion, the idea of accountability the latter. We answer to a person, but we answer for the moral content of our actions in the last resort to conscience.

OFFICIAL MISUSE OF POWER

It is not difficult to find many examples of the misuse of power by officials. Where these occur officials frequently defend their actions by arguing that what they did they did like soldiers under orders. Such was the claim made by war criminals after World War II. The Watergate incident in the USA (1972) and the Green Peace Incident (1985) which involved the sinking of a protestor's ship by French security service officers were significant modern examples of official abuse of power. States are presumed to act properly and at least honestly but, of course, individual officials may or may not perform to a high standard of public service. It is not easy to pin-point the abuse of power except by reference to a list of faults. Officials are in breach of their ethical duty where they are guilty of 'bias, neglect, inattention, delay incompetence, ineptitude perversity, turpitude, arbitrariness (R.H.S. Crossman, *cit.* Stacey: 516).

The Prime Minister of India, Rajiv Gandhi drew attention to serious cases of misrule in India. He argued that India's main political party, the Congress Party had departed from 'the high principles and lofty ideals needed to build a strong and prosperous India. But we obey no discipline, no rule, follow no principle of public morality, display no sense of social awareness, show no concern for the public weal' (*International Herald Tribune*, 10 January 1986). As India's official Congress Party has ruled the country for about forty years, the accusation was serious. Meanwhile, in the Soviet Union, a similar protest was made by Mikhael Gorbachov at the XXVIIth Party Congress of the Communist Party of the Soviet Union. In both cases however, the idea was that the lapses concerned were the product of human inadequacy inside systems.

Official misuse of power is seen by some organizations like Amnesty International as occurring when human rights are under threat. There is a tendency in many states towards extensive and entrenched violation of human rights. These include unlawful imprisonment without trial, torture, forcible movement, and political offences and a general or specific use of instruments of terror. Misuse of power is most dramatically observed in conditions of what might be called physical or criminal abuse.

For most of the time however there is a sense of unease about the more subtle exercise of power. This may be called the 'Actonian Principle', namely that 'power tends to corrupt and absolute power corrupts absolutely' (Acton). For many people the Actonian principle is undeniable. It is perhaps the most quoted aphorism of all, largely because it is so frequently observed a thousand citizens in official exchanges in a thousand offices daily. The official has knowledge, security and discretion which from the perspective of the humble citizen sets him apart from society.

LEGAL REMEDIES AND REDRESS

We may note several possible actions against maladministration. These actions include types of actions brought in the Common Law (British) system, actions brought where there are administrative courts (as in France) and the use of the Ombudsman (or complaints officer). In the first instance, common law actions may be brought by citizens, albeit at their own expense, in court. There are several ways in which an aggrieved citizen can ask to request redress of wrongs. An official may be challenged because his actions have been outside what the law permits; he may be challenged because he has exceeded the powers conferred on him by the law, and he may be challenged because his powers have been incorrectly or wrongly exercised. In this case, the usual courts may not suffice.

In the second instance, where there are administrative courts (as in France), the citizen can actually use special courts where he can pursue his grievance to obtain a solution. Unfortunately there is much hostility towards the notion of administrative courts in Anglo-Saxon countries and there are few defenders of the idea of a separate network of administrative courts.

The case of the Ombudsman is however particularly intriguing, given his role outside the administration. The Ombudsman is himself an official, but one with some a high degree of independence, provided with wide powers in the matter of the investigation of complaints. Originally conceived in Sweden at the beginning of the nineteenth century (1809), the office or some variant of it has spread to Finland (1910) Israel, Denmark, Norway, New Zealand and Britain. There are versions in a number of other western European countries. In Spain he is called Defender of the People (El Defensor del Pueblo) and, in France, Mediator (Médiateur). To be successful, the Ombudsmen must have extensive independent powers and powers of initiative, but often they do not act independently, but only when requested.

Sometimes the Ombudsman principle is widely construed and sometimes construed in a very narrow sense. The ideal might be for the Ombudsman to follow the New Zealand principle that where actions are 'unreasonable', 'unjust', 'oppressive' and 'wrong' that they should bring in the Ombudsman. A wide construction would suggest, 'the citizen has a right to expect not only that his affairs will be dealt with effectively and expeditiously, but also that his personal feelings no less than his rights as an individual will be sympathetically and fairly considered' (*Political Studies*, December 1974: 516–7).

The Ombudsman idea can indeed strengthen ministerial government. According to Sir Kenneth Wheare, 'it (the Ombudsman) strengthens the whole process of control within a department which, it would seem to me, should be welcomed by heads of departments and higher officials in a department, not resented. It gives some reality, some stuffing to the vague elusive notion of the single responsible minister' (Stacey, 1974: 516).

There may be a need in a ministerial structure to consider the role of the civil service, not to name possible offenders, 'but remove some of the restrictions on the matters with which they deal and to provide for direct access to them by members of the public' (Stacey, 1974: 516). In the 1980's several British civil servants, (including Clive Ponting and Sarah Tisdall) were prepared to challenge the system.

Public administration scholars are particularly concerned with the concept of maladministration, but the concept is not easy to define. Civil servants ideally should perhaps be anonymous, impartial and detached from politics. Being human however, they may not be any of these things. In a British-type system the amateur is all-important still and they may make amateurish mistakes, which are not always attributable to maladministration. Sweden, the home of the Ombudsman, is less secretive than Britain and, has in fact, been described as a 'goldfish bowl' society, because of its openness (Schonfield, 1965: 399). It is not therefore surprising that much attention has been paid to the Freedom of Information Act in the USA.

Developing countries operate under greater difficulties. They are unlikely to be able to ask whether their value schemes are appropriate. The attempts made to find rational bases for administrative action associated with many distinguished Western scholars appear decidedly ethnocentric. In other words, while it may be difficult to discuss the place of ethics in public administration in the West, it becomes even more difficult in non-Western countries. The cultures of developing countries present a degree of moral pluralism which makes Western administrative ethics only partly applicable to urgent problems.

Moral issues about, for example, the siting of a nuclear power station, do not have the same perspective, say, in China as in a Western country. Chinese administrators see problems such as nuclear power, capital punishment and educational curricula in vastly different 'moral' ways from their Western counterparts.

Justice in the West may be seen as a matter of 'fairness' to all groups, following on the writings of Rawls (Rawls, 1971: 10). Fairness may be seen as a matter of intuition or utility if we follow common Western thinking. However, justice in India or Indonesia, Guinea or Ghana, may be justice to the community rather than to the individual. Westerners often fail to see the point however that despite protestations that their scholarship is rational, very often the same or similar prejudices exist in Western countries. In short, the West may be less 'rational' than it imagines. What is different perhaps is that the West may be more 'secular'.

BIBLIOGRAPHY

Adamolekun Ladipo (1986), *Politics and Administration in Nigeria*, Spectrum, Hutchinson, London.

Adedeji Adebayi (1968), *Nigerian Administration and its Political Setting*, Hutchinson, London.

Baker R.J.S. (1972), *Administrative Theory and Public Administration*, Hutchinson, London.

Dibb Paul (1986), *The Soviet Union: The Incomplete Superpower*, Macmillan, London.

Downs Anthony (1967), *Inside Bureaucracy*, Little Brown, Boston.

Henry Nicholas (1975), *Public Administration and Public Affairs*, Prentice Hall, New Jersey.

Hodgkinson Christopher (1978), *Towards a Philosophy of Administration*, Basil Blackwell, Oxford.

Rawls John (1970), *A Theory of Justice*, Oxford.

Ponting Clive (1986), *Whiteball, Tragedy and Farce*, Sphere Books.

Parkinson C. Northcote (1958), *Parkinson's Law or the Pursuit of Progress*, Murray, London.

Parkinson (1960), *The Law and the Profits*, Penguin.

Peter Laurence J and Hull Raymond (1970), *The Peter Principle*, Pan, London.

7

The Problem of Bureaucratic Corruption

TERMINOLOGY

If administration were purely mechanical then there would be no problem of corruption. Administrators however exercise discretion. Discretion is a serious matter for administrators who are required to weigh up the various factors in any decision before actually making a decision. There are some things that no computer can achieve given that administration is a human activity (Hodgkinson, 1978, 3–4). For the most part to administer, like to govern, is to choose. Such is the essence of discretion.

The terminology associated with the subject of corruption presents many difficulties. For the most part, people use the general term 'corruption' to describe a very narrow concept. Corruption (bureaucratic) usually describes the situation in which an administrative system has become perverted by money. Bribery refers to the passage of cash from hand to hand. The term 'corruption' signifies a wider social implication.

However if a society is corrupt in a technical sense, it is probably corrupt also in a broader, moral sense. The fact is that in a society in which bribes are commonplace, a sense of hopelessness may subsequently develop. Citizens will come to learn that no administrative action can be expected unless a bribe is paid. In consequence, the state apparatus may cease to function effectively, and a 'higher' sort of corruption develop. Corruption (moral) follows closely and logically from corruption (bribery). Bribery may be seen as the prelude to corruption, which eventually becomes so prevalent that it is no crime, but part of the fabric of a generally corrupt society. The point was made by the Indian Prime Minister Rajiv Gandhi in late 1985, when he linked corruption in the narrow sense to corruption in the broad sense. He called for a new and better approach to his country's many problems.

The same point was made in Panama in 1988, when President Norriega was accused by the USA of profiting corruptly from the sale of drugs.

Corruption is an abstract word which can be difficult to define. Bribery on the other hand is a concrete term. Those found guilty of bribery can be punished simply by finding them to have broken such laws on the subject which exist. For the most part we will define corruption as bribery in the narrow material sense. However we must not lose sight of what we might call the classical idea of corruption.

THE CLASSICAL IDEA OF CORRUPTION

Political philosophers have normally approached the question of corruption in a moralistic fashion. Money in fact is not necessarily always the main problem. Rather corruption is often seen in relation to the abuse of power, an important interpretation which suggests something far broader than bribery. The classical idea is perhaps a biblical idea. The Bible argues that 'evil communications corrupt good manners', and states: 'For this corruptible must put on incorruption, and this mortal must put on immortality' (*Letters to the Corinthians*, xv. 53). At the end of life, the burial service for the dead states that the body of the deceased will be 'turned into corruption' (*Forms of Prayer to be used at Sea*). Eastern religions stress spiritual health and sickness.

Administrators may of course become intoxicated with power, and seek to derive satisfaction from its usage. Let us consider several quotations to illustrate the point. 'Unlimited power is apt to corrupt the minds of those who possess it' (William Pitt, 1790). 'Power corrupts, absolute power corrupts absolutely' (Lord Acton, *Letters*, 1904). Where they operate their office in an unfortunate or imperious manner, they may be seen as acting in a 'corrupt' fashion. Corruption, it must be stressed has more than one simple aspect.

THE POWER OF MONEY TO INFLUENCE DECISIONS: THE LUBRICATION THEORY

Shakespeare put the matter succinctly when he said: 'Gold were as good as twenty orators.' And a seventeenth-century proverb runs: 'A dog will not howl if you beat him with a bone.' Somewhat later, the poet Robert Southey saw two steps in the bribery process.

> But they wavered not long, for conscience was strong,
> And they thought they might get more,
> And they refused the gold, but not
> So rudely as before.

Tennyson's cynicism was undisguised. As he put it: 'The jingling of the guinea helps the hurt that honour feels.' In the present century, Brecht put the matter with further cynicism; 'God is merciful and men are bribable and that's how his will is done on earth as it is in heaven.'

Some say money enables public administration to flow freely. There is an argument that bribery in fact assists public administration to increase the efficiency of the state. As a result some people see bribery as a form of 'lubricating' the government machine. The lubrication theory is plausible and often quoted, particularly in aggressive capitalist societies. However, it seems to condone bribery and may have serious long-term effects. These may well be 'moral', but will surely tend to subvert the institutions of state.

Bribes are inevitably used in order to persuade people to make decisions favourable to the giver. The person who takes the bribe or 'taker', is presumed to take the bribe and give his favour. Of course he may take the bribe and still withhold the favour, but he runs the risk of complaint and exposure. Indeed, bribery for both sides is fraught with risks.

Moreover, there is a well-established psychological theory regarding the giving of gifts which is attributed to certain social anthropologists such as Malinowski and Mauss (Malinowski, 1922: 167, and Mauss, 1925). Mauss showed that gifts are never extinguished as he put it, that is gifts must be repaid eventually. A bribe is given in the clear expectation of some return in the future.

The prevalence of bribery and the difficulty of eradicating it is obviously a serious matter. Where it is known that the regular process of government is capable of subversion by money, or that procedures can be set aside by those designed to promote and protect these processes and procedures, then the state itself is likely to be placed in jeopardy. There are many examples of the correctness of this assertion, which can be found in every type of state. In the mid-1980's two examples from widely differing parts of the world, namely Haiti and the Philippines compelled attention. In both cases corruption actually produced conditions which ultimately led to the downfall of their respective government.

WHY DOES CORRUPTION EXIST?

Corruption (i.e., bribery) can be interpreted in a number of ways. It may most obviously be seen as on *economic* phenomenon. Officials may accept bribes because they want money, perhaps because their salaries are low or because they want certain immediate benefits which are the result of power to manipulate the system. If salaries are low and opportunities are many, then bribes will be taken. The risk will be worth taking whatever might be the associated penalties.

Secondly, bribery is a *cultural* phenomenon. Some cultures may see bribery as utterly unacceptable and even reprehensible. Others may take a much more relaxed attitude to bribery and corruption. Where political institutions are secure and public life is well-respected, then corruption may fail to develop. Where political institutions are weak and despised then corruption is likely to flourish. Of course cultures change substantially over time. In late eighteenth-century England, corruption in public life was widespread. By the end of the next century, corruption was illegal and gradually 'clean' government became the accepted norm. Thus corrupt societies today may subsequently become 'clean'. There could well be hope for a wide variety of states which today appear to be dangerously tolerant of corruption.

Thirdly, bribery may be seen as a largely psychological factor. To put the matter simply, bribery may be seen as an expression of greed. Human weakness may account for the existence of corrupt practices, though this may lead to a fatalistic acceptance of corruption.

The term 'nepotism' covers the idea that a public official rewarded his family with the fruits of office high or low. Nepotism is more likely to exist in societies of a *gemeinschaft* (face-to-face) nature than in *gesellschaft* societies (i.e., those which are 'rational' in nature). The origin of corruption may indeed be a family factor, but later corruption is more likely to be a marketable factor.

In other words, corruption probably begins as a cultural phenomenon and later changes to appear as a largely monetary matter, or bribery in fact. A modern corrupt public official will reward those who *pay* him irrespective of their family origins. A traditionally corrupt official may have a more mixed set of notives for his actions.

The developing world is frequently seen as a corrupt world. There is, however, no evidence to show that any society is immune completely from corruption. Where the opportunities for bribery exist in all territories they will be taken. The difference may however be that the developed states manifest rather less corruption in central government than in local government. Where a state is corrupt in *both* central and local government then its governmental (as well as its moral) problems are serious indeed.

WHERE DOES CORRUPTION EXIST?

Corruption may exist in some form or other in any state, irrespective of the region, state or nation being studied. Some people have argued that corruption is, for example, a product of a particular stage of development. If a country modernizes and develops then it will outgrow corruption. Corruption has been seen as a result of poverty, deprivation or any of the conventional ills which beset a developing country. Mature democracies such as Britain or the USA are seen to be founded on rational administrative principles, thus avoiding corruption. Weber stressed that rational-legal societies understand that public lives should not be consciously confused with private lives. A ruler's official income should not be confused with his private resources.

In developing countries some societies are often seen as extremely prone to corruption at all levels (Clapham, 1985: 50–54). In some states the whole of government revenue is seen as the legitimate property of the ruler, 'amounting in extreme cases to a system of government for purposes of personal enrichment, which has been described as 'kleptocracy' or rule by theft' (Clapham, 1985: 50). Rulers consciously or unconsciously see no need to make a distinction between what belongs to the state and what is their personal fortune.

In certain countries like Nigeria, the Philippines, India and Indonesia no tradition of non-corrupt political institutions has emerged on firm foundations. As a result, the political institutions themselves suffer. In socialist countries too, corruption is often widespread. Socialists cannot argue that only capitalist states are prone to corruption. China, the Soviet Union and numerous other socialist states have shown strong tendencies to corruption (see Chapter 10 below).

In advanced capitalist states even where central government is 'clean', very often, city, state and local government are highly prone to bribery and corruption. Local government everywhere has more than its fair share of corruption. In the USA, New York was supposed to have been organized by its 'machine', known as Tammanay Hall. The famous portrayal of New York and other cities in the twenties as being controlled by 'gangsters' allied with, or in opposition to, a Mafia as in (Mario Puzo's novel *The Godfather*) was not wholly far from the truth (Brogan, 1954: 123–73). In Miami in the 1980's drug-related corruption was believed to be rampant among the local police, according to many newspaper reports.

In Britain local government is notoriously less 'clean' than central government. In the early 1970's some of this was revealed as a result of a scandal in the north of England involving John Poulson, regarded as a 'Mr. Fixit'. Other parts of Great Britain have experiences of local government which indicate that local government in advanced countries may often be extremely corrupt. Bribes are in Britain likely to take the form of friendly gifts. An official may be given a house, car, clothes, and expensive travel — simply in order to exert influence in the awarding of valuable contracts.

Other Western countries have their own examples. In Holland, West Germany, Italy amongst others, we are aware of various forms of bureaucratic as well as political, corruption. They may exist in central or in local government, but the main fact is that few places are immune from government corruption of one sort or another in greater or in lesser degrees.

An interesting question to be asked is whether developing countries are more likely to be corrupt at the level of *central* government than are mature developed Western states. It is of course wrong to argue that Third World countries are corrupt and that Western countries are immune from corruption. It may be a matter of degree only. There is however a tendency by some political scientists to assert that ... 'the significant difference is that in the West corruption is regarded as abnormal and wrong, while in the Third World it is not' (Kempe Ronald Hope, 1985: 4). New states are frequently 'patrimonial' states (and a benevolent father requires to be recompensed). As a result the state's income is not distinguished from the personal fortune of the ruler. The patrimonial state is not the rational state. The godfather figure dispenses 'justice' as he sees it, as a father figure. Godfather figures are considerable figures because father-figures are necessarily considerable. In developing states they may be more significant than they are elsewhere.

Probably the most useful distinction to be made is between those governments which take the problem seriously and those which do not. In other words if a government accepts that corruption is likely to damage the state apparatus itself unless checked, it is in a different category from those which do nothing. The most obvious remedy open to a state is to make laws forbidding corrupt acts (however defined) such as the *Prevention of Corruption Act* of 1906 in the case of Great Britain. This Act made it illegal to take bribes 'corruptly', which proposition does not solve the problem however of what the law permits.

A more useful approach would be to consider states which have anti-corruption agencies already established. An anti-corruption agency exists to use its legal and policing powers to root out corruption by all legitimate methods. Examples include some US cities as well as some Australian states and certain countries such as for example Singapore, Malaysia, Tanzania, Hong Kong, Zambia, and Brunei. Where anti-corruption agencies exist, they at least show that a state at least has an official resolve to combat corruption. However information regarding anti-corruption agencies is difficult to obtain. A general answer would suggest that anti-corruption agencies have some successes and some failures. There is no anti-corruption agency, it would appear, which claims to have eradicated corruption entirely. Once it had done so it would have announced the main reason for its demise. An anti-corruption agency will naturally offer compelling evidence regarding the value of its work, but will naturally stress also the need to continue its work. In a sense anti-corruption agencies have a 'vested interest' in corruption.

A CONCEPTUAL MAP OF BUREAUCRATIC CORRUPTION

Corruption may be most conveniently analysed by reference to the following four-part *schema*. We may conveniently see all activities in the first part, No. 1 as honest business, but the suggestion is that the line between honesty and dishonesty as represented by No. 2, 3 and 4 is a matter of how business is regulated by law. Category 2 is sometimes called 'honest' graft in the USA because it is seen as general and even helpful by some commentators. Honest graft is an American notion that cities need 'machines' and 'bosses' which organize and manipulate people in large numbers. Denis Brogan defined it as follows: 'Honest graft was the utilisation of political knowledge and power to make gains in various forms of speculation and of business that could not have been made, or not made so easily, if political knowledge and power had not been made available. To know where a new road, a new bridge, a new school was to be built and to buy land, whose value would rise as a result of the building, was honest graft. To make sure that a road or bridge, or school or park was placed near property owned by you or your friends was also honest graft' (D.W. Brogan, 1954: 144).

The notion of 'honest graft' however is not so clear-cut or laudable. It may be distinguished only in degree from other types of corruption which are more plainly vicious, such as types of 'dirty' graft implication No. 3 and No. 4. The fourth type of bureaucratic corruption, is particularly cynical because the corrupt service is sold to the highest bidder. Corruption therefore becomes a marketed community.

Market graft is usually the most 'advanced' form of graft. It may be associated with drugs or prostitution in a syndicated form. It may even permit corrupt drugs dealers for example, to 'buy' police badges to send their agents in the guise of lawful police officers. Such sophisticated corruption may even take the matter one stage further. The bureaucracy and its symbols of office is for sale on a temporary basis. Where hundreds of millions of dollars are at stake as in the case of drug smugglers into the USA, bureaucratic corruption must inevitably become highly organized.

Corrupt Syndicates Usurp Legitimate Government

1 Honest Business Dealings (Buy and Sell to Make A Profit)	2 'Mild' or 'Honest' Graft (Bribes 'Lubricate' e.g., US cities)	3 Dishonest Graft Positive Bribes	4 Market Graft (Syndicates) Officials Protect and Sell 'Service' on a Commercial Basis
e.g., Stock Market legitimate	e.g., Insider Dealings on Stock Market	e.g., Police Ignore Traffic Offences	e.g., Drugs, Prostitution, Passports, etc.

IS CORRUPTION A PRODUCT OF ANY PARTICULAR TYPE OF IDEOLOGY?

Ideologies have little reference to corruption unless they apportion blame to others. The question of corruption is usually directed towards rival or hostile ideologies, viz., towards those whose ideological fundations are unacceptable. No ideology sees itself as corrupt. *Other* ideologies may be. Totalitarian states are particularly prone to corruption, not least because absolute power must corrupt those who exercise it. Liberal democratic states of the conventional Western variety will be pluralistic and will avoid the concentration and monopolization of power. A Stalin or Hitler will have cronies for long periods which an elected leader will not. In the short run, of course, liberal leaders may tend towards nepotism. In the long run those who subscribe to a liberal ideology must submit themselves to the test of an election.

Ideologies offer an explanation of the world as a structure and function. However no ideology accepts the continuing depravity of man after the ideology's triumph. In fact, no ideology can guarantee the success of values. Corruption appears to be possible under any ideological dispensation. For example, graft is likely to flourish where a 'command' economy becomes ineffective or inefficient. Socialist states may, moreover be more particularly prone to the temptations of corruption than are non-socialist states. The problem exists of course in China. 'Those who take advantage of the reforms to practise graft and embezzlement must be punished, but mistakes made out of a desire to help the people and the country must not be regarded as corrupt and unhealthy' (*People's Daily*, 3.6.85).

Hebei and Anhui provinces supported several guidelines or limits including distinctions between normal and unwarranted bonuses, reasonable and unacceptable price increases, services paid for and bribes, and necessary business expenses and using public funds to pay for gifts. Hu Qili (*China Daily*, 20 January, 1986) argued for death penalty for bad offenders including the relatives of party leaders (*Beijing Review*, February 24, 1986).

Socialist states are by nature, hierarchical, even feudal in structure. They are characteristically self-perpetuating oligarchies. New talent may be unwelcome and those excluded from power are often excluded from the perquisites of power. Planning, where unsuccessful may simply lead to bad or even falsified accounting. Socialist states are most frequently poor or undeveloped states. Their peoples may be deprived of consumer goods. In the Soviet Union it has been said that 'good food and especially meat (are) the yardstick by which most Russians measure their own prosperity' (Short, B.B.C. 1982).

The Soviet Union may be regarded as the home of the planned economy. Yet it is not particularly productive or efficient, and one close observer simply argued: 'the Soviet Union is infected from top to bottom with corruption ... each and everyone is afflicted with corruption' (Simis, 1982: 297). The concentration of power so characteristic of socialist states may assist in promoting corruption. However, for ideological reasons, no socialist would be happy in admitting a socialist form of corruption related to, and deriving from the system itself.

Capitalist corruption is, of course, the version found in North America, Europe or Japan. Capitalism obviously directs attention to consumer needs and the place of money in satisfying these needs. If 'money talks' in capitalism it may mean that clear temptations will always exist in situations of the market. Capitalism may be less prone to corruption than socialism because money and the market are naturally associated. In capitalist states many things take place which in a socialist state would be regarded as improper activity. If all economic activities were to be controlled by the state then administrative rules regarding state property will exist in abundance. These rules may be broken, or at least bent, by corrupt bureaucrats for money. If this happens then the system, at least in part, will be discredited. The bureaucratic network in a socialist state is dense; its probability for corruption, at least in some circumstances could be quite high. Capitalist systems are, according to fundamentalist socialist thinkers, inherently corrupt. They could be right if one defines corruption to include the use of money generally rather than rules and laws.

ASPECTS OF CORRUPTION AND BUREAUCRACY

Bureaucracies may have a tendency to create problems and to make manifest certain defects which already exist. If human nature is weak and is easily tempted, bureaucracies promote 'wickedness'. We may see some of these as the product of poor organization, some as the product of human frailty, and some as the product of a failure to understand the organization's objections. Under the first heading, poor organization, we may include such things as wasteful overlapping procedures, a failure to delegate responsibility, inadequate control over subordinates and poor levels of communication in a department. Under the second heading, human failings, we may include poor training, 'empire building', nepotism or favouritism. Under the third heading, failure to understand objectives, we may include problems of confusion of politics and policies, of administration and human need and of purpose, and of confusing *serving* the public and of *directing* the public.

From all these possible defects in organizations the road to corruption is at hand. Bureaucratic incompleteness may breed corruption and where there are internal organizational malfunctions there are very frequently to be found on the margin of corruption. In the developing countries a number of factors interconnect to make many states into 'soft' states to use Myrdal's term. The soft state, soft because it lacks self-discipline, 'makes corruption possible, and in turn the prevalence of corruption is a mighty influence in keeping these countries as soft states' (Myrdal, 1970: 208).

New states, it has been said, tend to bureaucratic corruption for several particular reasons. Administrators are seen to be lacking a work ethic and are prone to take from, rather than give to, the public; prone to follow the indiscipline of their political masters and tending to follow traditional views that tribal or personal loyalties transcend loyalty to a higher civic ideal (Jabbra, 1976: 673, 674 and Caiden, 1977: 303).

A particular problem relates to the concentration of administrative activity in towns, resulting in an urban bias. Rural populations tend to be disadvantaged in many parts of the Third World because political muscle is usually developed in the corridors of power in capital cities.

Administrative reform can help to improve performance and ethical standards. If the machinery is imported then the area of bureaucratic corruption will become minimized. If the machinery of government is efficient it is conceivable that the propensity for corruption would be diminished. Hence reform and enquiry into administrative practices is essential.

However, political factors often intrude. In the Philippines, for example, elections, party conflict and manipulation of the political process lead to a full politicization throughout the entire system. The main election issue between the two parties 'has been the shouts of the "outs" against the corruption of the "ins"' (R.S. Milne, 1969: 181–187). Politics in such a situation is about total power and those excluded from politics are also excluded from everything else. Where the state presides over and legitimizes corruption, then the state may be presiding over its own eventual decline as the case of Marcos shows.

SOME EXAMPLES OF THIRD WORLD CORRUPTION

There is much evidence of corruption in many if not most developing countries, a corruption which it must be stressed, is not necessarily a consequence of poverty, underdevelopment or political ideology. In assessing such corruption we must consider some specific examples chosen to illustrate some of the features of corruption, viewed internationally. There is a need to make a balanced appreciation of the state of corruption in non-communist states in particular (we have already considered socialist graft above).

AFRICA

In Africa certain states have a notorious reputation for corruption. Unfortunately corruption is prevalent in modern Africa, but some states are more prone than others. The case of Nigeria illustrates many of Africa's recurrent problems with corruption — or 'dash' as it is popularly known there. Nigeria is an interesting example because of the continuing pattern of corruption — military rule — civilian rule — corruption — military rule. Nigeria has had a particular struggle against corruption (Olowu, 1985: 8–12). Cases came before the courts in 1984 alone in large numbers covering every aspect of Nigerian society. From February to June 1984, 54, 701 public officers were dismissed or demoted, though this is a conservative estimate compared with the possibly more realistic figure of 150,000. Civilians and military were involved, universities, private and public sector officials and even such eminent persons as the Emir were suspected. A further coup took place in 1985 which some have taken to indicate the impact of unsolved corruption upon the state generally. A further unsuccessful attempted coup came late in 1985.

Examples of corruption fraud and embezzlement are reported with regularity in many parts of Africa. In 1985, the Government of Ghana uncovered large-scale bank thefts, and in 1987 found irregularities in the Treasury, the Auditor General's Department and other important state bodies. Twenty Ghanaians were executed for 'economic sabotage' including a cousin of Flight-Lieutenant Rawlings, the President of Ghana.

In Liberia the Foreign Minister was dismissed for corruption, as were two deputy interior ministers and even the Finance Minister was implicated. In Sierra Leone a number of senior ministers and officials were implicated, according to *Agence France Presse*. Millions of dollars are believed to be embezzled locally, while large sums have to be spent to pay off contracted debts.

The problem becomes worse when one recalls that, in 1980, for example, the salary of the lowest grade civil servant was ₦1,200 per annum, or four times higher than the nation's estimated GDP per capita. This figure excludes impressive fringe benefits, at least for some of the more fortunate civil servants. Of course politicians, too, were affected. Nigeria may well be a good example of the proposition that unrestricted corruption may well influence the political institutions generally. From corruption to coup may be not very far.

One of Africa's most notorious examples of corruption is Zaire, formerly the Belgian Congo. Zaire has gained a reputation for corruption which relates to the patrimonial theory of Third World politics, viz., that the leader in power treats the whole state as his private family. This is indeed Zaire's problem. Mobutu's rule in Zaire found a parallel in that of President Bokassa who systematically milked the resources of the Central African Republic in order to pay for his extravagently lavish coronation in 1976. Mobutu's cult of personality is intense and apparently rooted in patronage. By the late 80's, Mobutu controlled between 17 and 22 per cent of the annual national budget for his own use and a large portion of the rest was funnelled through the office of the president. Mobutu permitted a politics of appropriation which allowed for tolerated corruption for Mobutu's loyal supporters. Mobutu was the richest man in Africa, with 'two palaces in Kinshasa, an estate near the city (N'sele); chateaux in Belgium, Switzerland and France; presidential mansions in each region, cars, the presidential riverboat; the personal use of Air Zaire's 747 and DC-10' (Callaghy in Delury, 1983: 1199).

Kenya, Tanzania, Zimbabwe and Zambia on the East or South-East part of Africa have all been mentioned as experiencing various levels of corruption.

In Ghana, on the west coast corruption has been well-documented and appears to have gained hold shortly after independence. Cocoa production was the basis of the Ghanaian economy. Around the funds set up to organize the payment to cocoa farmers grew up a network of corruption (Dowse, 1969: 45). South Africa has had a serious problem which appeared to involve senior political persons and civil servants.

As a continent and on the whole one will find considerable evidence of corruption wherever one looks for it. Africa has experienced more severe economic difficulties than most other parts of the world. The situation may be all the more severe in that only three states in the whole of Africa (Mauritius, Congo and Gabon) have per capita incomes in excess of US$1,000 (Lancaster, 1985: 145).

ASIA

India has developed a vast network of corruption both in the legislative as well as in the administrative arenas. In the 1980's details were revealed of the sale of state secrets to foreign powers — a purely monetary transaction for private enrichment. The Prime Minister Rajiv Gandhi complained in public of the institutionalization of corruption at the highest levels. In a speech given at the end of 1985, Gandhi argued that corrupt officials were frequently honoured rather than properly denigrated. 'Corruption is not only tolerated but even regarded as the hallmark of leadership', Gandhi concluded. This situation applied to many levels of Indian society, but especially, he argued, to the Congress Party itself. In 1989, Gandhi was the victim.

The Party had no elections at all over a period of twelve years prior to 1985. It kept no accounts or membership lists or itemized expenditure with respect to elections. Election monies were known to have been the product of illegal contributions by companies and rich businessman, described 'as un-complicated as handing a suitcase full of cash over to a party functionary' (*International Herald Tribune*, 10 January 1986).

Corruption in India was often 'kickback' corruption about which countless complaints have been made and Party leaders and civil servants are often accused of accepting payoffs for foreign and domestic contracts. Some control is exercised by the National Institute of Public Finance and Policy, a semi-autonomous group in the Finance Ministry.

The Philippines is seen as a particular example of corruption, certainly so under the regime of Ferdinand Marcos. Some commentators argue that the Philippines lacks a clean bureaucracy, which has been deliberately 'politicized'. (Cariño, 1985: 13). The Philippines has been ruled by Spain, the USA and Japan and has had some difficulty in creating stable political institutions. Corruption has not helped the process.

Vast sums of money are involved in a form of corruption which is part of the system itself, as well as individual cases of bribery amongst government administrators. One case alone in 1983, as reported in the press, involved 700 million pesos. This figure 'was roughly equivalent to the 1983 national government budget for natural resources and was 183 per cent of that year's budget for social security, labour and employment' (Cariño, 1985: 15). Marcos may have expropriated US$10 billion.

Public goods are for sale in the Philippines, because the supply of many services from education to health are a government monopoly. However it should be observed that there are still many officials, especially at the lower levels who are dedicated to the public interest. For them life is difficult, especially when central government is seen to be corrupt, such as in the election of 1986 when the government was seen to be buying votes.

In Japan, corruption gravely affected the government in 1989, seriously eroding the power of the ruling Liberal Democrat party.

THE CARIBBEAN

In the Commonwealth Caribbean, bureaucratic corruption has been alleged for decades. Certain states like the Bahamas, under the premiership of Sir Lynden Pindling have for long been associated with charges of gross drug-related public corruption. In 1984, a commission of inquiry in Nassau revealed that between 1977 and 1983 the prime minister accepted US$2.8 million in gifts and loans and a further $240,000 unexplained (*Sunday Times*, 29 Sept., 1985: 24–49).

In Jamaica, a Commission of Enquiry (the Da Costa Commission, Jamaica, 1972) drew attention to many abuses, including the sale of offices, 'kickbacks' in the state, both at the political and at the administrative level officials were seen to abuse their powers of discretion. Bribes are used to cut through 'red tape', archaic rules and regulations and 'to transform the distant public administrator into a friendly patron' (Jones, 1985: 22).

LATIN AMERICA

Latin America's problem with corruption is never ending. Corruption and the drug culture are close companions in South America. Corruption there should be seen in the context of 'great inequality in distribution of wealth; (where) political office (is) the primary means of gaining access to wealth conflict between changing moral codes; the weakness of social and governmental enforcement mechanisms; and the absence of a strong sense of national community' (Nye, 1967: 418). Particular states where complaints were heard were Brazil, Panama, Ecuador, Argentina, Colombia, Nicaragua, and Mexico (Sloan, 1982: 323). In the latter, corruption has been compared to a 'cancer in a 'climate of virtual asphyxiation, a result of mordida' (the routine bribe). The military is an enthusiastic participant: 'There is no general that can resist a barrage of 50,000 pesos', argued General Alvaro Obregon several decades ago.

CORRUPTION IN THE DEVELOPING WORLD: AN ANALYSIS

Observers of the problem of bureaucratic corruption accept several conclusions about the prevalence of corruption in the developing world in particular. We might characterize these as follows: —

1. 'Soft States' are likely to become corrupt

Myrdal coined the term 'soft state' to refer to states lacking discipline and coherence. They are often artificial states with a poor appreciation of the public weal. They are characterized by a 'poor work ethic', a failure to appreciate the needs of the people they serve and the poor reputation with which political institutions are held generally. Perhaps the most important defect is ethical, however, which indicates the failure to have any civic sense or responsibility for promoting 'good' government in the state. Many of these states are likely to be taken over by the military or to have military men overthrow military men. In Africa, many such states exist — the Sudan, Chad, Ethiopia, Lesotho to name but a few.

2. Developing World Bureaucracies are Politicized

In many developing countries, the state is seen as having an 'extractive' role. The apparatus of the state 'extorts revenues from its people in order to provide benefits for a privileged group of government employees and hangers-on, (which) is very much more evident than in industrial capitalist or even socialist countries' (Clapham, 1985: 183). Politics cannot be separated from administration under these conditions. Public administration is supposed to be impersonal and to treat people equally; a soft or corrupt state cannot be impersonal. Of course administration can never be completely separated from politics, but clientelism (i.e., the bond established between superior (or patron) and inferior (or client)), is a very common feature of developing states.

The advent of computers in the West has tended to make administration more rational and more neutral. The US federal government spends about $10 to $20 billion yearly on computer-based information systems, sums beyond the capacity of most other countries. Computerization may mean less politics, the absence of computers may tend to make politics more prone to corruption.

3. Corruption is Normal and Clean Administration is Abnormal

In certain states corruption is tolerated because it is quite impossible to prevent it. As a result, a bargain may be struck as in the case of Zaire by which loyal supporters of the president are allowed certain types of personal benefits, albeit corruptly obtained. In return for these benefits, 'it is incumbent upon the recipients not to go too far in the direction of excessive gains. An official can be removed for indulging in so-called 'pervasive corruption which harms the nation'.

In many developing countries the political elite sees no obstacle to enriching itself and to turning the bureaucracy into a source of wealth. There is indeed no contradiction between avowedly socialist principles and personal wealth. A Ghanaian diplomat, Krobo Edusei became familiar to people as an official who shipped a gold bed from London to Ghana. He commented that: 'Socialism doesn't mean that if you've made a lot of money, you can't keep it'. As early as 1951, Ghana's Nkrumah warned that: 'Bribery and corruption, both moral and factual, have eaten into the whole fabric of our society and they must be stamped out if we are to achieve any progress.' However others have been more realistic, arguing that toleration is acceptable provided it is kept within bounds. At that level, corruption quite simply becomes normal.

POPULAR TERMS USED TO REFER TO BRIBERY

Baksheesh — (Asia generally) term of original Arab use to describe a tip, subsequently applied to bribery

La bustarella — (Italy) A little envelope, presumed full of money

La mordida — (Spain) The 'bite' taken by public servants in exchange for favours

Dash — (West Africa) — Payment to officials in a general almost systematic sense

Speed money — (India) — to allow a process or application to be expedited

Graft, grease, rakeoff, kickback, payola, five per-center — (USA) all terms to indicate illegal payment(s) for an administrative service

Fiddling — (Great Britain) — to describe the operation of manipulating

Bakku maaju — (Japan) back margin

paasenteiji — (Japan) percentage

ribeito — (Japan) rebate on a deal

tsu kiai — (Japan) relationships which lead to favours

guanxi — (Chinese) — relationships, i.e., corrupt relationships

makan swap — (Malay) — bribery

mooti garm karo — (Hindustani) — itching palm

BIBLIOGRAPHY

Brogan Denis (1954), *An Introduction to American Politics*, Hamish Hamilton, London.

Caiden Gerald (1981), *Public Maladministration and Bureaucratic Corruption*, American Society of Public Administration, Delroit.

Callaghy Thomas, *Zaire*, in George E. Delury (1983), *World Encyclopedia of Political Systems*, Longman.

Carrino, L.C. (1985), *The Politicisation of the Philippines Bureaucracy: Corruption or Commitment?*, International Review of Administrative Sciences, Vol. XLl, No. 1, 1985.

Clapham, see Chapter One.

Dowse Robert E. (1969), *Modernisation in Ghana and the USSR, A Comparative Study*, Routledge, Kegan Paul, London.

Harris Peter (1989), *Socialist Graft*, in Heidenheimer A, Johnson M. and Le Vine, (editor), *Political Corruption*, Transition Publishers.

Hodgkinson, see Chapter Six.

Kempe Ronald Hope (1985), *Politics, Bureaucratic Corruption and Maladministration in the Third World*, International Review of Administrative Sciences, Vol. L1, No. 1, 1985.

Jabbra, J.G. (1976), *Bureaucratic Corruption in the Third World: Causes and Remedy*, Indian Journal of Public Administration, Vol. 22, Oct–Dec 1976.

Jacques Barzun (1965), *Ràce: A. Study in Superstition*, Harper & Row, London.

Johnston Michael, *The Political Consequences of Corruption: A Reassessment: Comparative Politic*, July.

Jones Edwin (1985), *Politics, Bureaucratic Corruption and Maladministration in the Third World: Some Commonwealth Carribbean Considerations*, International Review of Administrative Sciences, Vol. L1, No. 1, 1985.

Lancaster Carol (1983), *Africa's Development Challenges*, Current History, April 1985, Vol. 84, No. 501.

Malinowski Bertrand (1922), *Argonaunts of the Western Pacific*, Routledge, London.

Mauss Marcel (1954), *Essai Sur le Don 1925*, trans by I. Cunnisan as the *Gift*, Cohen & West.

Milne, R.S. (1967), *Government and Politics in Malaysia*, Houghton Mifflin, Boston.

Myrdal Gunnar (1970), *The Challenge of World Poverty*, Penguin, London.

Oluwu Dele (1985), *Bureaucratic Corruption and Public Accountability in Nigeria: an Assessment of Recent Developments*, International Review of Administrative Sciences, Vol. L1, No. 1, 1985.

Scott James C. (1972), *Comparative Political Corruption*, Prentice Hall, New Jersey.

Simis Konstantin (1982), *USSR: The Corrupt Society*, Simon & Schuster, New York.

Sloan, J (1982). *Current History*, Vol. 81.

Part III
Comparative Public Administration

Part III

Comparing Public Administration

8
Comparative Administration: Developed Countries — Some Approaches, Styles and Methods

Social scientists need to use a number of approaches, methods and techniques for the better understanding of the various problems which they are called upon to handle. Some social scientists, learn much from studying history, some from the use of scientific, including mathematical, concepts. All however, have something to learn from a comparison of theories and practices in different places, times and cultures. As far as this brief account is concerned, we identify a number of approaches within the broad area of comparative administration. There will naturally be a number of possible approaches, but the scope and variety will depend upon the investigator and his individual judgment. In this short inquiry we will mention only three broad types: namely, the different countries' approach, the different ideologies' approach, and the type of systems' approach.

THE DIFFERENT COUNTRIES' APPROACH

The most obvious way forward is to consider bureaucratic styles in different countries and to take those in sequence. For example, we may study the method of recruitment to the civil service in a number of countries, Western or non-Western as the case might be. One example, not necessarily dated, is that found in the pioneer study by C.H. Sisson (1957). Sisson's book is entitled *The Spirit of British Administration: and some European Comparisons*.

Starting with Great Britain, Sisson moved to consider the *spirit* of administration in France, Germany, Austria, Sweden and Spain, though not the United States and developing countries. Sisson's approach was that of the Whitehall Civil Servant turned academic. In his analysis he considered a number of states and their civil services from the point of view of training, centralization, politics, administrative law and reform. However, the most interesting idea was that there was a difference in the mind of the administrator in different national traditions.

Sisson saw it necessary to dip into history in order to understand different bureaucratic styles — thus the Spanish Inquisition was still not too remote from the style of the Spanish bureaucracy. We may moreover detect real problems in the study of language. English is a more matter-of-fact language in administrative use than is French, Spanish or Chinese. Indeed, language can be an instrument of government, suggesting sometimes a command rather than a request. In French, Sisson argues, one can speak of the 'administrative sentence' (Sisson, 1959, p. 120). The way in which something is said by officials is almost as important as the rule itself.

In Asia perhaps we might further argue — though Sisson does not take the argument so far — some officials are by tradition, indistinguishable from the Western-type idea of political rulers.

In the USA on the other hand, officials are perhaps managers, without much sense of mystique. In fact, officials are everywhere subject to what might be call 'mental' or 'psychological' constraints. Administration in part relates to 'the mind', and each country or culture is a powerful source of bureaucratic style.

Where the culture of a state is arbitrary or tyrannical, the administration is likely to reflect such features. Administration is no mere managerial quality. For the most part, officials are likely to be unaware that their history, culture and philosophy make them see problems in a particular way — 'any more than is the member of a primitive tribe who nonetheless seems to the visiting anthropologist generally to be pounding around a narrow circle' (Sisson, 1959; 130).

Administration is often profitably analysed by adding countries like the layers on a cake (Brown, 1962: 2). But some people have objected, because if we study a hundred countries we may still be ignorant of any real understanding of the nature of administration. Yet one famous investigation carried on in the 1960's to advise the British Government and headed by Lord Fulton, did set out a country-by country approach, highlighting the major elements in the administrative practices in France, Sweden and the USA. It is hard to escape the common-sense conclusion that the study of governments comparatively, including the addition of new knowledge, must offer valuable insights all round. One cannot deny the benefits of knowing about the practices in other countries, unless one is convinced that administration is learned entirely by doing rather than by study.

Even at the level of performance, a knowledge of the practices successfully used in other countries can lead to considerable improvements. For example, we may be made aware of the *Freedom of Information Act* as in the USA, New Zealand, Canada and Australia. This Act may be seen to be an essential part of the right of citizens, for its objective is too allow citizens to have access to personal information kept on and about them. Yet, in some states where secrecy is the norm, or where the *spirit* of the bureaucracy is secrecy, such freedom of information is seen, by the civil service as unnecessary or even undesirable. That there must be some secrets is obvious, the point is how many.

The different countries' approach is valuable because it takes the bureaucracy in one country at a time, studies its major characteristics, cultural instincts and particular idiosyncracies — its 'idiom' perhaps. Other approaches appear to be relatively more systematic, analysing countries by 'task', 'role' or 'function'. The different countries' approach does see a

Japanese bureaucratic 'style' as significantly different from, say, a German 'style'. The way that a memo is written can in fact, in terms of language, be almost as important as the bureaucratic message itself.

Naturally, most people have a limited capacity to absorb large amounts of information about more than a few countries, just as few people can become proficient in more than a limited number of languages. At its most ideal, however, comprehensive, rather than superficial knowledge is obviously better.

THE DIFFERENCE OF IDEOLOGY APPROACH

In all countries which have recognized state systems, officials are appointed by the state act and through the law. In many other systems however, officials belong to a political party, and, in one-party states, membership of the party apparatus is crucial. In particular, communist parties stand out as many observers pay particular attention to the party bureaucracy. 'But here can be no doubt about the enormous power that the party apparatus and its officials wield' ... in the Soviet Union. Indeed wherever there is a communist mode of government there is according to some writers, an inherent tendency towards large-scale bureaucracies (Rizzi, 1985: 50) (Trotsky, 1972) (Djilas, 1957).

Traditionally, it is argued that a simple explanation of communist states is that they rely upon democratic centralism in administrative theory and practice. Democratic centralism suggests that power and responsibility flow two ways — from the bottom up, and from the top down (McAuley, 1978: 275). Most people however argue that it is 'centralism' rather than 'democracy' which is the truly operative principle in the well-known formula. The democratic centralism idea is found in most socialist states, including China. We may detect suggestions of cynicism about the principle of democratic centralism (Schapiro, 1984: 61). Other writers believe that 'democratic centralism' is a useful device towards the solution of certain complex issues (Churchward, 1968: 208). One writer, in his survey of Soviet constitutions believes that the second of the concepts is 'highly dubious' (Unger, 1981: 187).

Socialist states are ideologically distinct from non-socialist states obviously by definition. Those whose political credentials are reliable are appointed to key positions in party and state. The lists of such officials — called the *nomenklatura* — cover almost every important position in the Soviet Union, certain states in Eastern Europe, and in China, amongst others. Such 'devices' as 'democratic centralism' and the 'nomenklatura' are characteristic of socialist states, but not in liberal democracies in the West. While the Soviet Union is clearly characterized as a public administration in the 'nomenklatura' mould, China also runs a 'nomenklatura' system (Burns, 1987: 49). Ideology and organization clearly dovetail in socialist states.

115

THE DIFFERENT TYPES OF SYSTEMS APPROACH

Some writers approach the study of comparative administration as an exercise in types and systems. Countries with roughly or broadly similar 'systems' are often grouped together, especially in studies of comparative institutions which come from the USA. A well-known study is to be found in the writings of Gabriel Almond and G.B. Powell as part of one-time popular behaviouralist school of political scientists. Bureaucracies they argue, obviously appear everywhere, so it is merely a question of classifying them under appropriate headings. The types, forms and classifications used probably depend upon the personal interpretation of the scholar concerned.

For example, in the typology of Almond and Powell one can perceive several types of bureaucracy as follows: democratic, Marxist-Leninist, patriarchal, patrimonial, medieval and monarchical, amongst others (Almond and Powell, 1966: 144–163). Yet Almond and Powell argue that there is also merit in the classification of bureaucracy as set out by Merle Fainsod, namely: (1) representative bureaucracies, (2) party-state bureaucracies, (3) military-dominated bureaucracies, (4) ruler-dominated bureaucracies, and (5) ruling bureaucracies (Fainsod in Palombara, 1963, p. 233).

Other typologies may be found in other places, but because American studies dominated the scene during the sixties and seventies, many of the analyses tend to reflect the American view of political science (Caiden, 1982: 230–251).

A typical example is found in the writings of Ferrel Heady whose classification may be summarized as follows:
1. Classic bureaucracies (Germany and France)
2. Civic culture types (USA and Great Britain)
3. Successfully modernizing types (Japan)
4. Communist country types
5. Developing or Third World types (Heady, 1979, *passim*)

From the above list we can raise certain criticisms. For example, we may ask how certain states, for example, the People's Republic of China, may fit into the list, given its Third World status as well as a socialist-communist foundations. Moreover, socialism as a system (rather than as an ideology) may be found in a number of countries not necessarily ruled by a communist party. If a communist party dominates a socialist system inside a developing country, than we may clearly lack a clear focus of study and investigation.

The ideas contained in the systems-behaviour approach are not indeed new and offer certain benefits and certain intellectual costs. At a level of high generality the systems-behaviour approach can assist in our understanding of the broad comparisons between bureaucracies. But without detailed case studies and historical knowledge the technique of painting with a 'broad brush' may be far too general to be of much value. On balance a keen understanding of administrative history appears to yield considerable benefits to the student of public administration.

We are mainly concerned with public administration in states but the state bureaucracy in some countries is often of less importance than, say, the bureaucracy of the (Catholic) church, or the Communist Party, or perhaps the army. State bureaucracies are normally created by state law. In that case, state bureaucracies can also follow a legal mode of classification. The tradition of Anglo-American Common Law is widespread, extending to India, Pakistan, Malaysia and the anglo-phone states of Africa, amongst others. By contrast, the tradition of Roman Law stresses centralization of power as well as logic and structures. In a sense, communist systems link up, if somewhat uncomfortably, in the Roman Law traditions especially in regard to the concentration of power.

In the developing world, the state bureaucracy is relatively new, a post-colonial creation. There are other 'bureaucracies', in armies, communal groups, and above all in the party. Socialists speak, in a Soviet sense, of *apparachiki*, or members of the party apparatus, those persons who are in a very broad sense 'rulers' in their respective spheres. This tradition offer yet another and different perspective in contrast to both developing and, or, socialist states. Rather than stress law, they may tend to stress class, tribe, race and ideology. However, an efficient, honest and dedicated public service is surely a pre-requisite to any modern state. In practice, political consider-ations everywhere tend to predominate. However, administration in an ideal world would operate on a higher plane.

ADMINISTRATION: THEMES AND VARIATIONS

Administration is found everywhere but nowhere is it quite the same. Even the word 'administration' or the much-abused term 'bureaucracy' can mean different things in different places. In some countries administration is seen as an arm or a limb of the central government and must respond to, rather than make, policy. A good example of this proposition would be France. In other countries, administration is seen differently. In Sweden administrators are seen frequently as people who simply conduct the affairs of government without making policy. In Britain and her former colonies, administration is seen as a departmental matter with no clear separation between administra-tion and policy. In the Third World too, there are enormous variations of style and substance.

Despite these problems, it is certain that there is a 'bureaucratic phen-omenon' that suggests over the entire globe a tendency exists towards rule by officials. We have suggested that while some people find this tendency de-plorable, others take a more relaxed view. None doubt its pervasiveness.

One way of indicating the truth of this proposition is to consider the source of income of a population. In Sweden the state provides 57 per cent of all incomes (such as wages, pensions and unemployment pay). The USA's figures are 42 per cent. The figure in France is 55 per cent and in Germany

117

and Italy 51 per cent. Public sector employment in the USA accounts for about 20 per cent of the labour force. In a typical Western European state millions depend upon state benefits (the figures for pensions, unemployment benefits and related other benefits account for 14 million people in Britain alone). All of these benefits mean public administration on a large scale, even in an age of computerization and communications technology.

In all European countries, the public sector has increased enormously since 1945. At that time the largest employer was the armed forces; in 1986 on average almost half of all public workers are in the social services including education, health and their administration.

STRUCTURES OF ADMINISTRATION

For convenience, we may discuss modern administrative forms under a number of headings in order to proceed with a framework of analysis.

These headings are: (1) Recruitment (2) Structure (3) Central-Local Relations (4) Party Politics and the Administrator.

(1) *Recruitment*

All recruitments to Western senior levels civil services appear to be élitist in nature. The term *élite* of course signifies that *a few* specially selected individuals come to enjoy significant administrative roles. The fact of *élitism* does not necessarily imply that the civil services studied are anything other than concerned with the recruitment of the best available persons for posts. However the question of who are the 'best' potential civil servants is indeed difficult. In the British system, entry into the civil service at the senior levels (Administrative Class) appears to be the preserve of those who choose the civil service after attending public schools and Oxford or Cambridge Universities. British methods seem to favour liberal arts university graduates. In a survey carried out in 1969 by A.H. Halsey and I.M. Crewe, it was shown that at the most senior level of the British civil service some 73 per cent of the Administrative Class direct entrance appointees were Oxford and Cambridge liberal arts graduates. In 1979 a second survey showed little change in the intake of liberal arts graduates and some 60 per cent still came from Oxford. By the 1980's these proportions had changed and Oxbridge graduates constituted half of the intake.

In the USA recruitment to the federal civil service follows the British pattern but only for a portion of the civil service. The American concept is of a less confined and restricted catchment area than in the case in Britain. People are frequently brought in to the administration from outside the scope of the service itself. The British stress 'career staffing', that is people will spend their whole careers in the civil service, while Americans prefer 'programme staffing'. Hence in the USA a new programme or agency will take on new staff until the job has been completed.

The French bureaucracy operates from different premises, as we shall see.

118

Recruitment in the French case is an *élite* catchment area. French civil servants come from an *élite* social group and consciously see themselves as an *élite* body. Senior entrants into the French civil service join either the E.N.A. (Ecole Nationale d'Administration) which is the National Administration School, or the Ecole Polytechnique, which is the technical equivalent of the E.N.A. The graduates of the former, called *énarques*, are a powerful group of decision-makers who owe allegiance to the criteria of capacity and talent. Those who are recruited to the E.N.A. spend the first year understudying officials in ministries or perhaps embassies. In their second year they receive instruction in drafting laws and government decrees. In the final year, students are put into groups to try out ideas along the lines of the Harvard Business School, for example, where they develop skills of team work and group analysis. Many, perhaps most, French top decision-makers today are *énarques*.

The French approach implies that public officials can form a meritocracy based on a common intellectual training and understanding of a code of behaviour and discipline. The Swedish approach on the other hand is very much more 'open'. Bureaucrats are not a caste or particular élite, and Sweden prides itself on having a highly 'democratic' public administration. Recruitment at least in theory, is open to all.

If we turn to consider the case of Japan, we find a similar *élitist* manner of recruitment to that found in Britain and France. Many young Japanese prize a career in government service, so competition to enter the service is keen.

Students begin early to climb up the educational ladder towards a career in government and they need to succeed in a series of examinations which are set from an early age. Elite and prestigious institutions as much as academic ability, offer the way to success in the bureaucracy. In Japan it is important to have been to the 'right' schools and universities, with Tokyo University as the summit of the entire system. Most would-be civil servants will attend Tokyo University, and at least three-quarters the major Japanese universities. The Constitution of 1947 makes a specific reference to the role of public officials, declaring them to be 'servants of the whole community'. Japanese tradition sees officials as masterful and authoritative. They certainly constitute an *élite*. Out of about 250,000 civil servants, those belonging to the first grade constitute about one thousand, many the products of Tokyo University. Japanese students are required to pass through a series of examinations, the passing of which with high honours in an indispensible prerequisite to advancement in the civil service (*Current History*, December 1985).

The Japanese civil service has grown impressively, but it still retains its dominant central *élite*. In 1940, the Japanese national government had 231,898 employees. In 1960, this figure was about 3,000,000 or one per fourteen of the entire working force. In the late 1980's Japan's civil service constituted about 17 per cent of the work force. Entrants to the Civil Service are still expected to show 'loyalty and obedience to superiors, tact, anonymity, patience and a capacity for the endless details and rituals of administration...' (Ward, 1963: 101).

Recruitment is a complex question. The ancient Chinese who first considered it, devised a method of selection which required a combination of a knowledge of ancient texts as well as a strong moral (Confucian) sense. In some ways, the British mode of recruitment was in harmony with this approach. There must still today be some criteria for recruitment which of course depend upon circumstances. The fact is that recruitment criteria invariably suggest *élitism*.

(2) Structure

The internal organization of government in any state reflects not only the national psyche or mood, but the history of the organization of government in the country concerned. Organizations in fact, have a life of their own.

Parliamentary states have an untidy organizational structure. The government machine, both central and local, gives the appearance of a decided lack of system. There is no attempt at structural coherence. The Minister, who is appointed by the Prime Minister, is a party politician and a Member of Parliament. All the other people in the department, except for the Parliamentary Private Secretary, are civil servants. It has been said that ministers are on top, and civil servants are 'on tap', which suggests that civil servants merely obey orders and execute policy. The truth may be somewhat different. Ministers are temporary heads and senior civil servants will serve many ministers as a life-time career. Hence civil servants are able to gain much knowledge and, in consequence, an associated power of and over particular subjects.

In the British parliamentary system, civil servants are in theory 'anonymous' agents of policy. The theory is that ministers are responsible, technically, for mistakes errors and shortcomings, having to answer usually to the House of Commons. Civil servants must be impartial, according to the theory, offering their skill, expertise and advice to all ministers in equal measure, irrespective of party loyalties. In fact, many of these old 'truths' have been shattered in the eighties (Wright, 1978: 293–313).

The British Departmental Structure

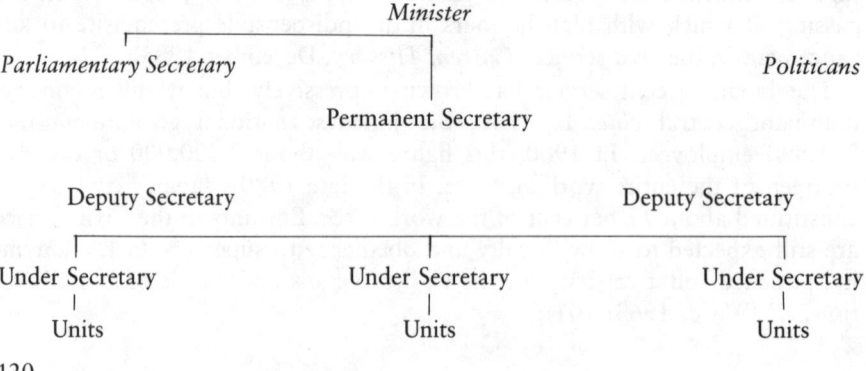

In the British system, the department as can be seen from the above diagram, is a single-unit organization designed to produce a service or undertake a task, for example, transport, education and defence. Politicians have a very limited role to play in a typical British ministry. The Minister is, of course, a politician and a Member of Parliament, but the organization of the ministry is left to the permanent secretary and his staff. The minister may be seen to be the 'intruder' by the civil servants (Wass, 1984). The British ministry according to the textbooks stresses procedure and faithfulness to precedent. It tries to avoid ideological positions and usually attempts to adopt a neutral position. In the period of Margaret Thatcher's government, however, the textbook analysis has been modified.

The French Departmental Structure

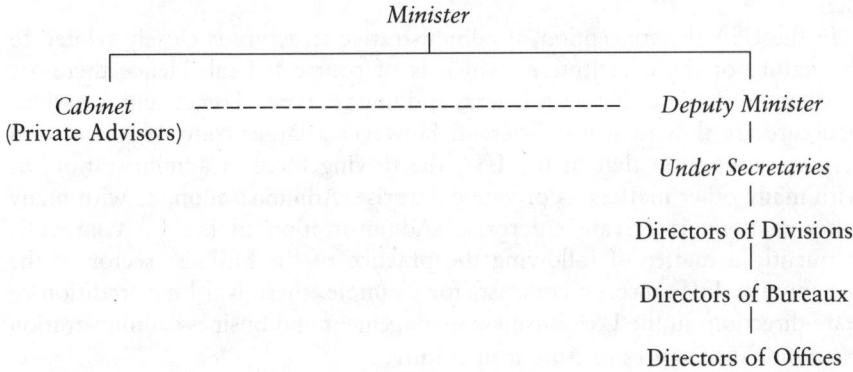

In many important ways, French administration is noted for its clarity, centrality and intellectual vigour. There are very special French ways of looking at the world (Sisson, 1959: 49–59). French departments differ from the British model in a number of ways. While the French ministry usually acts as a single-purpose organization, it is a decidedly more 'political' at the top than is the typical British ministry. In Continental Europe generally, ministers create for themselves a group (called a *cabinet*) which is usually connected with, or even is part of, the minister's political party.

Essentially, however, Europeans feel the presence of the *State*, largely because of centuries of understanding and grappling with it. The civil servant of today may even see himself as the inheritor of the *etatist* tradition in very large measure. In Europe generally (unlike the USA, for example) the state is a meaningful and significant feature.

The structure in Sweden is different again. In Sweden *policy* is often distinguished from *execution* of policy by the creation of many special agencies to provide for services on the ground. In Sweden the national ministries are very small and so the agencies are the 'working parts' of the system. The Swedish notion of public administration structure has a quite unusual appearance to those brought up in the British or French tradition. The attraction of the Swedish system is that it allows particular enterprises to be decentralized. The conventional view of Swedish administration is that it plays only a small part in the central government machine, which interpretation is questioned by some writers (Schonfield 1965: 203). Swedish public administration does however make possible a situation in which 'large blocks of work that would be done by government departments in Britain are entrusted to autonomous agencies in Sweden' (Fulton, 1968: 138). Hence the Ministry of Education has a central staff of only about 120 persons. The reasons for such a special system in Sweden are in fact historical and would not appear to be the result of some pre-conceived plan (Heckscher, 1955: 6). Sweden however does share an administrative tradition which distinguishes it to a large extent from that of the USA and links it closer to models elsewhere in Europe. This is once again, the tradition of the European conception of the 'state'.

In the USA the conception of administrative structure is closely related to the nature of the constitution, which is of course federal. Hence there are profound differences between federal and unitary types. French and American structure are thus radically different. However a larger contrast relates to a certain assumption that in the USA the driving force in administration, as with many other matters, is private enterprise. Administration, as with many other matters, is private enterprise. Administration in the US context is frequently a matter of following the practice of the business sector of the community. In France by contrast, for example, there is a long tradition of state direction; in the USA business management and business administration are dominant features of American culture.

The USA is above all a society which believes that government administration has much to learn from the private sector. Hence the idea of the business school has flourished in the USA (and beyond) because business schools are seen as innovators. Government is seen as a follower of business, given that the USA has developed in accordance with a 'national myth' that capitalism is the guarantor of the freedom of the individual from oppression by the Government (Schonfield, 1965: 321).

One observer commented: 'It is clear to the most obtuse observer that there is a much more distant relationship between business and government leadership in the United States than, say, Britain, France or the Netherlands.... A Britain businessman can say, 'Some of my best friends are civil servants', and really mean it. This would be rare in the United States' (Mason, *cit* in Schonfield, 1965: 334).

If we consider the case of Japan we see a pattern of administration which suggests certain aspects of Japanese social history. 'Within Japan', said one writer in the *Economist* (November 28, 1987), 'the ministry's role is often likened to that of a village elder who decides the shape of the annual harvest, and then shares it in the way that is best for the village as a whole so as to preserve social order and cohesion'. The important ministries, for example, the Ministry of Finance, will have senior civil servants whose authority exceeds that of many politicians, even, if they choose, being able to challenge the Prime Minister.

Japanese civil servants acquire great influence in policy-making which gives them access to many aspects of Japan's vast economic enterprises. At the age of 55 or earlier, however, Japanese civil servants retire from the public service to take up positions in the private sector. Japanese civil servants in fact begin new careers as members of the lobbies with which they negotiated previously. Others seek to enter politics, usually right of centre in alignment. Civil servants often succeed as politicians, attaining Cabinet and other high office. From 1947 to 1984, of fourteen prime ministers, seven were former public officials, generally having served either in the Ministry of Finance or the Ministry of Foreign Affairs.

Japan's civil service faces problems similar in nature to those faced by Western states. The growth of state intervention in certain key areas has led, as elsewhere, to a state of 'overloading' of government. Pressures for subsidies, social welfare and defence remain strong. In particular, problems have arisen over the rice subsidy scheme, Japan National Railways and the national health service. Japan has implemented various schemes of privatization, including that of Japanese Air Lines.

(3) Central-Local Relations

Each Western state approaches the question of central-local relations differently. For some it is the great complex issue of public administration. French revolutionaries spoke of *la République, Une et Indivisible*, stressing the indivisibility of the state and the need to foster and strengthen unity and central direction. Hence Paris was (and is) the focal point of the French State. During the French Revolution 1789–1799, the revolutionaries appeared to have a taste for uniformity and regularity. France was (1790) divided into departments of approximately equal size and roughly square-shaped. The idea was that the region could be covered comfortably in one day on horse-back. The departments were later strengthened by Napoleon who installed officials (called Prefects) whose task it was to act as local agents (Machin, 1977: 18–22). The Prefect was seen as the representative of the State itself.

Recently, however, departments have been complemented by larger modern regions. In the mid-eighties, President Mitterand attempted to restore the importance of the departments in the electoral process. Mitterand also changed the title of 'Prefect' to simple 'Commissaire', but obviously the Commissaire, like the Prefect, is the spokesman for the state in the provinces. The system is nonetheless unchanged in its essentials.

Neither the American nor British administrations envisage an identical perfectoral structure relating the centre to the localities. The American federal tradition functions very loosely with 50 diverse states co-existing often uneasily with the centre. Washington is seen as a distant centre of compromise

123

far from the perspective of the various state capitals. Washington is not Paris. Relations between Washington and the states and localities are often contentious. Yet Washington is the capital. But it is a capital of a very fissiparous country.

In Britain, London is the dominant partner in local government, partly because of the central government's control over finance, and partly because Parliament (centred in London) can make and unmake local government structures at will. Moreover, political decisions are taken (in London) by professional politicians who are also Ministers of the Crown. English local government is operated through a system in which local officials (appointed) work with political figures (elected). Professor Laski pointed out 'that the whole difference between efficient and inefficient administration lies in the creative use of officials by elected persons' (Laski, 1938: 425). At the local government level however, the elected persons are not generally politicians in the strict sense in which they are at the central government level. Ultimately central government exerts strict controls over local authorities through financial controls. In 1984 the Greater London Council was penalized because it proposed to spend 33% more than it was allowed. In 1985, eighteen local authorities were 'rate-capped' (or given fixed limits to their spending by the central government).

In Japan, a centralized form of government has always been evident. Before 1947, all institutional and state power was concentrated in the Emperor, and, even after some measure of local government decentralization, Japan's form of government is still highly unified. Hence, 'This pronounced degree of fiscal dependency plus the long-ingrained bureaucratic habit of looking to Tokyo and the national government for guidance detracts greatly from the actual degree of autonomy enjoyed by the prefectures, cities, towns, and villages of Japan' (Ward, 1963: 103).

(4) Administration and Party Politics: Western States

In a sense, all public administration is conservative. In few countries is public administration sympathetic to radical change and radical politics. The *élitist* character of officials is obviously significant, because they are attracted to order, regularity and continuity above all. Nethertheless the ideal is one of neutrality. Public officials everywhere are supposed to offer impartial advice to their political superiors. A civil servant is distinguished from a party politician albeit at a theoretical level. Many complain that this situation is 'unrealistic' and has everywhere broken down in practice (Dror, 1984: 80–81). Dror sees only 'rulers' to include politicians and civil servants.

The classic guidelines were set out in the *Report of the Committee on the Political Activities of Civil Servants*, (the Masterman Committee) in 1949, which saw 'the political neutrality of the Civil Service (as) a fundamental feature of British democracy and is essential for its efficient operation. It must be maintained even at the cost of some loss of political liberty by certain of those who elect to enter the service.' These principles imply certain rules in national politics as civil servants should abstain from any public manifestation of their views which might associate them prominently with a political party. They should not (a) hold office in any party political organization; (b) speak in public on matters of party political controversy; (c) write letters to the Press, publish books or articles, or circulate leaflets setting forth their views on party political matters; (d) convass in support of political candidatures' (Masterman Report, 1979: Cmd 7718).

Western states see these guidelines as reasonable and even perhaps desirable (H. Finer, 1949: 614–617). The difficulty is with policy-making, as Dror demonstrates. Public administration scholars often believe that policy-making in all countries is the responsibility of policy-makers and that the distinction between politicians and civil servants is false. In the United States in particular, Republican Presidents tend to favour Republicans in the senior ranks of the public service. Even in Great Britain, the home of the concept of political neutrality, Margaret Thatcher has tended to prefer civil servants who are sympathetic to the Conservative Party's philosophical position.

In Japan, the top levels of the civil service are heavily politicized. The reason for this is historical — service to the Emperor was all-important — and because the national legislature is a much weaker body than the collective bureaucracy. Hence the civil service has much to say about monetary and fiscal matters and location of industry, and can hold up implementation of new policies such as privatization (*Economist:* November 28, 1987: 74–5).

Perhaps the safest approach is not to distinguish between politicians and civil servants but to talk about 'policy makers' or even Dror's preferred (if somewhat old-fashioned) term, 'rulers'. Dror argues a case saying: 'The term "Ruler" is used in the clinical and technical sense of real heads of government, never mind their formal titles. With some adjustments, the concepts "Ruler" also covers collegial and collective ruling bodies, such as Cabinets' (Dror, 1984: 79).

Comparative administration is a subject of some complexity. It is not simply a question of borrowing aspects of one system to be incorporated into another. It is obviously necessary to take into account ideology, history, culture, geography and economic factors in order to understand why a particular bureaucracy has evolved why, where and how.

At the same time however, certain questions need to be asked about the role of political institutions, the efficiency of the current administrative arrangements, the neutrality or otherwise of the civil service, and indeed the whole range of questions asked by Weber. Many of these are still relevant to the modern observer in the developing world administration, especially in regard to patrimonialism. 'The theory of modern public administration, for instance, assumes that the authority to order certain matters by decree — which has been legally granted to public authorities — does not entitle the bureau to regulate the matter by commands given for each case, but only to regulate the matter abstractly. This stands in extreme contrast to the regula-

Comparing Bureaucracies

	Recruitment	Structure	Central-Local Relations	Party Politics
GREAT BRITAIN	Elites. Oxbridge. Public Schools. Career Staffing	Amateur. Learn by doing, muddle through	London mainly predominant, Local loyalties strong	Neutrality in theory. Disposition — conservative
FRANCE	Elitist (intellectual), Social exclusivity	Unitary State. Rigorous training.	Paris totally dominant	Support for order and stability
SWEDEN	Open	Division into policy and execution	Stockholm — a neutral centre	Civil Service has a neutral political approach
USA	Enter for long or short periods; Open. Programme staffing	Federal Government. Assumption private enterprise should show the way	Washington Federal, State Capitals for 50 States	Constitution excludes them
JAPAN	Enter after a long period of educational competition and elimination	Senior civil servants exercise considerable power both during and after tenure	Tokyo is the centre of power, despite a well-structured local government	Top levels of the civil service are highly politicized

tion of all relationships through individual privileges and bestowals of favour, which is absolutely dominant in patrimonialism, at least in so far as such relationships are not fixed by sacred tradition' (Gerth and Mills, eds., 1946: 196–8).

In some respect these words of Weber still point the way to many contemporary dilemmas in the field of public administration, namely, how to find a compromise between cultural diversity and the modern principles of public administration.

BIBLIOGRAPHY

Almond Gabriel A. & G.B. Bingham Powell (1966), *Comparative Politics: A Developmental Approach*, Little, Brown & Co., Boston.

Blondel Jean (1972), 'Contemporary France: Politics, Society, Institution' in D.G. Charlton, France: *A Companion to French Studies*, Methuen, 1972, London.

Brown B.E. (1962), *New Directions in Comparative Politics*, Bombay, Asia Publishing House.

Burns John P. (1987), *China's Nomenklatura System, Problems of Communism*, Vol. XXXVI, Sept–Oct 1987.

Churchward L.G. (1968), *Contemporary Soviet Government*, Routledge Kegan Paul, London.

Crozier M. (1964), *The Bureaucratic Phenomenon*, University of Chicago, Chicago.

Cummings William K. & Victor N. Kobayashi (Dec. 1985), *Education in Current History*.

Djilas Milovam (1957), *The New Class*, Praeger, New York.

Dror Michael (1984), 'Policy Analysis for Advising Rulers', in Rolinson and Istvan Kiss, eds., *Rethinking the Process of Operational Research and Systems Analysis*, Oxford, Pergamon Press, 1984.

Hill and Frank, see Chapter One.

Fulton John (Chairman), *The Civil Service, Vol. I., Report of the Committee 1966–1968* (H.M.S.O.) Cmnd. 3638.

Heady Ferrell (1979), *Public Administration: A Comparative Perspective*, Marcel Dekker, New York.

Heckscher Gunnar (1955), *Swedish Public Administration at Work*.

Laski H.J. (1948), *A Grammar of Politics*, 5th edition, Allen & Unwin, London.

Howard Machin (1977), *The Prefect in French Public Administration*, Croom Helm, Kent.

McAuley, M. Mary (1977), *Politics and the Soviet Union*, Penguin.

Palombara, see Chapter I.

Ponting Clive (1986), *Whitehall: Tragedy and Farce*, Hamish Hamilton (Sphere Books), London.

Rizzi Bruno (1985), *The Bureaucratisation of the World*, Tavistock, London.

Report of the Committee on Political Activities of Civil Servants, the Masterman Report, Cmnd. 7715, 1949.

Rush Michael (1984), *The Cabinet and Policy Formation*, Longman, London.

Schonfield, see Chapter Ten.

Schapiro L.B. (1984), *The Government and Politics of the Soviet Union*, Hutchinson, London.

Trotsky Leon (1972), *The Revolution Betrayed*, Pathfinder Press, New York.

Urger L. Aryeh (1980), *Constitutional Development in the USSR: A Guide to the Soviet Constitutions*, Methuen, London.

Ward (1963) (ed.), *Japan: Political Systems, Asia*, Prentice Hall.

Wass Douglas (1983), *Reith Lectures*, The Listener, B.B.C., London.

Weber in Gerth and Mills (eds), see Chapter One.

Wright Maurice (1978), *Ministers and Civil Servants*, Parliamentary Affairs.

9
Comparative Administrative Systems: The Developing World

Many commentators point out the differences between post-colonial states on the grounds of their inherited colonial tradition. They speak of anglophone versus francophone traditions, for example, as English administrative theory and practice is often contrasted with French administrative theory and practice. It is believed that the colonial influence in these matters was decisive. In India, the British tradition of educated amateurs lived on in the Indian Civil Service, whereas the French have continued to see their colonies as something akin to administrative regions (departments) integrated in the greater structure of metropolitan France. The French colonies were peopled by French citizens who elected representatives to France's Parliament. Special cases can be made out for the Spanish and Portuguese traditions which stressed the assimilation of the respective peoples to the metropolitan culture.

The French approach to colonial administration differed in significant ways from that of the British.

1. The French notion of administration at home as well as for colonies was that administrators were selected after an examination only. British administrators were selected largely by personal interview on their presumed 'personal qualities'.

2. French administrators tended to perceive a colonial career as a second-best to a career in France itself. In 1943, for example, in French West Africa, a quarter of the officials, including four governors, were actually Corsican. Others were from the West Indies and provincial France generally. British administrators, however, were often administrators of high quality in themselves, having *chosen* a career in the colonies. It would be true to observe, however, that it was the home rather than the colonial civil service, which attracted the élite.

3. French training for the colonies consisted in special training at the *Ecole Coloniale*. French cadets were introduced to the concept of *France d'Outre Mer*. There is no equivalent in English colonial theory of the idea that the colonies were no more than an extension of England. The words of the Ghanaian ambassador to the United Nations sum up the difference between the French and British. 'The French set out to assimilate their subject peoples by sharing with them the highest known form of civilization ... the French, the British made no such effort with theirs, but left them free to pick up such Anglo-Saxon attributes as they saw fit to

embellish the African personality' (*Observer*, London, 25 September 1960).

4. The British saw administration as a matter for individual territories, whose individual units developed in an *autochthonous* fashion (lit. from the soil itself). The French view was that an élite would develop to administer a centralized empire. Francophile colonials were sent to Paris to absorb French culture and to serve where appropriate on French bodies, including the National Assembly.

5. The British saw local colonial peoples as members of a territory who would nevertheless always remain, realistically, 'foreign'. The French (and the Portuguese) envisaged assimilation of the local culture into French (and Portuguese) culture. Macau was able to survive long after the age of colonies in part because it saw itself different from China, that is, essentially Portuguese.

6. French, Portuguese, Belgian and Dutch colonial civil servants all followed a pattern of civil administration rather more broadly similar to each other than to that of Great Britain. For the most part, British official thinking failed to generate a comprehensive philosophy of colonial administration. British administrative practice leant in large measure towards nurturing an indigenous administration rather than on conferring the benefits of a metropolitan culture. Naturally the British encouraged locals to admire British institutions, and in sport, for example, they were successful.

7. The British colonial administrators were chary of theorizing about policy. They were prepared to transfer institutions, legislatures and courts of law, for example. They were uninterested in questioning the reasons for, or the underlying philosophy of, their presence. Many British institutions have however persisted long after the departure of the British themselves. Those institutions have merged, to some extent, with local needs, so that it has become quite difficult for observers 'to distinguish between British and indigenous elements in political traditions which have come down from pre-independence times' (Heussler, 1963: 218).

British practices, classically revealed a tradition of 'muddle-through'. French and also continental attitudes generally showed (compared with the British) a far greater concern for administrative logic and central control. British attitudes were known for stressing the *differences* between states and a desire to 'trust the man on the spot' (McIntyre, 1967: p. 70). Of course, ultimately both the British and French assumed the superiority of their own systems over those whom they were charged to administer. Later writers were to refer to 'imperialism'. Disraeli believed that 'imperial characteristics' were part of the 'destiny of man' and included the United States in this categorization. Gladstone on the other hand believed that the 'lust for territory was one of the greatest curses of mankind' (McIntyre, 1967: 19).

However as far as most non-Western states were concerned, administration required to be a part of overall development. There could however be no development without sound administration. Weber's rational bureaucracy was necessary. It was hardly correct, however, to see ideology, even the rhetoric of nationhood, as a substitute for administration. Whatever the political complexion of the government in power, an efficient, incorrupt administration was essential for the purposes of development. This was true both of times before, as well as after, colonial rule.

Other traditions have also emerged such as those of the Netherlands and Belgium. The largest Dutch colonial territory was Indonesia, but it never accepted the proposal to continue any form of association with Holland after independence. Belgium ruled the Congo until independence in 1960. Today the Congo has become Zaire with a massive problem of administration but little sign that even modern Zaire can evolve administrative coherence. The USA is not normally seen as a former colonial power, but in fact the USA has perceived a 'manifest destiny' to expand its frontiers. Whatever impulses drove European nations to acquire colonies, made Americans turn to the West. If one excludes American Indians, then this process of expansion had a limited effect upon the number of persons involved. The US is most evidently a former colonial power in respect to the Philippines, Hawaii and Alaska, as well as Puerto Rico.

Despite all these numerous but important historical qualifications which can be made about administration in developing states, there are certain features which they share in common. We draw attention to these as follows:

1. THE CHANGING RELATIONSHIP OF IDEOLOGY AND ADMINISTRATION

Colonial civil servants were, because of their 'foreign-ness', often far removed from the lives of the people. After independence (often fought on a platform of independence) the 'values' of the administrators became important in a way not in evidence when the neutral foreign administrators were rulers of a colony. The new administrators became politicized very quickly by accepting new ideologies, necessary to survive in a post-colonial society. The classical notion of separating 'politics' (or more properly 'ideological politics') from administration was not pursued. New states rushed to develop new ideologies such as *pantasila* in Indonesia, *consciencism* in Ghana, *ujaama* in Tanzania, *humanism* in Zambia, and numerous others. As a result administration has become ideological almost as did theology in western Europe during the Middle Ages. In modern Islamic states religion dominates almost everything and no possibility of a separate autonomous and neutral administration exists. In many states civil servants are seen as spokesmen of tribe, caste, class or regional group, duty bound to serve their original loyalties. The distinction between party or ethnic loyalty and professional neutrality has become blurred.

2. COST OF THE PUBLIC SERVICE IN DEVELOPING STATES

In developing states, the civil service is a major source of new jobs. In many states the cost of maintaining the public service is considerable, relative to the national income. The following figures indicate the extent of the problem:

	1960	1979
Zambia	11 per cent	27 per cent
Jamaica	7	20
Kenya	11	20

(Cost of civil service relative to National Income: Source: *World Bank)*

Many bureaucracies in the developing world tend to become large and purposeless empires, often self-seeking and unable to provide the needs for the fulfilment of which they exist. In effect, the performance of the bureaucracy does not always measure up to expectations. Officials are effective only when they are personally beneficiaries of the system (Downs, 1967: chap 17). Relations between the centre and localities are often strained and even fall short of the dictum of John Stuart Mill in *Representative Government*: 'Power may be localized, but knowledge, to be useful, must be centralized' (Mill, 1910 ed: 357).

In short, there are administrative costs for most new states which are partly financial and partly emotional. The powers which all bureaucrats everywhere exercise are fully enjoyed in developing countries. Many developing states are hindered, when they should be helped, by their bureaucracies. In China for example the problem of the relations between administration and the administered is centuries old. Both communists like Mao Zedong and Deng Xiaoping as well as their opponents have found fault with a bureaucratic style of government (Freedman and Morgan, 1982).

3. THE RELATIONSHIP OF THE BUREAUCRACY TO THE MILITARY

The military state — a state controlled by soldiers — is sometimes run by them. There are close resemblances between military and civilian organizations. The latter requires a hierarchy to be effective; an army certainly is characterized by 'the forcefulness, extensiveness and explicitness of its hierarchical structure' (Nordlinger, 1977: 44). Since 1945, the military has intervened in two-thirds of non-Western states. To rule a civilian population, however, an army needs officials to run the post office, water supplies and keep transport, power and supplies running, among many other things.

An army may take power in a coup, but it is hardly likely to be interested in mass popular participation (Feit, 1973). A network of obedient officials serves its purpose much better. However there is a difference between a civilisan and military administration. No civilian would accept military discipline willingly without some compelling reason. There are important family resemblances between military and civilian administrations in the public sector. Indeed one of the arguments of the military is that it is the guardian of the national purpose when civilians become corrupt and law and order breakdown.

After a coup, however, a new military government will have to face the same problems as a civilian administration (Clapham, 1985: 149). A coup give way to another coup, the problems however remain. The civil service usually benefits from military intervention because the army *protects* administrators from politicians (Clapham, 1985: 153). The result is that soldiers and civil servants (including technocrats) get along very well together, while politicians get along with neither.

CHARACTERISTICS OF PUBLIC ADMINISTRATION IN CERTAIN DEVELOPING REGIONS

There is no one single formula or discernible pattern which allows us to summarize the conditions for bureaucracies in the developing world. The best approach, therefore, is to describe the regional characteristics, on the assumption that the geographical approach is most fruitful in these circumstances. Those countries chosen within various regions are usually fairly typical of the region as a whole.

AFRICA

In the immediate years after independence, say perhaps in the 1960's, Africa relied upon foreign administrative support. In Botswana, for example, a significant number of foreigners have played a role in senior policy-making, assisting the Prime Minister and the Ministry of Finance and Development Planning. In Botswana, Swaziland and Lesotho as well as in most former British-administered territories, British residual institutions are still important. In West Africa, legislatures and state government appear to have claimed more attention than formal administration. Traditional native administration has been much less disturbed than many observers claim. Tanzania and Zambia have even attempted to utilize traditional structures, with indigeneous ideologies to back them up. Unfortunately these ideologies have not been conducive to the need to modernize and develop. Former British territories however have kept much of the basic infrastructure including the tax structure which they inherited from colonial times.

Similarly in former French African territories, French influence, including use of French, remains profound. In the Central African Republic, Chad, Gabon, Senegal, and Upper Volta the French influence is still somewhat evident, in military organization, for example. In some cases francophone (French-speaking) African states have closely modelled themselves upon the French model. In Senegal, for example, the constitution appears to follow that of the French Fifth Republic. The bureaucracy too is modelled upon the French pattern. Senegal has prefects in thirty departments and an Administrative Staff College. The civil service is an *élite* as in France in both local and central administration.

Francophone Africa has retained extremely close ties with France. The example of the Ivory Coast is perhaps instructive in this regard. French experts are very much in evidence and courts exist on the French model for controlling administrative matters. The Supreme Court for example, has an administrative section which is the final court of appeal for those cases which relate to administration. There are also audit and control sections which check state revenues and income. Government officials are also subject to the jurisdiction of the National Assembly. In the Ivory Coast, too, the local government is similar to that established in France, with some 25 departments each controlled by a prefect appointed by the president.

France has been fiercely protective of its former colonies. France has continued to influence policy choices for these new states, including such things as the monetary system, the organization of military schools and the nature of national development. Central government, including its power to tax has always been much more pronounced in francophone than in anglophone Africa. More recent developments however show a greater sense of the responsibilities of local communities in francophone Africa. In Chad and Senegal, personal taxes imposed by central government have been reduced or abolished (Wozny, 1984: 81).

ASIA

Perhaps the most important case anywhere of a post-colonial bureaucracy is to be found in India. Ministers in India are, as in the British system, important political figures who oversee large ministerial portfolios both at central level and in liaison with the individual states. While the British ruled India they effectively reproduced a class of administrative officers which paralleled the British model. The result is the Indian Civil Service may be seen as a modern *élite* derived from both Indian and British traditions. Thus while responsibility for policy is a political, not administrative matter, senior civil servants nevertheless are close interpreters of policy.

India has immense public administration problems. In part these have been inherited from the previous administration, the former British *raj*. In the early part of this century the administration of India was already large enough to astonish Lord Curzon as he took up his appointment as Viceroy of India. Britain then saw its administration as the 'steel frame' holding India together. Britain's administrators administered India's railways, canals, salt, carpet and tea production, and even managed the opium trade.

The 'steel frame' of administration built up by the British over centuries has continued to operate. Its long-term effects have not been wholly beneficial. Industry has not been able to develop in face of a mass of controls and licences. Administrative decisions have held back many industries; in other cases unnecessary subsidies have sustained over 100,000 'sick' industries. (*Asian Wall Street Journal*, November 19, 1986). Added to these problems are those belonging to pure 'bureaucracy' in the popular pejorative sense. Thus licence applications for industrial development take several years to process. The Department of Industrial Development requires details of the applicant's passport and an authoritative letter of introduction before it will release its annual report.

India's administrative steel-frame has been frequently attacked and many attempts at reform have been made, especially by Rajiv Gandhi. Some of these reforms have in fact followed modern Western public administration. For example, courses on resource management in the public sector have been introduced, as well as concepts such as management by objectives. Thousands of civil servants have been returned to the classroom and India's universities have made a number of fundamental studies in public policy analysis (Ganopathy *et al.*, 1985). India's huge public administration has been scaled down in many areas but the combination of history and culture is difficult to combat effectively.

India itself of course is a vast sub-continent and local government administration is pertinent to the mass of the people (Maddick, 1970: 319). Each state, region and area however sees the problem in a different way, but local administration is concerned with, such mundane but necessary services as agriculture, education, health, irrigation, public works, social welfare and finance. If the Indian Civil Service symbolizes the British legacy, the rural life symbolizes the traditional devotion to the village. The former tradition is less than 300 years old, the latter tradition is more than 5,000 years old.

There are of course a number of different India's from the perspective of public administration. There is the central government level, the lowest rural level (*panchayati raj*) and the middle tier of states. In India, however, pressures to make the administration a *political* force were strong and were even encouraged by Prime Ministers Nehru and Indira Gandhi. India is, of course, immensely pluralistic, scattered and politically diverse. Above all, it is extremely hard to govern, as the continuing conflict with the Sikhs demonstrates. The idea of a single organization for a country with India's complexities is difficult to contemplate.

The case of colonial Malaya suggests in some measure, that of India. The Malayan Civil Service corresponded to, and indeed sprang from, the Indian Civil Service (Milne, 1967: 149). Both of these, in turn reflected the outlook of the British 'Administrative Class'. However, unlike the British Administrative Class, both Malayan and Indian members of the higher administration were, perhaps somewhat paradoxically, 'district officers'. In fact, both ICS and MCS were generalists expected to serve as magistrates (judges), agricul-

135

tural officers, health inspectors, school supervisors and any such jobs as may be offered to them. Local government in Malaysia is further dominated by the problem of federal-state relations, and in the 1980's certain parts of Malaysia, Sabah for example, have often indicated irritation with the central government in Kuala Lumpur.

After independence in 1963 and the Malayanization of the civil service, great concern was shown regarding reform and increased 'efficiency'. Plans were devised to modernize management approaches including the use of management consultants who recommended training and modernization. However everything depends upon political leadership in Malaysia given the federal structure (Montgomery and Esman, 1966).

Indonesia's civil service, from independence in 1945 to the end of the Sukarno era (1966) was renowned for inefficient performance at best, and unrestricted corruption at worst. Indonesia consists of some 6,000 islands and its geographical configuration together with its cultural and ideological peculiarities make it a particularly difficult study for any precise science of public administration. The Dutch, of course, saw Indonesia as a colonial problem which required order rather than development (The Dutch East India Company was wound up on 31 December 1899). Indonesia has had particularly difficult problems with administrative reform since 1945. Sukarno was uninterested in reform, and Suharto has not fully succeeded in creating a unified Indonesia, even after two decades. Indonesia has been under some form of military rule since March 1966, when President Suharto took over the executive power following Sukarno as head of state.

Bangladesh has been independent (from Pakistan) since 1971 and has been under military rule since 1982. Bangladesh is significant to students of public administration because it at first consciously rejected the inherited model of an administrative generalist class of public servants. After the 1982 coup a 'partnership' between the civil administrators and military developed. In a state like Bangladesh, consisting of about ninety million people, the civil service tends to reflect internal divisions and an ambivalence regarding the role of the military.

The Philippines has demonstrated a similar tendency of balancing martial law and normal administrative needs. Departments, bureaux, agencies and divisions were reduced in size especially after the removal of Marcos in 1986. Nevertheless grave problems remained including those of graft, political uncertainty regarding the future and lack of administrative direction. Thailand is also ruled by a combination of military men and civilian officials. Attempts made to reform the system have failed where corruption — widely reported to be rife — exists. Singapore by contrast is more like an 'administrative state', which ensures that political factors, including corruption, are kept to a minimum. The concept of the 'administrative state' is most clearly in evidence in Hong Kong where the civil service has for long been the policy-maker *par excellence*. Hong Kong, of course, has been, under British rule, the supreme example of an administrative state. It will become a special administrative region of the People's Republic of China in 1997, when it is quite likely that it will be as depoliticized as it has been under British rule for a century and a half. China appears to desire Hong Kong to remain an administrative state, without political ambitions until the middle of the twenty-first century.

LATIN AMERICA

In Latin America, the over-whelming presence of the military in certain states has a depressing effect upon the structure of public administration. The public official may be taken into the military bureaucracy and the military men may find themselves administering civilians. In a wholly militarized state such as Chile or Uruguay the military may control many aspects of life. They do so by allowing techocrats to concern themselves with narrowly prescribed levels of expertise (Clapham, 1985: 153). In Latin America, too, there are different forms of economic philosophy. Some of these espouse free enterprise (such as Chile) perhaps rather unexpectedly, but such freedom does not extend to politics. Others, such as Cuba and Nicaragua are hostile to capitalism. The public administration of Cuba in particular, follows the traditional socialist model of planning and control, under a socialist folk-hero to pursue profit where this is feasible.

In a state like Haiti there has been no effective clean public administration. Public security is paramount and local government follows the prefectoral system. Other strongly authoritarian states such as Paraguay or Peru see the role of the civil service as that of upholding national order.

MIDDLE EAST: ISLAMIC STATES

The role of the official in Islamic states is close to the role of the mullah. Thus, in Algeria, which is a single-party Arabic-speaking socialist state with Islam as the official state religion, the idea of the administration is perhaps best seen as a foreign importation. Indeed in many Islamic states, government is largely a matter of religious organization. The method of government may be called *shura* (consultation). Western administrative forms are often very shallow in Islamic states, depending upon the length of contact with Western Europe, as these examples suggest.

In Egypt, for example, the fundamentalist challenge, has been gathering momentum. Egypt is more 'modern' than many Islamic states though it has a highly developed 'old-boy' network of peer groups which has come to influence the structure of officialdom in the country. In 1986, Egypt experienced serious riots. Iran provides (1986) an excellent example of a theocracy in which modern public administration is suspect — where it is not heretical, and religious governance is deemed wholly adequate to all modern needs.

In Libya, too, Western notions of public administration are seen as an intrusion, that is to say where they are in fact permitted. Libya operates on the basis of revolutionary committees — as Qaddafi expressed it: ... 'the People's Committees exercise administrative responsibilities while the Revolutionary Committees exercise revolutionary control'. This suggests a separation of administration and politics, but Libya has neither (to Western eyes) rational administration nor rational politics.

THE ADMINISTRATIVE NEEDS OF DEVELOPING STATES

Developing states above all need development, which seems a circular argument. However well-constructed the plans, and however well-intentioned the ideology, there can be little progress in a developing state when there are faults in the conduct of public administration. Hence 'the success or failure of the development effort may hinge on the effectiveness efficiency and responsiveness of public administration' (Ibrahim in Robinson, 1971: 181). It is unwise for governments to adopt the attitude of an ostrich with regard to sound administration simply because the developmental priorities have been set.

Many obstacles to growth can be traced to the deficiencies of public servants who require to be motivated as well as everyone else. The various criticisms of civil servants as produced by Parkinson, Downs and others apply equally as much in developing areas as in mature states. Expenditure on administrative education is probably a fundamental necessity for progress.

Developing states have come through a series of stages and sequence since emerging from colonial status. Colonies originally had three basic developmental roles — peace-keeping, revenue collection and some basic public works projects such as reservoir and road construction. After independence these tasks became more complicated. Civil servants learned on the job and occasionally in Western universities. Their capacity to undertake their new tasks was taken for granted. Plans were drawn up without proper recognition of administrative responsibilities and skills. We may or may not agree that 'All administrative obstacles to growth may be finally traced to public servants, and measures to improve their quality are, therefore fundamental' (Ibrahim in Robinson, 1971: 192). However the role of the civil service is critical in developing countries today.

Planning is a case in point. Many plans are hindered because of the incapacity of administrators. Targets are poorly understood because administrators have a poor perspective, or because plans cannot be achieved. Administrators faced with a daunting set of required goals may simply resort to time-honoured tricks. These include 'going by the book', 'passing the buck', 'empire-building', 'using obsolete rule-of-thumb methods', and all the supposedly conventional sins of administrators everywhere.

In developing countries the situation, given a scarcity of resources, could be critical. Advice given to developing states may be of limited use if the administrative and technical capacity of the community is unequal to the task. Where military intervention takes place the situation may be more serious. Military men may be poor administrators or they may make serious administration difficult. In due course states under the control of the military may, if there are no elected politicians, see no other way forward than rule by force.

REMEDIES FOR ADMINISTRATIVE DEFECTS

The creation of new administrative attitudes may go a long way towards remedying defects.

(1) Psychological

People in organizations may often lack the will to reform the administrative structure under which they live. Incentives may however be provided to stimulate activity because 'bureaucracy' does not create anything; it administers. Thus plans in developing countries work best when people both inside and outside public administration have the will to implement them. 'In other words', argued a conference group at Cambridge (1966), 'the state should wherever possible rely on providing incentives for private men to do desirable things rather than trying to do everything itself' (Robinson, 1966: 195). In Asia and Latin America, such incentives may be easier to develop than in the case of Africa (*Economist*, June 18 1988). It remains true that development may fail where the administration is defective, in structure or function, but the will to reform the system must also be present. In this respect, socialist states score badly.

(2) Organizational

We have already spoken of 'hiving-off' as a possible method of separating tasks and organizations from larger organizations. In both developed and developing states, organizational changes, like 'hiving-off' may be valid administrative reforms. Development often consists of schemes (devised by economists) which merely create new administrative agencies and which divert resources from the project in hand.

Other organizational devices may be valuable. These include the use of an ombudsman where appropriate. Government by 'goldfish bowl' (as in Sweden) may be more desirable than government in secret: anti-corruption agencies have a normally beneficial effect — as in Hong Kong and Singapore. Teams of efficiency auditors can be set up to monitor the progress and performance of departments and may be used where appropriate.

Training is frequently used to upgrade administrative skills and may be developed along the lines of the Administrative Staff College idea (Taylor,

1970: 8). All governments which require trained personnel will normally use training extensively. To a large extent senior personnel will be given management training, while more junior civil servants will receive specialised 'hands-on' instruction.

(3) Use of Traditional Forms of Government

Many complaints are made about the inappropriateness of using Western governmental forms for developing countries. Administrative units may be wrongly conceived or even inappropriate for development. Even whole states (like Uganda) are often an amalgam of quarrelling 'tribes' and cannot cohere for the purposes of public administration. New ideas are not always appropriate, hence the call for 'intermediate technology' (Schumacher in Robinson, 1971: 85). Modern Western public administration is a form of Western technology, but it does not export without modification. Developing states which do not make the effort, however, may forgo modernization.

(4) Financial/Fiscal Reforms

The cost of administration is high if this includes public training at universities and other colleges as well as finding employment for them. It sometimes makes much sense to employ expatriates who can be given short-term contracts after which their services can be relinquished. The training costs are not met by the recipient country but rather by the country from which the expatriate comes. Administration can be made cost-effective in a number of ways. These include use of better manpower in tax offices, monitoring of tax, rate and rent collection. Value-for-money exercises are useful, even when the labour supply is plentiful.

Above all is the question of local-central relations. Where a locality is totally dependent upon financial support from the central government, it is obvious that local government must be weakened. Case studies of Kenya and Nigeria have demonstrated severe conflicts over systems of taxation (Wozny, 1984).

We may illustrate all these points by reference to the case of China. Public administration in China is a problem of immense proportions, given the huge population of over one thousand million people, whose average annual income is about US$1 per day. China has a bureaucratic tradition so ancient that it appears a natural phenomenon to millions of Chinese. To take the psychological level first, since the Cultural Revolution, Chinese leaders have offered incentives to the workforce which have been highly successful in stimulating production. From about 1980 on, elements of the free market were permitted which has increased peasant incomes by 70% in real terms. Before these incentives were re-introduced (i.e., during the period of Mao's hegemony) 'growth was slow, consumers dissatisfied, workers bored, bureaucrats overwhelming and often corrupt' (Economist, December 21, 1985).

Secondly at the organizational level, China has reduced many of the bodies which appear, to the Western eye, to be sensible reforms. The number of ministries, boards and agencies was drastically reduced in the 1980's, but with an extra ten million workers entering the labour market annually, there must be limited administration. In any case, as in the Soviet Union, in China, the key to understanding is not so much formal structures as in contacts (*guanxi*) or backdoor operations (*houmen*) (Seymour, in Curtis ed., 1985: 423). The Chinese may very closely adhere to strict administrative procedures where necessary but can also rely, perhaps more characteristically, on personal networks and family alliances.

Mao Zedong was opposed to over-reliance on formal administrative procedures and he had reason to complain. At the centre is the State Council which, as late as 1982, had half a million officials and 18 vice-premiers. Until the 1982 reforms, there were in China 108 ministries with perhaps 20 vice-ministers each. Shensi had 108 departments which corresponded to the 108 at the centre. Metallurgy alone was a huge department with 28 vice-ministers. The steel plant at Ma On Shan was mentioned as a company where one out of three workers was described as an 'executive' and five out of six security officers were described as 'chiefs' (*New China News Agency*, 8 December 1981).

Deng Xiao Ping made his own criticism of the public administration in China saying that it was devoted to an 'ossified bureaucracy blindly observing absurd regulations, creating redundant organizations, employing more people than needed, and avoiding decision making'. Overstaffing had created in China a party (state) administrative hierarchy of 20 million, controlling a third of the G.N.P. The inevitable outcome was corruption which in fact did not diminish after the reforms were implemented (Harris, 1988).

Traditional forms of government, our third category, have also been the subject of change. The basic administrative unit developed by Chinese revolutionaries was, from 1958 to 1982, the commune. The commune represented a whole living complex for hundreds of grouped millions of Chinese peasants. Instead the Chinese government has returned to the traditional idea of the township.

Criticism of the communes began in 1979 because of their economic (productivity) as well as their administrative, 'failures'. As in the USSR and other socialist states, command economies produce severe administrative tensions because of the burdens imposed from over-centralization. An added burden in the Chinese context has been the integration under the commune system of farm and local government administration so that the communes have been responsible for education, welfare, the local militia, small-scale industry and trade, as well as for agriculture.

The number of communes rose to 81,000 in 1963, but by the early 1980's the system of communes was politically unpopular. The Fifth People's Congress decided in 1982 to reestablish village and township governments. The traditional levels in the P.R.C. are the province, the county and the township.

Controls over individuals are however maintained at the lowest levels by *danwei* seen as a control mechanism akin to a form of industrial feudalism (Butterfield, 1982: 41). Traditionally there existed mutual protection agencies in China so that families who grouped in tens and hundreds or the *bao-jia* system. Chinese administration perceives the linking of persons as a fundamental traditional need which the *danwei* system merely institutionalizes.

Finally China's need for financial and fiscal probity in its public administration is all important. However it is the case that corruption is all-pervasive. The costs and benefits of public administration in China are not perhaps evaluated enough, but they clearly exist. Thus increased productivity in agriculture is not so clearly paralleled by increased productivity in public administration. Complaints are heard in China about the paucity of administrative skills on the part of China's millions of officials — a centuries-old complaint. Officials are to be avoided and feared: traditionally 'Never in the whole of your life go into the house of the mandarin'.

The size of the public administration could be criticized in the state, if not the party, sector. The party of course was, and always will be, sacrosanct. The old Latin tag is still, in many developing (including socialist developing) countries very appropriate: 'Who will control those who control us?'

BIBLIOGRAPHY

Butterfield Fox (1982), *China, Alive in the Bitter Sea*, Times Books, New York.
Clapham, see Chapter One.
Feit Edward (1973), *The Armed Bureaucrats*, Houghton Mifflin, Boston.
Freedman Ann and Morgan Maria Morgan (Chan) (1982), *Controlling Bureaucracy in China*, New York.
Harris Peter (1988), 'Socialist Graft', in Heidenheimer, Johnson and Levine, *Political Corruption*, see Chapter 6.
Heussler Robert (1963), *Yesterday's Rulers: The Making of the British Colonial Service*, Oxford University Press, Oxford.
Ibrahim in Robinson, see Chapter 4.
McIntyre W. David (1967), *The Imperial Frontier in the Tropics, 1865–1875*, Macmillan, London.
Nordlinger Eric (1977), *Soldiers in Politics: Military Coups and Governments*, Prentice Hall, New Jersey.
Schumacher E.F. (1964) in Robinson, see Chapter 4.
Seymour in Curtis, see Chapter 4.
Taylor A. (1970), *The Administrative Staff College*.
Wozny James (1984), *Personal Taxes in African States*, Occasional Papers No. 81, Metropolitan Studies Program, July 1984.

10
Public Administration in Socialist States

SOCIALIST PERSPECTIVES ON BUREAUCRATIC MORALITY

One of the most striking features to the analyst of socialist systems is the simplistic view which socialists have of bureaucracy. The overall message is that bureaucracy is a product of the bourgeois order, and that in socialist states administration should be a reasonably straightforward matter. It was Lenin who argued that under socialism the 'housewife will learn to run the state'.

However the lesson has been reluctantly learned that under socialism, no less than in so-called bourgeois states, there exist bureaucratic problems. We cannot simply reduce public administration to the simplistic levels as set out by the authors of the *A.B.C. of Communism* (1920). Hostile statements about the role of bureaucrats have been made ever since Marx produced his classic denunciation of the bourgeois state. Marx made frequent references to the bureaucracy without ever seeing a constructive role for it in any of his writings. Marx's single essay on the bureaucracy, *Kritik des Hegelschen*, (1843, published 1927), is an early work. In the *Critique of the Gotha Programme* and in the *German Ideology*. Marx failed to see bureaucracy in anything other than a pejorative light. 'The general spirit of bureaucracy is secret, a mystery, safeguarded inside itself by hierarchy and outside by its nature as a closed corporation' (*Marx*, ed McLellan, 1977: 31).

For Marx as for many other writers, bureaucracy in a bourgeois state is seen as inherently unethical. Bureaucracy is an integral appendage of the bourgeois order and can have no life of its own. Bureaucracy in general for Marxists is not an autonomous factor and was tarred with the brush which soiled the bourgeoisie itself. However, Marx never lived to see the day when, as Weber put it, charisma became routine. Marx's legacy was that of an unremitting hostility to the bureaucrat as the lackey of the capitalist state.

In his turn, Lenin looked ahead to a different aspect of the concept of bureaucracy. While agreeing with Marx that bourgeois bureaucracy stands as a support of the bourgeois state, Lenin looked to the future in a way Marx did not. Lenin believed, as he argued in *State and Revolution* (1917), that: 'Under Socialism *all* will govern in turn and will soon become accustomed to no one governing' (Lenin, 1952 edition: 140–41). This point was taken up by Bukharin and Preobrazhensky in the *A.B.C. of Communism* (1920) using the classic phrase already made famous by Saint-Simon. 'The government of men will be replaced by the administration of things — the administration of machinery, buildings, locomotives, and other apparatus. The communist order of society will be fully installed' (Bukharin and Preobrazhensky, 1920: 240). Bureaucracy, in short, could be seen as a mass, not an élite, activity in a socialist state.

The *A.B.C. of Communism* popularized the conventional Leninist thought at the time that 'if all are bureaucrats, none is a bureaucrat'. What results, Lenin argued, is 'the *complete withering away* of every form of state in general' (*State and Revolution*, 1952 edition: 141). Lenin's ideal was that of a state in which managers were subject to recall and in which officials received the pay of the workers.

Stalin for his part, had no time for 'recall' and 'equal pay'. It became clear that the facts of power in Russia, later the Soviet Union, made the 'withering away of the state' very unlikely. Bureaucrats became, enphemistically, *cadres*, *apparats*, or 'organs of soviet power' (Fitzpatrick, 1982: 93–102). Trotsky tirelessly pointed out that the Soviet Union was a bureaucracy, on a par with that created by the Tsars. To most communists however, the Soviet Union was not a bureaucracy in the pejorative sense. It subscribed, so it was believed, to a different, higher, ethic, not to be judged by bourgeois terminology. Bourgeois bureaucracies were bad; communist bureaucracies by contrast were the proper organs of state. In the party (as opposed to the government bureaucracy) the proportion of workers was initially high. However, in fact, workers were less in evidence in top government jobs (Fitzpatrick, 1982: 97). A huge bureaucracy built up (and was, on occasions, dismantled by whim) under Stalin (Schapiro, 1963: chapter 13).

The Soviet Union was described by some writers even during the early Stalin years as an unquestioned bureaucracy (Rizzi, 1939, Trotsky, 1937, 1965). In due course, critical attention came to be paid to the Soviet Union viewed as an organizational phenomenon. The most celebrated critic was probably Milovan Djilas, who was a former Vice-President of Yugoslavia, and who made strongly derogatory preferences to communist organization in *general*, i.e., not merely to the Soviet Union. Socialism for Djilas is therefore government of the bureaucrat, by the bureaucrat and for the bureaucrat. There thus emerged for critics and non-critics alike a socialist bureaucratic morality (or immorality, according to taste) (Djilas, 1957: 151).

The introduction of planning in socialist states and the rapid evolution of the concept of the planned economy made the whole bureaucratic process more complex (Carr and Davies, 1974: chapter 23). Western critics of the planning concept believed that planning created an intolerable bureaucracy which would ramify *ad nauseam*. Hayek characteristically disapproved of a situation in which 'government has to decide how many pigs are to be reared or how many buses are to be run, which coal mines are to operate, or at what prices boots are to be sold ...' (Hayek, 1944: 55).

Europeans and Asians it must be remembered, socialist and non-socialist alike, have a far stronger sense of the bureaucratic ethic than Americans (Self, 1972: 236). One might see this as a product of political culture and history.

144

But it is important to realise that a socialist bureaucratic morality is not necessarily solely the product of socialist ideology. Other factors are involved in various proportions, including political culture and experience, leadership, and an indeterminate number of fortuitous residual factors.

However, we may perceive a distinction between bureaucracy and bureaucratic morality. All systems except one-man 'Robinson Crusoe' systems are to some extent bureaucratic. It is the *ethos* of bureaucracy which disturbs many people, namely the sins of perverted bureaucracies. So all socialists can acclaim a socialist order on moral grounds while denouncing any tendency to selfishness. The top rulers themselves are seen as above reproach while able to complain of 'bureaucratism' below (Deng Xiaoping, 1983: 287).

Socialist perspectives on bureaucratic morality may of course be approached from a number of angles. Generally, they appear to be over-simplistic. Only occasionally do socialist leaders criticize socialist (as opposed to capitalist) bureaucracy. It is however important to add here that the most senior officials in a number of *socialist* countries, do, from an Olympian position, criticize shortcomings. Gorbachev (1986) is of course an important example. Most lesser communist leaders tread rather more circumspectly.

1. The Ideal

'In the Soviet Republic, the masses do not merely elect (electing not venal lawyers but their own folk) but they participate in the work of administration, for the soviets and other organizations of the working masses are actually engaged in administrative work' (A.B.C. of Communism, 1920: 232).

It is quite possible to imagine a quite positive and constructive bureaucratic morality particularly in the early days of socialist states. Where bourgeois rule is bureaucratic rule, it is arguable that a new bureaucracy which serves the worker can do nothing but good.

Later, of course, other justifications for socialist rule multiply. Rhetorical statements and apologia increase a hundred fold and outside critics are informed of the benefits of socialist rule. Much of this rhetoric is seen as barren, even false, (for example, Leszek Kolakowski described communism as founded on lies) (Kolakowski, 1969, 1986). However, it may be argued that there *is* an apparently ideal bureaucratic morality in socialist systems. Naturally socialist rulers insist that socialist bureaucratic morality is sound.

This morality is built on several very well-known socialist administrative devices. Two examples will be briefly discussed, namely democratic centralism and planning. Taken at their face value socialist administrative devices should be seen as altruistic, rather than as intentionally repressive or dictatorial. As Aryeh L. Unger put it: 'Translated to the realm of the state and stripped of its rhetorical flourish, "democratic centralism" was said to combine centralized decision-making with democratic accountability and local autonomy' (Unger, 1980: 19). It could also be argued that in the context of a poorly educated society (as late as 1920, two-thirds of the Soviet population was illiterate), democratic centralism was a constructive and realistic alternative.

Democratic centralism had its origins in early Bolshevik thought and indeed in 1920, democratic centralism was argued at the Ninth Party Congress as a counterweight concept to bureaucratic and by implication, 'authoritarian practices at the party centre' (Schapiro, 1961: 199). While many Western commentators condemn democratic centralism as a euphemism for central dictatorship, it may be more altruistic than is commonly supposed. Clearly, Soviet policy-makers interpret their decision-making process as such, namely altruistically.

The Rules of the Communist Party of the Soviet Union (October 31, 1961) set out a bureaucratic morality of apparently high-sounding ideals. Article 19. . . . 'The guiding principle of the organizational structure of the party is democratic centralism, which signifies:

a) The election of all leading Party bodies, from the lowest to the highest;
b) The periodical reports of Party bodies to their Party organs and to higher bodies;
c) Strict Party discipline and subordination of the minority to the majority;
d) The decisions of higher bodies are obligatory for lower bodies.'

In administrative terms a dual subordination was envisaged which applied to every executive organ. The duality refers to the vertical level. In consequence the body which elects the executive has a responsibility to the electing body. The duality also refers to the horizontal level with its numerous connections. Local authorities could argue for a measure of control over local affairs (Vyshinsky, 1948: 230–31).

Democratic centralism is the centre piece of socialist administration, on the basis of the need to reconcile direction and control with the rights of the masses. Indeed, taken at its face value, and according to one observer, democratic centralism would not be out-of-place as a 'description of the British Conservative Party' (Robertson, 1985: 81). Others admit that democratic centralism has both negative and positive aspects (Hill and Frank, 1981: 72). Indeed, democratic centralism, 'lends a coherence and unity that such a diffuse organization (as the CPSU) might otherwise lack'. Moreover, it is unlikely to be abandoned in the search for political reform (Brown, 1979: 151–4).

Since 1961 when the Party rules set out the concept of democratic centralism, there have been more ideological than bureaucratic reforms. Socialist property has created more concern than socialist bureaucratic morality (Shlapentokh, *Asian Well Street Journal*, April 18 1986).

What Soviet apologists argue is that (for socialists) democratic centralism is the ideal and the reality, and that *democratic* centralism is not *bureaucratic* centralism. Socialism does not have antagonistic contradictions as a variety of observers have pointed out, including Andropov, Mao Zedong and Anatoliy Butenko (Kux, 1984: 1–27).

The apparatus of the Chinese Party (but more especially the Chinese state) is immense, but like the Soviet and East European versions of socialism, the actual administration claims to be altruistic.

The Chinese political culture is of course a bureaucratic culture, and has been for centuries. However, bureaucrats have always been unpopular, both in classic literature and in the opinions of Mao Zedong and Deng Xiaoping. At its most ideal and altruistic level, the Chinese were ruled by a scholar-gentry. The urge towards bureaucracy in China appears to be very strong. There is a saying that whatever one does in China the long-fingernailed mandarins come creeping back! Nothing that Mao's mass-line produced could shake this fundamental fact, and he failed to break the tradition of centuries. China's *ethos* was bureaucratic, not democratic (Freedman and Morgan, 1982: 229–264). However, at best, China's bureaucrats aspired towards certain ideals, whether cultural or egalitarian. That they did not fulfil these ideals is a matter for the record.

THE CONCEPT OF ADMINISTRATIVE LEVERS: PLANNING THE ECONOMY

If the market pricing mechanism is unavailable, or even perhaps illegal, then we may conclude administrative 'levers' may be the only alternative. Resources may of course be allocated administratively. The basis of this allocation may be according to a scale of points, targets, physical quantities, coupons, vouchers or other species of entitlement. The use of administrative levers calls into discussion the whole of bureaucratic morality. In a socialist state, currency exchanges and financial management, for example, are bureaucratic phenomena. In a market state, such matters are minimally administrative.

Socialist states naturally make extensive use of bureaucracy in which levers are pulled and the system works largely through bureaucratic discretion. With the concept of the plan, for example, a particular altruistic morality emerges. Targets have to be set, but they are set by human beings rather than by the market in which 'money' takes the decisions. In economic matters such as planning, administrative levers are essential given the imperatives of the plan (Nove and Muti, 1972). However the use by administrators of such levers places a burden upon those who take necessary decisions. The pricing system is 'objective' in the sense that administrative levers can never be. Bureaucrats in a full socialist planning system must decide how levers are to be pulled, when they are to be pulled and when the pulling has to stop.

Thus in 1984, in Beijing a group of 11,000 government price inspectors were deployed to monitor price levels. The objective was to see develop in China a system of prices which promoted a stable society where prices would not be too excessive for hundreds of millions of Chinese. There is an altruistic aspect to this approach. Officials are servants of the people and in socialist countries, as everywhere else, they are supposed to exist for reasons related to the higher ethic of socialism. The use of administrative levers (i.e., the use of the bureaucracy) can be reasonably justified under socialism as an alternative to the implicit Darwinism of the market. The use of administrative levers however implies a different higher ethic from the market-place with its survival-of-the-fittest mentality. Hence experiments in Hungary to utilize together both economic and social levers have had some, albeit limited, success.

While it is easy to draw attention to the inadequacies of the administrative lever approach, it is not without some merit. For example during wartime, resources are allocated by points, coupons and the bureaucracy of rationing. However sceptical one may be regarding the allocation of resources in a so-called command economy, it is at least conceivable that at its best and working well, altruism can form a part of general approach to bureaucratic morality in a socialist state. We next consider a more realistic model.

2. The Reality

'No process has been discovered by which promotion to a position of public responsibility will do away with a man's interest in his own welfare, his partialities, race, and prejudices' (James Harvey Robinson, *The Human Comedy*, 1937).

The assumption made in this part of the analysis is that socialist bureaucrats will tend for the most part to behave egoistically. Socialist states are unquestionably bureaucratic states, and some seventy years after the 1917 Revolution, it is unrealistic to expect routine socialist administrators to behave according to the heady ideals of 1917 and later. We must not even expect them to perform in an altruistic fashion. They may not in fact perform according to their rhetoric. It is more fruitful to see the internal 'politicking' of socialist states in their huge internal corporations rather than a crusade to establish equality. In socialist bureaucracies as everywhere else, the rewards go to those who play the bureaucratic game, empire building, horse-trading, striking bargains, alliances, promising rewards, favours and sundry privileges. For example there may be rivalry between parts of the military and parts of the party. Factions are ubiquitous.

There are many points of similarity. Socialist and non-socialist bureaucrats alike react to many of the same stimuli. Fringe benefits are as acceptable as they are in Moscow, Manchester or Madrid. All administrators agree that one of the key points in the bureaucrat's catechism is: 'I want that bastard's job' (Lord Thomson, *Times*, January 2, 1976). There are differences between Western bourgeois bureaucrats which may be as great as between socialist and non-socialist officials. It has been pointed out that a British businessman can say: 'Some of my friends are civil servants and really mean it. This would be rare in the United States' (Mason in Schonfield, 1965: 334).

Officials in socialist states, as Downs has pointed out for the USA, may well identify the interests of their departments with their own personal interest (Downs, 1967). Socialist egoism faces the extra difficulty that the rhetoric of ideology and the value system of socialism itself places special burdens on administrators. Thus the bureaucrats' natural egoism is constantly being reconciled to the conventional wisdom of socialist ideology. The overall impact on the community at large however has been the clear expression of self-interest and even privilege, a 'stifling conformity' as well as resistance to change by officials together with a bureaucratic insensitivity to the needs of those served (Harding, 1981: 329–59).

The natural egoism of the bureaucrat is more obviously institutionalized in the Soviet Union than in many other socialist states, though it is in Poland also. Perhaps the most well-known example is the recruitment device known as *nomenklatura*.

The *nomenklatura* is perhaps one of the most widely discussed features of Soviet established lists of positions governmental and non-governmental, but which can be filled only by certain persons designated by responsible Party organizations and as such there is some distant relationship to the idea of an Establishment in Britain, but of course whereas the British Establishment is subtly unspoken, the Soviet *nomenklatura* is defined (Voslensky, 1986).

For some critics, the *nomenklatura* is 'a monstrous labyrinth of preferment, patronage and privilege' (*1986 Problems of Communism*: 65). The numbers involved in the Soviet *nomenklatura* system are 'close to several million persons'. They constitute 'a class unto themselves that manifests a highly developed sense of vested interest in self-preservation'. The bureaucracy moves on tracks created by the nomenklatura system, and no reformer even Gorbachev could do more than remove a few incompetents or gerentocrats from its midst. The *nomenklatura* thus ensures that the party bureaucracy remains the heart of the party. From being merely 'the schedule of positions that can be held only by party members, subject to sanctification by the party *obkom* or the Central Committee' (Simis 1982: 61), the *nomenklatura* system generates a characteristic socialist morality.

The whole bureaucracy is influenced by the recruitment process. Perhaps some 3 million executive positions in Soviet society are *nomenklatura* controlled. These positions cover *inter alia* the party apparatus, the administrative positions in the state, the soviets, the trade unions, education, science, the arts, and youth organizations (*Komsomol*).

In Soviet Georgia, bureaucratic egoism is notoriously well-established. One report indicated that about one-third of *nomenklatura* officials were unqualified professionally. These were, to use the Chinese expression, 'red' (Russian, *partinost*) without necessarily being 'expert' (Hill and Frank, 1981: 87).

Many Western commentators see the Soviet Union and many other socialist states, such as Rumania and North Korea, as riddled with egoism. Voslensky's detailed examination of the structure of privilege in the Soviet Union emphasizes the entrenched egoism of the ruling class. Egoism has become the kernel of a once-idealistic creed, making Soviet bureaucrats remote from the people whom they serve. This remoteness is summed up with the frequently-made comment that the late President Gromyko did not walk in a Moscow street in the past thiry years.

Western writers have for long made jaundiced comments about bureaucracy in general. A favourite cynic is C. Northcote Parkinson, described by Self as writing in a 'cruder but wittier manner' than say Anthony Downs and Gordon Tulloch (Self, 1972: 234). As regards Parkinson, it has been reported that Mikhael Gorbachev has taken up the message of Parkinson's 'law' with some enthusiasm. The Soviet Secretary-General is reported to have urged, in pure Parkinson-fashion, that Parkinson was alive and well and living in Moscow (*Observer*, London, 23 December, 1984). Gorbachev saw the moral weaknesses of the Soviet bureaucracy in direct speech towards his officials. He stated that: 'Many heads of ministries wish to wrest as much capital investment and resources as possible while getting as small targets as possible. Enviable persistence in trying to get additional funds and having planned target figures reduced is shown by K.N. Belyak, Minister for Mechanical Engineering for Livestock Farming and Fodder Production'. After delivering these words Gorbachev sacked Mr Belyak.

Downs produced a more serious set of bureaucratic norms, essentially amoral, arguing that prosecution of public programmes depended upon the self-interest of the bureaucrat. It is possible of course that socialist bureaucrats *believe* in the ideology of socialism but no more perhaps than colonial empire-builders believed in the *mission civilisatrice* of European colonisers.

Nevertheless, socialist bureaucrats argue that officials are builders of communism, thus conveniently associating ethics and self-interest.

Socialist bureaucrats do of course constitute a large body of people. In the Soviet Union the ruling bureaucratic group in fact consists of 'those who from regional level and above sit on the committees, praesidia, or bureaux and those who lead the ministries, State committees, and Secretariat Departments and sections. It is one which includes party officials, industrial administrators, diplomats, journalists, generals, secret-policeman, trade-union officials, artists and the occasional worker or peasant' (McAuley, 1977: 298–9).

By contrast a Western bureaucrat is an official paid by a clearly-defined legal entity to administer certain state functions. The bureaucracy in a socialist state will routinely include professors, diplomats and ballet-dancers. There are perhaps 20–30 million people recognisably bureaucrats in the Soviet Union, in the sense that their whole existence is in pushing paper. Many millions of others are state employees. In such conditions administrative egoism is a *sine qua non*.

In primarily economic matters, the socialist bureaucrat is compelled to pull levers — which may not necessarily work. Khruschev showed in the fifties some of the pitfalls. He argued a telling case.

'It has become traditional to produce the heaviest chandeliers possible rather than just beautiful chandeliers to adorn homes. This is because the heavier the chandeliers manufactured, the more a factory gets since its output is figured in tons. So the plants produce chandeliers weighing hundreds of kilograms and fulfil the plan. But who needs such a plan?'

'Furniture factories have plans stated in roubles. Hence they find it best to make a massive armchair since the heavier the chair the more expensive it is. Formally the plan is fulfilled since the furniture makers add various details to the armchair and make it more expensive. But who needs such armchairs? Everybody knows this. Everybody talks a good deal about this, but still the armchairs win' (*Pravda*, July 2 1959, p. 2).

The pricing system is of course 'objective' in a way in which the administrative level is not. Western economists lack sympathy with the administrative levers argument, contending that bureaucrats 'cannot convey the multi-dimensional opportunity-cost information needed for efficiency of operations' (Prybyla, 1986: 23). Administrative planning it is claimed, moreover, encourages 'irrational' egoism in a way in which the 'rational' pricing system avoids. Entrepreneurs are according to this logic, even more moral than bureaucrats 'where the entrepreneur is bold and adventuresome, the bureaucrat is obedient and staid. Where the former seeks to maximise gain, the latter tries to minimise loss' (Prybyla, 1986: 37). The Western economist relies not on bureaucrats but a mixture of utilitarianism and Darwinism.

Twenty-five years after Khruschev's 'reforms' there are still administrative levers to pull to keep over 175 million people at work in the Soviet Union. There are 700 administrative organs (including 100 central ministries) handling economic planning with 15–20 million bureaucrats involved. Some 850 billion different documents are issued annually on the economy in the Soviet Union, according to *Isvestiya* (Dibb, 1986: 91).

Administrative egoism in its socialist guise takes on characteristic forms. Because most, if not all, resources belong to the 'state', everybody is potentially a bureaucrat. In China, which has the largest state and party *apparatus* in the world, the ethic of the machine is often the machine itself. The system exists because it exists. Reform therefore becomes a risky enterprise. Bureaucrats tend to resist the operations of the natural pricing system because such a system destroys bureaucratic interest. In socialist states egoism is therefore powerful because the bureaucracy like the ideology constitute pillars of the system (Schapiro, 1972: 44;. In 1990, Gorbachev undermined party hegemory.

The bureaucratic spirit may encompass, such phenomena as *Shturmovshchina* ('storming the target'). Thus a factory can produce *when* it needs to meet the targets of the plan. A factory may be active or inactive over given periods. The 1975 Nobel Economics Prize winner Leonid Kantorovich estimated that a more efficient use of resources would eliminate the 'storming' and increase national income by 50 per cent (Kaiser, 1976: 316). Some enterprises use experts in the location of raw materials known as a 'fixer' (or *tolkach*). The whole concept of the Five-Year Plan (*pyatiletka*) is part of bureaucratic ethic itself.

ORIENTAL VARIANTS OF SOCIALIST BUREAUCRATIC MORALITY

Western socialists, that is, principally socialists in East European states, obviously differ culturally from their Asian counterparts. Political culture is a vital but often overlooked ingredient in bureaucratic morality. Behaviour, especially bureaucratic behaviour, is situational in the East. In short, a system of ranking is instinctive in many Asian cultures. In Korea, for example, there are multiple levels of politeness according to perceived rank, which may account for the personality cult associated with Kim Il Sung. Earlier influences such as Buddhism have had a great impact upon the oriental *psyche*. A Polish bureaucrat, steeped in a Christian tradition is heir to the idea of a universally understood code or set of standards. An Asian bureaucrat, socialist or not, has not experienced these traditions.

For the modern oriental bureaucrat in a socialist state, in particular China, Burma, North Korea, Vietnam and Kampuches, the Roman civic tradition is not relevant. Underneath modern performance are layers of history. The family is universally both the focus of loyalty and also the model for social organization. Nepotism in many contexts is a virtue not a vice, because the supreme loyalty is to family or clan. Thus Confucius was once approached by the Duke of She who said to him: 'In my part of the country there is a man so honest that when his father appropriated a sheep, he bore witness to it'. Confucius replied: 'The honest in my part of the country are different from that, for a father will screen his son, and a son his father. That is honesty indeed' (Confucius: *Analects*). Hence Chinese attitudes to the bureaucracy naturally derive from Chinese history. The Chinese after all, invented bureaucracy, and the characteristic notion of the scholar-official who knows the fruits of office as well as the pains of imperial (or party) rejection. It has been well said: 'The Chinese are Confucian when in office, Taoist when they are thrown out, and Buddhist when they are about to die' (Ronald Eyre, 1977). The only modern difference is that the party has replaced Confucius.

Centralization, too, in the Chinese context, may be a socialist tradition, but it may also reflect the Chinese tradition that 'father knows best'. Disturbance of hierarchical patterns may have quite undesirable consequences. A modern example may be cited. After 1984, industrial enterprises in China were allowed to make certain policy decisions at the enterprise level. However, these reforms were either ignored or challenged by government departments at the local level. Neither provincial governments nor Beijing at the centre could disentangle the bureaucratic complex. Output, taxes, profit-levels, personnel, energy needs and sales were all handled by different government departments or units. Critics of the command economy itself began to appear in China in 1986.

Bureaucrats operate manually and deliberately, taking on tasks which the market performs, as it were, automatically. Bureaucrats are producers of more work for bureaucrats, supervising, planning, controlling and enforcing work made by other bureaucrats. In China until 1982 the State Council consisted of 100 agencies, 52 ministries and commissions, 43 general bureaux and 5 general offices. There were also 40 *ad hoc* agencies which coordinated the work between different ministries and general bureaux. The State Council had internal divisions and additionally all the ministries, each with its own status. The State Council had a staff of 51,000 people, and 500 on average in the various administrative units. Some ministries had dozens of ministers and deputy ministers.

After 1982 it was possible to reduce this mammoth system by about one-third but still the problem remained of an uncontrolled bureaucracy, poorly educated, elderly and inefficient. The bureaucratic work ethic remains poor and in China complaints constantly recur about *jingshenwuran* or spiritual pollution. Briefly, the Chinese leadership held that: 'The substance of ideo-logical contamination consists in spreading bourgeois and other exploiting, corrupt and decadent thoughts, spreading distrust of socialism, communist undertakings and leadership of the Communist Party. Spreading such thoughts and feelings is ideological pollution' (*China Talk*, Vol. IX: No. 1, Feb 1984).

Elsewhere, socialist bureaucratic morality is still perceived to be a superior morality to any other. Of course, one is supposed to consider the intentions rather than the results. However, the consumers have to accept a society in which the heels are stitched on the toes of boots, where an entire exhibition of faulty goods is necessary and where a Moscow journal is running a com-petition (1986) for the worst item of shoddy goods, where there is nothing new, and everything is of poor quality, restricted choice and non-existent styling (Tusa, 1986: 7, 14).

Socialist bureaucracy above all, finds it very difficult to cope with the moral imperatives of change. The cumbersome process of decision-making is above all unable to react quickly. Crisis management is particulary difficult where local officials are reluctant to act. The nuclear 'incident' at Chernobyl in the Ukraine in May 1986 illustrates the point. Earthquakes in China are not reacted to because no-one knows how to make other than routine decisions. As well demonstrated in Poland, the party hierarchy had only the party-military *apparat* to use against Solidarity.

SOCIALISM AND THE MARKET

The behaviour of bureaucrats in socialist states is particularly interesting when they are suddenly confronted with the demands of a market economy. The critical and new factor in socialist states in the past decade has been a tentative and hesitant flirtation with alternative economic systems. When approaching the market's bureaucratic problems many socialist bureaucrats have tended to behave in strange ways.

Not knowing how to manage the market, many have merely seen money as a commodity to appropriate to personal use. Socialist systems, in so far as they are able, routinely allocate resources administratively. 'Thrust into a

153

market environment, bureaucrats tend to behave not like capitalists, but like black marketeers, lining their pockets, stealing and generally acting not according to the rules of the market, but according to the street-smart corrupt codes of the underground economy' (Prybyla, 1986: 38).

Opportunities exist, and are all too often taken. Again the reasoning advanced is simplistic. The high points of communism, it is argued are pure, but the purity of the idea is sometimes impaired by the failings of the executants. China's problems and those of the Soviet Union, Romania and other socialist states have been the object of much attention. In China, the leaders of the politbureau speak of 'spiritual pollution', caused by the 'sugar-coated bullets of the bourgeoisie'.

Certain Chinese leaders saw corruption as the result of so-called reforms, that is, as a departure from the strict ethical standards of communism — Chen Yun in particular spoke at the Party Congress, and denounced the abuse of power by officials. Hu Qili told graduates at the Central Party School on 18 January 1986 that officials should be punished, if necessary, by death.

Party ethics have been a matter for grave concern in China in recent years. In 16 February 1982, *Red Flag* discussed the matter, setting out a number of ethical imperatives. 'Every Communist Party member should firmly re-member that the basic tenet of our party is to serve the people with all our hearts.' Rhetorically, the question posed was: 'How can we allow all kinds of poisons to continue to infest our party?' The answer was not forth-coming. The five elements in such materialism (*tzu xu*) were listed as money, better houses, attractive wives, children and face.

Nonetheless in Shanghai and Guangzhou, economic crimes reached severe proportions. In 1982 many thousands of bribery cases were reported in Shanghai, Sichuan and Guandong. Huge amounts of money were involved. A notorious case was reported at Hainan Island where officials were implicated in importing thousands of cars, motor cycles, television sets and then re-selling than elsewhere at up to treble the price. One commentator held that 'corruption exists at every level of the political system on mainland China and among the militory as well' (Liu, 1983: 602–623).

China: Opportunism-corruption

Place/Date	Crime	Amount Involved
Shanghai 1982	Smuggling and bribery	17,000,000 yuan
Sichuan	Smuggling and bribery	260 cars
Guandong	Smuggling and bribery	23,000,000 yuan
Shenzhan	Smuggling and bribery	205,000,000 yuan
Shenzhen	Embezzlement for house-building	50,000 yuan
Anhui	Electricity fraud, bribery	1,500,000 yuan
Liaoning	Smuggling, fraud, bribery	3,111,700 yuan
Hobei, 1983	Smuggling bribery, fraud	unknown
Beijing, 1981	Embezzlement	8,000,000
Kirin, 1979	Misappropriation	26,000

154

| Hainan, 1984 | Import fraud, bribery | 500,000,000 yuan |
| Fujian | Embezzlement, bribery | Unknown |

N.B. bribery is *huilu*, embezzlement is *tanwu*.

The meaning of such massive bureaucratic fraud is best understood as a commentary on the fallibility of socialist bureaucrats. Uncontrolled bribery, theft, illegal speculation and misuse of public funds have dented the efforts of the Chinese leadership to modernize the bureaucracy. The children of important officials have not been readily prosecuted for their misdeeds. An exception was that of Ye Zhi-feng (daughter of Ye Fei, Vice-Chairman of the National People's Congress). She was sentenced to 17 years in prison on a charge of leaking 'state secrets' on vehicle imports to Hong Kong and foreign businessman, as well as taking bribes. In January 1986, former party organization head, Qiao Shi was promoted to a new anti-corruption unit. The Discipline Inspection Commission previously set up in 1975 under Chen Yun was able to see the extent of moral decline in the public life of the People's Republic of China.

In a communist state virtually any attempt to circumvent the workings of the planned economy at some point involves an illegal act. Andropov discovered this fact in 1983 when he instituted his anti-corruption campaign. In June 1984, two large purges of officials took place, one in Latvia and the other in Uzbekistan. In Latvia, more than 100 senior officials were expelled from the party for abuse of their position for personal gain. In Uzbekistan, 16 high officials were dismissed, as well as 56 cotton industry officials and 155 rank-and-file policemen. In July 1984, the former director of Moscow's celebrated food store, Gastronom No. 1, was executed, for what the official news agency Tass described as 'various illegal machinations with food products' (*Foreign and Commonwealth Office Brief*, London, March 1986).

Gorbachev removed a number of senior officials, including the Chairman of the USSR State Committee for the Supply of Oil Products. His dismissal was explained on the grounds of 'abusing his official position for personal gain'. In Juanuary 1986, Vladimir Sushkov, a deputy Minister for Foreign Trade, who was also co-Chairman of the USA-USSR Trade and Economic Council, was dismissed from both posts on grounds of corruption. When the 27th Soviet Communist Party Congress was opened in February 1986, a number of dismissals was announced and also some executions for corruption.

During the latter years of the Brezhnev era, corruption was well entrenched and has been well documented in many places including, in particular, by Konstantin Simis who was well-placed to observe corruption, crony-communism and nepotism (Simis, 1982).

Socialist states have tended to build up considerable disparities of many kinds, especially in access to services and privileges. The new class of which Djilas wrote in the Jugoslav context has established itself in many socialist states and the bureaucrats lead the way. In a speech made to the Party

Congress on 26 February 1986, Boris Yeltsin, the First Secretary, attacked the privileges accorded to party and state bureaucrats, but the matter was partly played down by Geidar Aliev and Yegor Ligachev.

In China, nepotism (*guanxi*) was denounced and cadres asked to observe exemplary discipline where the promotion of their own offspring and relatives to leading posts is concerned (*Beijing Review*, February 24 1986, Vol. 29, No. 8, p. 5). A particularly bad case occurred in Shanghai. The children of high officials were accused of gang-rape. They were sentenced to prison and in three cases were given the death penalty (*Beijing Review*, March 3 1986, Vol. 29, p. 5).

In Rumania, the nepotism built around Ceaeusescu was notorious. Some of the jokes about this nepotism are telling. One example is that: 'Ceaeusescu has succeeded in achieving socialism in one family.' The weaknesses of Eastern Europe in 1989–90. Eastern European rulers were shown to be corrupt, despite their socialist credentials.

CONCLUSION

'*If to do were as easy as to know what were good to do, chapels had been churches, and poor men's cottages princes' palaces*' (Shakespeare, *Merchant of Venice*, ii (13)).

Deng Xiaoping and Mikhael Gorbachev appeared during the eighties to share a common hostility to something called the 'bureaucracy'. In this they would be joined by Mao Zedong, Margaret Thatcher and Ronald Reagan. In fact these leaders are on record as opponents of their respective bureaucracies. Yet what disturbs them is the bureaucratic *ethos* of bureaucratic *morality*. Quite obviously the modern state needs a civil service, but the spirit of the bureaucracy may be inimical to plans and policies laid down by the leadership.

Weber's conception of the spirit of the bureaucracy was positive. All too often, in socialist countries particularly, the bureaucratic *ethos* is the organizational millstone around the neck of their hopes. The *apparat* is a brake on social change and political scientists have assessed its role as such (Ionescu 1967, McCauley and Carter, 1986: 5). But not all have realised that the *apparat* is necessary and potentially creative. Administrative levers are potentially neutral. There are legitimate offices of state (*jigou* or *jiguan* in Chinese). Moreover even democratic centralism may be an ideal, and far removed from bureaucratic centralism, which is its antithesis. On a purely Weberian reading, an administrative culture may not be ethically different from a market culture.

However, bureaucratic morality can be viewed differently. If the Chinese speak of *jigou*, they also speak of *guanliao zhuyi*, which suggests the more sinister, unethicial aspects of bureaucratic morality. The popular usage of bureaucracy is pejorative, 'with all its routine of tape, wax, seals, and bureauism' (Williams, 1976: 41). The problem for socialists is that they above all are not supposed to act according to their self-interest (Letowski and Muranowski in Kernaghan and Dwivedi, 1983: 91–95). All too obviously however, socialists do.

On the basis of recent history however there is little chance that the bureaucracy in China will seriously reform itself (Harding, 1981: IX, 335). The *nomenklatura* system in the Soviet Union, too, is well-entrenched. In a socialist state, moreover, resources are allocated not in accordance with the wishes of the consumers, but for the benefit of the planners. Crony-communism, favouritism, and nepotism become the classical attributes of socialist-style bureaucracy. The bureaucratic spirit prevails because the bureaucracy, acting as guardians of morality, generally as well as of public decision making, has much to lose (Harasymiw 1984, Carrere d' Encausse, 1980: 233, 236).

The final stage is that of opportunism-corruption. In most socialist countries a pent-up dam of corruption has built up, and in some, such as the Soviet Union, Rumania and China, the barriers have already broken. Opportunities exist and are readily taken. Hence the extensive documentation of cases of the abuse of office for private gain. Socialist bureaucratic morality will find it difficult to move towards the altruism which the rhetoric all too often proclaims. Marx argued of capitalist bureaucrats: 'But within bureaucracy the spiritualism turns into a crass materialism, the materialism of passive obedience, faith in authority, the mechanism of fixed and formal behaviour, fixed principles, attitudes, traditions. As far as the individual bureaucrat is concerned, the aim of the state becomes his private aim, in the form of a race for higher posts, of careerism' (Marx, 1977: 31). Marx could well be describing many socialist states in the 1980's.

BIBLIOGRAPHY

Brown Archie (1979), *Eastern Europe: 1968, 1978, 1998*, Deadalus, Winter.

Bukharin Nikolai and Evgeni Preobranzhensky (1920), *The A.B.C. of Communism*, Penguin, London.

Burns John (1983), *Reforming China's Bureaucracy*, Asian Survey, June 1983.

Carrere Helene D'Encausse (1980), *Le Pouvoir confisque. Gouvernants et Gouvernes en USSR*, Paris, Flammarion.

Deng Xiao Ping (1983), *Selected Articles*, Renmin Chuban She, Beijing.

Dibb Paul (1986), *The Soviet Union, The Incomplete Superpower*, Macmillan.

Djilas Milovan (1957), *The New Class: An Analysis of the Communist System*, Praeger.

Downs Anthony (1967), *Inside Bureaucracy*, Boston, Little Brown.

Eyre Ronald (1977), *A Question of Balance*, Dec. 1, 1977, The Listener.

Fitzpatrick Sheila (1982), *The Russian Revolution*, Oxford University Press, Oxford.

Freedman Anne and Morgan, Maria Chan (1982), *Controlling Bureaucracy in China*.

Harding Harry (1981), *Organising China: The Problem of Bureaucracy, 1949–1976*, Stanford, California.

Hayek F.A. (1944), *The Road To Serfdom*, Routledge, London.

Hill Ronald J. and Peter Frank (1981), *The Soviet Communist Party*, Allen & Unwin, London.

Ionescu Ghita (1967), *The Politics of the European Communist States*, Weidenfeld & Nicolson, London.

Kaiser Robert (1976), Russia; *The People and The Power*, Secker & Warburg, London.

Kernaghan Kenneth and O.P. Dwivedi (1983), *Ethics in the Public Service: Comparative Perspectives*, International Institute of Administrative Sciences, Brussels.

Kolakowski Leszek (1969), *Marxism and Beyond*, Paladin, London.

Kux Ernst (1984), *Contradiction in Soviet Socialism*, Problems of Communism, Vol. XXXIII.

Ilych Vladimir Lenin (1952), *The State and Revolution*, Progress, Moscow.

Letowski Janusz and Wlodzimierz Muranowski (1983) (in Kenneth Kernaghan and O.P. Dwivedi) *Ethics in the Public Service: Comparative Perspectives*, Institute of Administrative Sciences, Brussels.

Liu P.L. Alan, *The Politics of Corruption in the P.R.C.*, American Political Science Review, Vol. 77, No. 3.

McAuley Mary (1977), *Politics and the Soviet Union*, Penguin Books.

McAuley Martin and Stephen Carter (1986), *Leadership and Succession in the Soviet Union, Eastern Europe and China*, Macmillan, London.

Marx Karl (ed. David McLellan 1977), *Selected Writings*, Oxford University Press, Oxford.

Muti and Nove (1972), *Socialist Economics*, Penguin, New York.

Prybyla Jan (1986), *From Mao to Market*, Problems of Communism, I, Vol. XXXV.

Robertson David (1985), *A Dictionary of Modern Politics*, Europa, London.

Rizzi B. (1939), *La Bureaucratisation du Monde*, Hachette, Paris.

Schapiro Leonard (1963), *The Communist Party of the Soviet Union*, Methuen, London.

Schapiro Leonard (1972), *Totalitarianism*, Macmillan, London.

Schonfield Andrew (1965), *Modern Capitalism*, Oxford University Press, Oxford.

Self Peter (1972), *Administrative Theories and Politics*, Allen & Unwin, London.

Simis Konstantin (1982), *U.S.S.R.: The Corrupt Society*, Simon & Schuster.

Simis Konstantin (1982), *U.S.S.R.: Secrets of a Corrupt Society*, Dent, London.

Smith Hedrick (1975), *The Russians*, Time Books, New York.

Davidovich Trotsky, Lev (1937), *The Revolution Betrayed*, Faber & Faber, London.

Tusa John (1986), *At the Twenty-Seventh Party Congress*, The Listener, March 13, 1986.

Unger L. Aryeh (1980), *Constitutional Development in the U.S.S.R.: A Guide to the Soviet Constitutions*, Methuen, London.

Voslensky Mikhael (1986), *Nomenklatura: The Soviet Ruling Class*, Doubleday, London.

Williams Raymond (1976), *Keywords: A Vocabulary of Culture and Society*, Fontana/Croom Helm, London.

Part IV
Policy and Policy Problems

11
The Meaning of Policy

Governments can do nothing, and may simply encourage a sense of drift. The famous British Prime Minister, Lord Salisbury once said: 'British foreign policy reminds me of a man floating downstream in a boat and throwing out a boat-hook from time to time to avoid a collision.' In this sense policy is all improvisation and guesswork. Policy-makers accept inertia and inaction. Salisbury also held that the commonest error in politics is sticking to the carcass of dead policies (Letter to Bulwer Lytton, 1878). Innovation in other words, is nearly always mistrusted.

Other statesmen too have complained that they find it difficult to grasp the right moment to act. 'I claim not to have controlled events', said Abraham Lincoln, 'but confess plainly that events have controlled me.' There could even be a virtue in uncertainty, argued Cromwell somewhat earlier for, 'No one rises so high as he who knows not whither he is going.' Countless politicians have attempted to guess what the public wants and adjust their thinking accordingly. But at its very best, politics and policy-making still involve a systematic effort to move other human beings towards a grand design. Governments are on this reading the agent of the 'grand design'.

In the twentieth century, governments everywhere spend much of their time talking about policy. Even where they try to avoid policy-making, they are constrained so to do. There are few who would argue as did Locke that, 'Government has no end but the preservation of property.' It suggests that there is *no* other role for governments except protecting property and hence, no need for policy-making as such. The essential fact of the present century is that governments *are* in the business of policy. Naturally the term 'policy' is itself one of great complexity which is used frequently and perhaps inaccurately in a number of contexts.

POLICY: SOME DEFINITIONS

1. Policy is 'a set of decisions taken by a political actor or group concerning the selection of goals and the methods of attaining them, within a given specified situation. These decisions should be within the power of the policy-maker to achieve' (Roberts, 1971: 152).
2. 'Policy may be defined as a deliberate course of action or inaction taken by those in office under the influence of values and pressures on the way resources/expenditure and coercion are to be used in pursuit of objectives or in support of other policies' (Smith, 1976: 15).

3. Policy is: 'A purposive course of action followed by an actor or set of actors in dealing with a problem or matter of concern' (Anderson, 1975: 3).
4. '*Policy* is a projected programme of goal values and practices: the policy process is the formulation, promulgation and application of identifications, demands and expectations' (Laswell and Kaplan, 1950: 71).
5. 'A term as nebulous as "policy" requires initial refinement. A public policy is here considered as the structure and confluence of values and behaviour involving a governmental prescription' (Kroll, 1969: p. 9).
6. 'A major guideline for action directed at the future' (Dror, 1971: 12).

The following are commonsense 'rule of thumb' definitions by persons appearing before a commission (the Maud Commission):

'a matter of great significance'
'not administrative detail'
'important issues'
'issues involving significant political or social reaction'
'issues involving political significance beyond a certain extent'
'the determination of a general guide to action arising out of particular problems'
'a principle'
'a precedent for a line of similar cases'
(Dunsire, 1973: 157)

It appears that policy is not one unified single phenomenon. Weber said: 'One speaks of the currency policy of the banks, of the discounting policy of the Reichsbank, of the strike policy of the trade union: one may speak of the educational policy of a municipality or a township, of the policy of the president of a voluntary association, and, finally even of the policy of a prudent wife who seeks to guide her husband' (Weber, 1970: 77).

Weber would have added others to his list were he alive in the 1980's. He could write of monetary policy or modernization policy, as in the case of China. He could observe the attempts made in the developing areas of the world to make policies with a minimum of resources, or where social, psychological or political constraints offer obstacles to the policy-maker. Africa offers many examples of this situation.

We need to ask however, whether we can find any systematic study of policy, to observe what scholars have said or are saying on the subject. We begin with asking what ideas exist about the craft of policy-making in the minds of administrators. We discover that there are 'proverbs' of administration.

The 'Proverbs' of Administration

Because there are so many self-taught administrators in the world they tend to practise the art, craft and perhaps, science, of administration on the basis of certain unexamined suppositions. The noted writer on administration, Herbert A. Simon, spoke of the 'proverbs' of administration (Simon, Public Administration Review 1946, 57–61). Just as we learn proverbs while young, so administrators may cling to a few simple rule-of-thumb guidelines for action. 'Proverbs' are, for Simon, a particularly undesirable phenomenon. In developing areas of the world there is perhaps a great temptation to offer 'proverbs' about development, seen as a great good in itself, but one which is often unrealistically appraised and which may not always be sensible or desirable. Too often administrators appear to engaged in 'casual unreasoning action by ordinary men in positions of extraordinary power' (Kelly, 1951: 1).

The administrator who wishes to excape from a built-in tendency to think in terms of proverbs may wish to take on a more rational approach. The more far-sighted administrator may want to see more system and more science in the way in which he makes policy. If policies are to be made from first principles then the administrators needs to be rational in his approach to the problems which face him. It is perhaps a curious fact of history in colonial (and post-colonial) states that the opportunities for administrative novelty have been most marked. To give one example, in the case of Singapore, the British founder of Singapore, Raffles, literally built up a city from nothing. Raffles found a site for an outpost at the southern tip of the peninsula of Malaya. After negotiations with the Sultan he proceeded to lay out an entire city from scratch, looking, as he said, a century ahead. Raffles then, 'drafts a constitution alone, without lawyers or books to consult. He himself plots every detail of the place, harbour regulations, law courts, post office, land registry, botanical garden. The detail amazes — even down to the width of the roads' (*Listener*, July 9, 1981). Raffles states: 'I trust I shall be able to lay the foundation of a new orders of things' (Collis, 1966).

Raffles was one of those rare people in history who was able to make a fresh start. Because virtually nothing existed before (i.e., no Singapore) every policy was, by definition, a *new* policy.

Most modern administrators are unable to make such changes as those contemplated by Raffles. But Raffles may be seen as the perfect 'administrative' man. He could choose the policies as he saw fit using private reasoned judgment.

Some observers like Herbert Simon, see that there is a need to bring reasoned judgements into administration wherever possible. We may be prisoners of the past and of circumstance. We have little opportunity to reflect, to ask questions and go back to first principles. But there may be good reason to try to use our reason if possible. A colonial official, an extremely busy administrator in Tanganyika, indicated the extent of the pressure by informing one enquirer that he 'enjoyed' periodic bouts of fever, as these allowed him precious time in which 'to think out his next moves' (Heussler, 1963: 173).

Herbert Simon is associated with a rational approach to the process of policy-making. Simon did not believe, as is sometimes suggested, that policy was a simple matter of being 'rational'. There were a series of steps in his argument which we need to follow. If we begin with a very important idea, (perhaps the key idea in social science) we will distinguish between *facts and values*. *Facts* suggest administration, an undertaking more or less different from policy, which we considered previously.

Decisions, Simon argued, contained elements partly factual and partly evaluative. Facts suggest administration; values indicate the higher reaches of policy-making. The decision was the centre-piece of Simon's thinking. Decisions however implied choice. How can we make good decisions untroubled by the legacy of the administrator's past successes and failures?

If we were to arrange to place our objectives in order of priority understanding their consequences, costs and benefits, we might arrive at a 'rational' answer. Decisions have to be thought out, the various alternatives considered and a reasoned choice arrived at. Simon concluded: 'A complex decision is like a great river, drawing from its many tributaries the innumerable component premises of which it is constituted' (Simon, 1965: xii).

We know however that men are not rational and that they have tended to make reason the slave of the passions. Simon suggested that our reason is limited (the concept of bounded rationality) and accepted a compromise approach. Decision-makers might be expected to see what was good enough or what was just about satisfactory. So people could be expected under the best conditions to adopt a 'satisficing' model. Because our information and powers of endurance and application are necessarily limited, the administrator will most generally be satisfied with lesser ideals. In the rationalist model, the modern applications are likely to be found in such areas as operations research, critical path analysis, system analysis, and performance evaluation and review technique (P.E.R.T.). These approaches try to solve problems by use of logic, reason and proceeding from first principles.

ARGUMENTS AGAINST THE RATIONALIST APPROACH

1. Simon's approach, it must be stressed, is not Utopian or irresponsibly abstract. Nevertheless, it has been described as a 'rational' model because it does make some steps in the direction of a science of administration (Storing, 1962, 123–150). Conventional political philosophers have thrown considerable doubt upon the possibility of any place of reason anywhere in politics.

   Michael Oakeshott disputes the power of reason in politics. 'In order that a man's conduct should be wholly "rational", he must be supposed to have the power of first imagining and choosing a purpose to pursue of defining that purpose clearly and of selecting fit means to achieve it; and this power must be wholly independent, not only of tradition and of the uncontrolled relics of his fortuitous experience of the world, but also of the activity itself to which it is a preliminary' (Oakeshott, 1967: 86).

Oakeshott's view was that those political philosophers such as Plato and perhaps Hobbes and Hegel (at times) were both wrong and dangerous. Reason in public life cannot be separated from tradition and experience and reason may be an insecure guide to policy. Those political philosophers who have tried to construct political systems out of the fancies of their mind have produced schemes either fanciful or impossible. The best guide was experience and tradition. But in Africa and Asia the weight of tradition may be too heavy.

Of course, Simon is not the creator of a grand political theory but rather the latest commentator regarding the role of reason in a branch of public administration, that of decision-making.

2. Simon's method is largely intended to counteract the idea that sensible men using commonsense ('proverbial') methods could be satisfactory administrators. According to one assessment of Simon's work: 'He believes that men ought to act rationally and that their preferences should at least have that degree of consistency and stability necessary to the exercise of rationality' (Storing, 1962: 150). The some commentator had doubts, believing that Simon's rational approach fails, 'both for its definitions and for its standards of significance and relevance, on a commonsense grasp of the phenomena to be investigated' (Storing, 1962: 150). In short, if administrators cannot be persuaded to be rational, they may still rely upon irrational prejudice, common sense as they see it, and hallowed proverbs. It is therefore not so easy to dethrone commonsense and administrators may continue to use wrong-headed over-simplistic guidelines to action.

3. A further demerit of the Simon approach is that he cannot separate the facts of a case from human values to understand that rational administrative behaviour is a mirage. Simon's attempt to separate means from ends is unrealistic for the most part. Above all, it suggests an organization which has little capacity for change. If, generally, administrators can solve their problems by the use of reason the result may be somewhat static organizations. Moreover, his conception of an administrative man is perhaps 'too simplistic, rational, narrow and instrumental for senior public policymakers and more suitable for junior public managers, planners and technocrats working within well defined public programs already depoliticised, routinised and technically stagnant' (Caiden, 1982: 67).

A lesser change may be that Simon's approach may reinforce the *status quo*, acting as a brake upon much needed change. There are times in a nation's history when it needs quite fundamental reform. Reason tells us that *apartheid* in South Africa cannot be changed by mere tinkering with the system. Similarly the French and Russians could argue that in 1789 and 1917 respectively, a revolution based on reason was necessary. In other words, the lessons of history suggest that drastic changes take place when minor changes cannot solve major problems.

165

MERITS OF SIMON'S 'RATIONAL' METHOD

Before Simon's attempt to discover whether there was a science of administration, it was perhaps taken for granted that administrators 'ran' an organization. Administrators thought that they learned by doing, acting according to a few ill-understood maxims. The idea of delegation was a case in point. It was clear that one who delegates too much is too weak while one who delegates too little is too autocratic, even dangerous. But delegation remains an 'unscientific' principle. Other maxims would be the so-called 'span of control' theory, and delegation itself.

Simon called upon administrators to accept the need for a set of conceptual tools to understand 'how an administrative organisation looks and exactly how it works' (Simon xlv–xlvi). At the heart of the theory is the related study of decision-making. Simon believes that if the decision-making process is broken down into its elements, 'students may better understand administration, legislators may choose among alternatives more wisely, and administrators may achieve correct decisions' (Storing, 1962: 69).

Simon's objective in writing was, as he saw it, the need to find a set of practical tools for administrators so that they could see some way to substitute rational decisions for snap judgments. The value of attending to the decision-making process lay in the development of a better informed choice in the hope of arriving at 'correct' decisions on matters of public concern.

At the end of the argument the fundamental conclusion is that Simon's approach must be commended because man must, as far as possible, try to see whether reason, rather than prejudice or guesswork may be useful in the solution of problems. Reason is man's most precious gift. It has a fundamental role to play in policy-making.

THE INCREMENTAL APPROACH

An increment is a small addition to some activity. An incremental policy is one which makes only a small departure from the present. The idea is not on its own either apologetic or pejorative. It merely indicates, by contrast with rational changes, that there is an alternative. It argues that a small change in policy is preferable to a fundamental or drastic change. Policy-makers are not free to make large-scale changes, even if they should wish to intervene at certain times and in certain places.

What are the major constraints upon policy-makers? Those include a variety of factors of which a few examples may be given. These include the activities of interest groups, apathy, the actions of forerunners, financial restrictions, the personalities of the participants, the weight of history, as well as aspects of culture both in the broad, and in the narrow, sense.

Incrementalism naturally accepts that nothing is static, that change is inevitable even desirable. However, such change must be gradual, not allowing too much play to the imagination. Many people describe incrementalism, not always accurately, as 'muddling through'. Thus, when Raffles arrived in Singapore, on a tropical swamp, nothing was established; there could be no 'muddling through' in such a case. For most other cases, however, incrementalism appears to be both necessary and desirable. It is certainly easier to understand, as well as comforting.

One of the public policy analysts associated with incrementalism is Charles Lindblom who has argued the case against the rational approach and the case for incrementalism. Lindblom argued that step-by-step change is realistic, relevant and understandable. He argues that: 'Limits on human intellectual capacities and an available information set definite limits to man's capacity to be comprehensive' (Lindblom, 1959).

The following diagram expresses the incrementalist position.

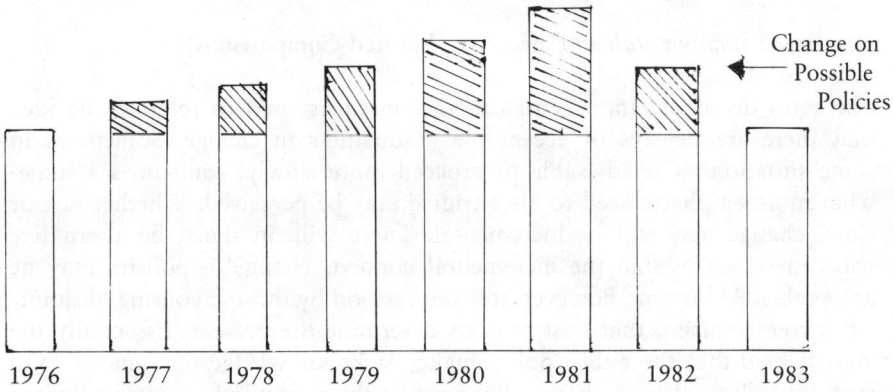

The Incrementalist Model of Public Policy-Making

Other Names:
    Bounded Rationality
    Organizational Drift
    Limited Cognition
    Intuitionism
    Line-item Budget.

A number of changes may gradually lead to a quite substantial change over a period of time. However within a period of years the first or base position may be reaffirmed. An example of this may be found in economic policy. Interest rates may increase for some period but later on may be reduced as part of an incremental move down as well as up.

In one sense incrementalism supplies what is missing in the rational policy model, namely those factors which derive from history, politics and culture. Reason strikes out to discover new ways forward. Sometimes one needs to

167

survey a problem as would a man in a ballon, floating over a valley seeing a road or river, but whose view is perhaps obscured by clouds. That is the general rational view. By contrast, policies must also be a concern of those who build roads and dam rivers who improve an environment piecemeal, step-by-step.

Incrementalists follow an approach which refers to experience, tradition and caution. Growth, for the incrementalist, must be slow sure and steady. As a matter of course, administrators do not feel inclined to take risks. There is little reason to expect policy-makers to innovate where they can get by, merely making moderate or few changes. Developing countries naturally want to make great leaps forward (as did China in 1956). These attempts to hurry development in developing countries may perhaps be seen as an over-rational or over-zealous approach. *Politicians* in developing countries may of course be more inclined to want large-scale changes immediately; *administrators* may well prefer the path of caution.

Disjointed Incrementalism (Successive Limited Comparisons)

The term disjointed incrementalism is sometimes used to refer to the idea that there are degrees of acceptable gradualness in change. Sometimes in some situations it is advisable to proceed more slowly; sometimes a somewhat more emphatic need to alter course may be perceived. Whether fast or slow, change may still be incremental. There will, in short, be alternative ways in which, within the incremental context, change in policies may be acceptable. At bottom, however, it is understood by those favouring 'disjointed' incrementalism, that past policies determine the present. Essentially the view is held that the public policy-maker lacks knowledge time, money and even the will to effect a change, but even so the method of successive limited comparisons *describes* reality. Whether this method should also *prescribe* a method for practising administrators may be more controversial. In new states policy-makers may wish to follow a given course of action, for example, in economic development — perhaps socialism. In due course economic reality may make incrementalism appear to be both sensible as well as workable.

The Demerits of Muddling Through

Organizations which 'muddle through' may be very good survivors. Policy-makers may find it on the whole sensible to muddle along from problem to problem using guesswork, gambling and intuition to guide them. Some incremental policy-makers may live according to what Simon might describe as a proverb: 'If it isn't broken, don't fix it.' In short, *any* interference with an organization may be counter-productive. A policy, practice or procedure may nevertheless require attention whether it is 'broken' or not. For example, people may be prepared to queue for long periods for a service with a minimum of complaint. The administrator may see this as inevitable delay, and, as such in a sense, on occupational necessity. There may appear to be no need to shorten a waiting period. Nevertheless if a remedy exists it may be important to use it. The proverb could be rewritten 'If it isn't broken, it may still require attention now with an eye on the future.'

Muddling through is often associated with the benefits of intuition, of getting a 'feel' for an organization. There is no doubt that people develop a sense of how an organization should work from knowing how it works. A British Labour Prime Minister, Harold Wilson, once said of his attitude to 'running' the government, that he wanted to 'fly the plane by the seat of his pants'. In short he trusted little except his general knowledge of men and their probable actions in the machinery of government.

Muddling through may be a quite dangerous approach when it sees all problems as equal. For example in every area of public administration there are some very difficult issues, in particular housing and transport. These two matters, particularly in developing countries, may in fact often lead to controversy.

Muddle through may also be a formula for successful interest groups. If policies are formulated in a cautious and predictable manner, interest groups may very well be able to 'target' their activities and, in order to protect themselves, may be able to control the state's policy-makers. An example of this is to be found in higher education (Mann, 1976: 168–20). Policy-makers have to accept what they are told by interest groups and adjust (or compromise) accordingly. Incrementalism may in fact compromise away the possibility of meaningful change. Incrementalists believe in a balance of probabilities, with no more than an expectation of modest gains. Incrementalists may in fact tend to rely upon a safe 'proverb', namely, that the best is the enemy of the good. To put it in another way, incrementalists worry that we may fail to do what we can because we are guilty of concentrating on what we might. All forms of incrementalism are prepared to settle, perhaps for second-best. Incrementalism is the art of the possible.

THE RATIONAL AND INCREMENTAL APPROACHES COMPARED: THE CASE OF NEW AND DEVELOPING STATES

States which were formerly colonies often enter the international community with high aspirations for change. Many policies in the new state will appear to the close observer to follow the old policies of the former colonial power. For a variety of reasons, not the least economic, the room for manoeuvre is small. When making demands for independence however, the local anti-colonial group may suggest rapid change and a whole range of new policies, particularly in the field of economic development. For example as in many parts of Africa, it was suggested some twenty years ago that 'capitalist' free enterprise would be replaced by some form of distributive 'socialism'. In many cases however, Western businesses continued to supply much of the capital for development. Distributive socialism where it was tried, as in Tanzania, has had little conspicuous success. In other places it has been a disaster.

While independence might have suggested a whole range of rational solutions to the problems of colonialism, within a short period of years, it was clear that the scope for radical change was somewhat limited. An important example might be India. In India, for example, policies may be made in some areas more by rational analysis of the relations between alternative policies and goals, and in other areas more by incremental trial and error. India is after all a country of about 800 million people. India's agricultural policy for example has changed little for two decades. This policy implied that farmers pay no tax and receive subsidies together with guaranted prices and output (*Economist*, December 21, 1985). This policy may have to change if India is to meet all the pressures of a growing economy in the last part of the twentieth century. The Indian government might opt for radical change or incremental change.

In China, new agriculture policies were fundamental not incremental. Since 1978, as a result of the 'production-responsibility' policy, agricultural production has risen by more than 7½ per cent per annum. Average incomes in the rural areas have increased by 70 per cent between 1979 and 1983. China, unlike India, is more accustomed to large shifts in policy, especially in economic policy.

•————————————————————————•

Incremental Change	Large Change
Continuous Improvement	Innovation (Raffles)
(*It works, don't mend it*)	War
	Revolution
	(*Let's change everything*)

MIXED SCANNING AND DEVELOPING STATES

Not everything is amenable to a rational approach just as muddling through may be an inadequate way to solve serious problems. Incrementalism can be realistic, but there are occasions when a certain degree of Utopianism can be appropriate. 'Without vision, the people perish' might be a retort to the committed incrementalist. On the other hand, too much Utopianism may be too rich a diet for many of the mundane problems which beset modern societies. In China the idealism of Mao was followed by the realism of Deng Xiaoping, to give but one example.

The hope that both rational and incremental approaches could be combined was the hope of Amitai Etzioni, and from a somewhat different perspective, of Yehezkei Dror. The need for an appraisal of all strategies by 'scanning' is self-evident to many policy analysts. There may be a merit in combining several model alternatives.

Dror looked towards a better public policy and public choice aiming at combining all relevant approaches. Decision makers should, as a matter of prescription, aim to be rational in so far as it can be shown to be applicable. Dror is attracted to the rational model but with an eye on training, think-tanks and 'the art of the possible'. Dror also considers the question of developing countries. Dror notes that developing states are attracted by planning and 'science'. They wish to break away from 'colonialism'. They require a 'maximum effort to arrive at better policies' (Dror, 1964: 156).

POLICY MAKING: THE BRITISH CASE

The British version of policy-making, as well as that of most parliamentary states, is apparently highly concentrated. The victorious party after an election crystallizes its 'victory' by capturing the cabinet. Cabinet ministers, under the prime minister, are policy-makers in the broadest possible sense of the word. Collectively they make, keep and break policy. Individually a minister, assisted by his political deputies, usually junior ministers, shape departmental policy. Departmental policy will reflect cabinet policy in general, but at the departmental level the minister is dependent upon the professional advice and assistance of his civil servants as well as other advisers.

Policy and administration usually interact constantly at departmental level, more at the top level than lower down. Where policy needs to be implemented however, we tend to speak more of administration. Within departments there is internal organization as well as the more routine business of resource administration. Some of these tasks can be described as those laid down by law, or which are devolved on other bodies such as public corporations or local government.

Sir Douglas Wass, in his Reith Lectures (1984), outlined the interlocking arrangements 'between a permanent politically neutral and meritocratic civil service and the small political directorate of ministers which oversees it' (*Listener*, 8 December 1983). Policy can be more or less 'political'. Obviously the higher one goes in British-style administration, the greater the element of politics and the less the routine. But civil servants do make a good deal of policy. The line between politics and administration at the upper reaches of government is not always easy to draw.

Many of the old ideas about British policy-making are under attack. Ministers cannot plead 'Crown Privilege' when asked to explain policies (as was the case until 1968). The diaries of Richard Crossman offered frank disclosures of the vagaries of policy-making. These solemn matters became the object of fun in a popular television series known as 'Yes Minister'. The focus has however been on policy *mistakes*, rather than on policy *achievements*. As a result the policy orthodoxy has come under scrutiny, and, 'Nobody really believes that senior civil servants are faceless, pliable, sexless creatures without fixed ideas, or intellectual eunuchs impartially proffering advice with all deference and humility to the great man in the minister's office' (Chapman, 1963: 39).

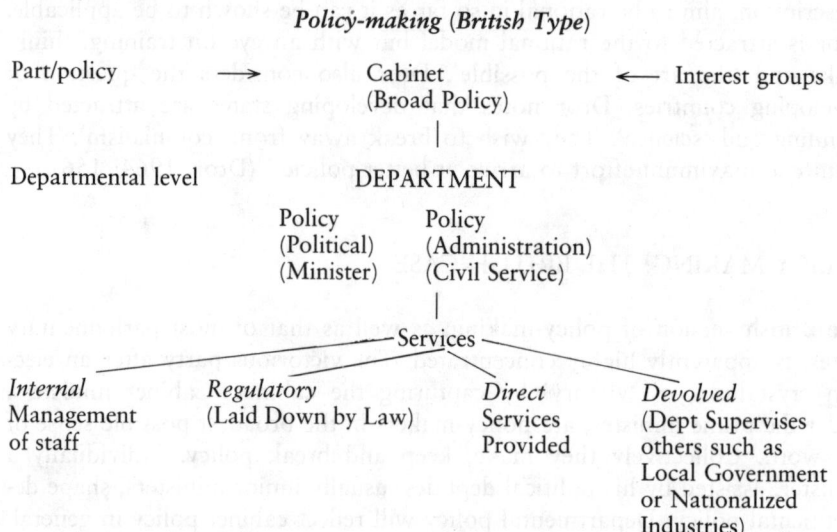

Policy-making (British Type)

Part/policy   ⟶   Cabinet   ⟵ Interest groups
(Broad Policy)

Departmental level   DEPARTMENT

Policy   Policy
(Political)   (Administration)
(Minister)   (Civil Service)

Services

Internal	*Regulatory*	*Direct*	*Devolved*
Management of staff	(Laid Down by Law)	Services Provided	(Dept Supervises others such as Local Government or Nationalized Industries)

POLICY-MAKING (JAPANESE TYPE)

Policy-making in Japan in some ways suggests the British model. Policy is the responsibility of the Japanese cabinet but individual ministers are concerned with the work of their own ministry. Civil servants in Japan, as in Britain, advise their political masters, and their power is even larger than is the case with civil servants in Britain. Japanese civil servants have a reputation for efficiency, and for thoroughness. The best brains in Japan find their way into the civil service and remain there until they reach the early to mid-fifties at which point they will enter business and politics. A career at the top in politics is often forged within the civil service. About one-third of all cabinet members since 1945 have come from the civil service. Japanese civil servants, described as 'sons of the samurai' are a district élite. They are also proportionately fewer in number than in a number of other countries. On the basis of per 1000 of population the relative figures at national government level are:

Japan: 17.1
Great Britain: 20.2
USA: 22
France: 84.5

(Dahlby, 1981, *Far Eastern Economic Review*, 34–40)

Japanese public administration like British public administration is bedevilled by similar dualities — by cleavages between more and less prestigeous universities, between central and local government, between 'specialists' and 'generalists' and between 'administration' and 'politics'. Policy-making in Japan is therefore an apparently complex matter. However there is a strong sense of national identity and national interest which means that groups perceive a need for a national consensus. For example Japan's energy policies led to savings in oil utilization in the 1970's partly through administrative guidance and also through the efforts of the Ministry of International Trade and Industry (MITI). In Japan, interest groups see the need for a national consensus and may complaints are ritualistic. Japan groups in the labour and government sectors work towards common goals as 'it is undeniable that the compulsion for conformity spontaneously felt and acted out by the Japanese is extraordinary by international standards' (Taira, 1983: 393). As a result Japan looks from some angles like a command economy, from others like a highly competitive yet vague mixture of various types of public administration.

Issues are 'processed' in part through characteristic 'independent representative' advisory bodies which include groups from all sectors of Japanese society often determined to avoid confrontation and reach a consensus (Elliot, 1983, 766). Certain matters were particularly contentious, for example the 'three K's', the rice subsidy scheme, Japan National Railways (JNR) and the national health service (*Kome, Kokutetsu, Kokumin Kentohoken*). These are processed with the need for compromise constantly in mind, stressing the avoidance of conflict and radical reform.

The Japanese bureaucracy is highly élitist and highly scornful of groups of lower ability or values than those found in other groups. Reform is difficult however and former Prime Minister Nakasone's attempts to penetrate the powerful Japanese civil service and control its operations (1983–5) were regarded by some observers with scepticism (Taira, 1983: 382).

Japan: Policy Process

Diet (Parliament)	Ministries	Courts
	Prime Minister's Department	
	Departments (Ministries)	

POLICY PROBLEMS AND POLICY PROCESS

Private persons hope to make private decisions and provided their actions do not contravene the law, it has been accepted by liberals, writers like John Stuart Mill, that this privacy is sacrosanct. Policy problems which are by implicating public problems must be a matter of wider concern and are often regulated by law. In the West, individuals have recourse to the law to solve their problems when these cannot be solved in private. In developing countries, on the other hand, it is probably true to say that many more things are 'public' then is the case in the West. Civil actions are both unseemly and expensive.

In all governments, certain processes are concerned to a large extent with the formulation of the 'will of the state' — which could be described as policy processes — while others appear to be concerned rather more with the execution of that will — or the administrative process. Policy is intellectually different from administration. Administrators therefore may ideally carry out a policy made elsewhere. However, many people have pointed out that administrators have goals too. A group of people will create a collective will for 'it would be fallacious to assume that only they (i.e., groups) make policy, and it would be naive in the extreme to pretend that ranking administrators within organisations do not make policy' (Hodgkinson, 1978: 67).

The term 'policy process' has claimed the attention of a number of commentators. One definition states that 'policy analysis is creating and crafting problems worth solving' (Wildavsky, 1979: 389). Problems have to be capable of some solutions or near-solutions with available resources. Some problems may be so difficult that they may have no solution other than fundamental revolution. A certain degree of realism is therefore necessary. Where solutions can be devised which satisfactorily resolve highly complex and contentious matters then high levels of statesmanship are evident. An example might be in the case of pollution.

Policy making is an *art* because it is creative; it is also a *craft* because the policy maker needs to have professional and administrative skills. Those who are engaged in policy analysis normally study cases, as do lawyers. They begin with an analysis of problems, and they compare and contrast similar policy matters before they recommend solutions.

Problem solving and policy analysis may be particular Western approach. Problem solving is possible only where there are no impossible barriers. Amongst these might be mentioned a firm and unshakeable commitment to Marxism-Leninism or fundamentalism in religion. Whatever solutions are devised in a scientific and critical spirit should not be frustrated by non-rational factors including ideology or tradition.

In socialist states for example, policy analysis must not produce solutions which run counter to Marxism-Leninism as interpreted by the party.

Similarly in developing states which are committed to 'socialism', economic policies which depend upon the 'market' may be unacceptable. In short, solutions which depend on *dogma* are sometimes doomed from the start, when the solution proposed runs counter to the prevailing dogma.

Assuming that political leaders accept policy analysis there are several steps which will normally be followed. Firstly, a problem is identified and examined. Secondly analysis takes place in a critical and rational spirit, and thirdly, procedures are devised that can work, allowing the policy to be implemented.

In the United States, where policy analysis is popular and well-developed, a distinction is sometimes drawn between policy analysis and planning, policy analysis studies problems like higher education. Pollution, and local finance, for example, which help us to see how people interact spontaneously. The conclusion might be that these things have been badly planned and require detailed planning. However in the USA, planning of public policies is regarded as suggesting too much governmental activity.

To take the case of pollution, some writers believe that the private, not public, sector could be made responsible for the control of pollution. Governments could ask the private sector to pay in advance, somewhat like an auction, for the right to create pollution. Later, 'the sum paid by the firm would theoretically equalise the extra cost to its consumers with the amount available for compensating present and future pollution victims' (Self, 1980: 12).

In developing states there may be a need to think differently and governments may desire to make *general* improvements in education, health or city environment. Where a uniform improvement is needed, the operations of the 'market' may be inadequate, as Lindblom suggested. There will often be a need to find *minimum* standards such as those relating to basic needs of a whole community. The operations of the 'market' may lead to a deterioration in standards. The operations of the black market, and possible bureaucratic corruption may involve heavy social costs in, for example, Africa. The latter's governments could see Western public policy analysis as culture-bound scientism, or, rhetorically, as 'imperialism'.

In the West, everybody in *general* is relatively secure largely because of welfare state policies. Policy analysis can help to explore areas of improvement which have special relevance to the community.

Western states are *modern* already, they may improve themselves in particular ways. Developing states seek modernization and the agencies of modernization are governments, and governments are frequently ideological. If they are ideological, however, they cannot solve the problems and thus frustrate themselves before they even start. Moreover, in a simple economy community, development can often be effected by means of a few simple decisions (Passmore, 1971). In a complex industrial society, policy decisions require massive organization. A dam may be built in Tanzania without large-scale planning. The building of a nuclear power plant, however, is a highly intricate operation, involving much preparation on such matters as siting, safety, system integration to grids, and the whole area of politics and public relations. Large multi-national corporations even in capitalist countries have developed complex, perhaps socialist-like, planning mechanisms.

POLICY ANALYSIS

Policy analysis has a number of component parts — 'problem identification, options development, comprehensive inpact evaluation, alternative future guesstimation, goal development and so on' (Dror, 1971). In developing areas, an objective policy analysis may be difficult to achieve and so most of the analyses apply to the developed world. The policies are capable of being rational modern and scientific, but all analysts realise with Simon, that, they will have to be content with 'satisficing'.

We may take the case of Japan, where a study of a number of policies shows why Japan has been the success which it is acknowledged to be. When policies are seen to be sound, attention is shifted to tackling those which are not so sound (Pempel, 1982: 301). In other Western countries certain areas of policy-making are particularly difficult to enter, the question of trade-union reform and higher education are cases in point. Naturally the political culture is relevant, as well as the political institutions to define the area. Japan's stability is also impressive, involving a long period in office by a cohesive conservative coalition together with a strong administrative structure.

These lessons derived from a study of Japanese *Kambatsu* (administrative élites) indicate that policies can be examined most fruitfully on a case-by-case basis. The arguments for the so-called case-study approach are strong, because it keeps us in touch with reality.

While the governments of most OECD countries spend about 40 per cent of national income, the Japanese figure for public expenditure was below 30 per cent. In Japan taxes (1980) represented only 19 per cent of national income, compared with 29 per cent in the USA, 37 per cent in France and 53 per cent in Sweden.

Think-Tanks

The idea of think-tanks has its origins in the USA, a history of some forty years. As Dror defines the concept as 'policy research, design and analysis organisations....' He distinguishes think tanks from policy analysis units which merely improve organizations or processes. Think-tanks have no party affiliation and may contain some twenty-five full-time professionals. 'Think-tanks are select units of high quality professionals grouped in islands of excellence to make cardinal contributions to public policy-making' (Dror, 1984: 219).

Examples of think-tanks have been found in the Rand Corporation and, for a short period in the past, the Brookings Institution in the USA. In Britain, a think-tank was set up in 1970 under the title Central Policy Review Staff (CPRS). The CPRS studied a wide variety of subjects, including regional policy, the supersonic aircraft Concorde, energy conservation, counter-inflation measures and the car industry.

POLICY IMPLEMENTATION

Most people are aware of the very obvious truth that a policy programme will not work if it is not properly implemented. Those who have to carry out policies are frequently officials such as judges, policemen, probation officers, and all other types of civil servants. In many circumstances, the persons who have to execute a badly conceived policy may receive criticism, hostility or even abuse from the general public.

Implementation is therefore a crucial part of the whole process of making, and then keeping to a given policy. While a policy begins as a reasonable objective, it may, in its execution become irrational and biased. Thus a housing policy or university admissions policy may in practice be discriminatory, because of the attitudes of the officials administering the policy. We may often see a tendency to present officials with highly complex even insoluble social issues. When solutions are not found, it is the official, not the intentions of the policy who is criticized. In particular, the search for scapegoats is a common feature of poorly-conceived policies. Political science is keenly interested in the question of policy implementation because it looks upon policy making in the context of what is in reality truly the art of the possible.

Policy Implementation: Western Problems

In the West much attention has been given to the need to make the public service more responsive to the needs of the public. Civil servants must be both civil and servants. Public administration can be explained in a functional or geographical way as we indicated in Chapter One. How a department is organized is not necessarily of much consequence to the individual citizen who is mainly concerned with his or her own personal affairs (OECD, 1987: chapters II and III).

Experts in public administration have pointed out that individual citizens can be caught between government departments, government policies and even the performance of clerks whose work is routine and unimaginative. The collection of a passport or a traffic licence however can be a complicated exercise. Three elements are involved in the implementation of policy — the policy itself (e.g., on what basis the policy is made, say, about passports) the administrative department (say, immigration) concerned, and the client (OECD, 1987). This is a very simple example. Other examples would be more complicated, say, in the field of foreign policy formulation and implementation. But above all, however, is the problem of the cost and benefit of the modern welfare state, especially in western Europe.

By contrast, in the USA, policy 'is implemented primarily by a complex system of administrative agencies' (Anderson, 1975: 99). There are in fact entire 'networks' — offices, departments, consumer organizations and numerous associations which may all be seen as part of the general apparatus of implementation. 'Quasi-governmental' agencies (such as quangos) can be involved as part of the 'network' as well as private bodies which are often largely independent. The prevention of cruelty to children can be the responsibility of government as well as a voluntary agency (in Britain the NSPCC). The growth of privatization has encouraged the use of non-governmental bodies to carry on tasks according to 'market forces'. There may be wholly private companies and enterprises which carry out such duties as refuse collection, running hospitals, providing data, security and services of every description. Government departments may in fact implement policies at the basic grass-roots level, merely via conventional business contracts. The provision of public services and public goods may further be sub-contracted out in such a way as to avoid the use of trade union labour. In some cases, dirty and dangerous jobs (such as the removal of asbestos) may be given to low-wage migrant or poorly-educated workers. Government can itself ignore the asbestos removal problem, despite the fact that the law itself may prohibit the use of asbestos in public buildings.

Implementation studies in Western countries have concerned themselves with the very obvious Western questions of unemployment, crime, transport facilities, development of education and social services generally. In the West and in an ideal world, policy-makers, themselves elected to responsible office make clear and unambiguous policies which they then hand over to civil servants for implementation. This is, of course, far too simplistic a model, because there is often no clear solution to difficult problems and also because those who implement policies are frequently called upon to interpret and explain the intentions of the policy-makers. A good example would be welfare state benefits (Brown, 1975: 211–247). In Britain, millions of pounds are unclaimed by potential recipients, for despite welfare policies, claimants are actually unaware of their full entitlements.

Policies in the West have outputs, outcomes and impacts. Policy outputs can be measured — number of roads built, numbers of graduates produced and number of patients cured. Policy outcomes are more long-term and are concerned with the quality of schools, the levels of technology in hospitals and the prospects for a decline in infant mortality. Policy impacts might relate to the long-term effect of policies, say on trading patterns or the 'war' on drugs or the result of building an underground, metro-railway (Fox in *Policy Science Review* 1987: 128–139) (Pressman and Wildavsky, 1973). In Western states, scholars stress the importance of clearly understanding definitions and objectives. As Parkinson suggested: 'It is not the business of the botanist to eradicate the weeds. Enough for him if he can tell us just how fast they grow' (Parkinson, 1962: 21). Policymakers would accept the need to be clear but without worrying too much provided the results are achieved.

Policy Implementation: Developing Countries

Developing countries present the Western exponent of public administration with a complex problem. Given that there has been some attempt in the West to develop what might be called a value-free method of public administration, we might consider in this context some of the problems of implementation of policy in developing countries. At a human level the eradication of the poverty of the developing world is without solution. The cutting of public expenditure is however often a matter of strict government policy. Structural adjustment involving the further depreciation of living standards has presented many problems.

The political and human costs of policies made at the central government level are often unacceptably high. We might mention the policies of Stalin in the Soviet Union, or Mao in China. It may not always be possible to implement policies where the people cannot accept the rigours of a particular policy as the above cases showed. In the case of South Africa, however, race policies are implemented in spite of the hostility of the population.

The major problems of developing countries in the implementation of policy appear to be as follows:

1. A Conflict between Aspirations and Reality

Developing countries have high hopes, and aim to conquer poverty, disease and illiteracy quickly. How this may best be done depends to a large extent upon both their own efforts and help from overseas' experts. The reality is however full of constraints. The legacy of the former colonial power (the use of a foreign language, for example) may be a particular problem. It may be useful to know French, Portuguese or English to secure benefits, if the laws are written in one of these languages rather than in a local language. Particular problems exist in India and Hong Kong.

2. The Nature of Developing States

Nation building is a central feature in the first years of new and developing countries. Subsequently follow hard choices of policy-making. States assume much responsibility for policy, while the private sector is often seen as hostile, exploitative or foreign to the new state. Policy-making may be a product of bargaining in capitals, and implementation may be left to regions, tribes and local rulers. Benefits may be allocated at the furthermost parts of the state in ways quite different from those at the centre. Federal states like Nigeria and Malaysia offer good examples, but in China, too, the coast is better served with resources than is the interior. The newly developing Third World state is often institutionally fragile and frequently has a much less well-established basis in the hearts and minds of the inhabitants than has the tribe, regional government, church or mosque. The civil service sometimes remained faithful to the practices learned from their former colonial rulers. Sometimes officials in new countries became the mouthpiece of their ethnic or regional base. Often they are sucked up into the political debate.

3. The Intermediate Technology

The developing world has a need to fit political institutions to needs, so that grand policies can actually be seen to lead to improvements in living standards. For example, there exist massive housing problems, urban overcrowding and rural deprivation. Policies may seek to remedy these things but without noticeable success. Policies designed to create employment may produce unemployment. Policies designed to develop the economy may distort the economy, leading to a waste of the community's valuable resources.

The Western economist E.F. Schumacher argued that policies should be framed to take account of their correct implementation at the grass-roots level. Thus, for example, policies should provide for the needs of the villages, not the towns of the developing world. Production should be seen in terms of local resources without a need for large injections of capital. Finally, production should be based upon simple ideas without a need for specialist training and skills.

Policies should be capable of being implemented. Thus housing policies should be related to what can realistically be done. In Africa, coconut fibre roof tiles have been produced for roofing; windpumps have been developed to provide water; fishing boats have been made from locally available plywood. All of these improvements can be implemented within the local resources of the community (Schumacher, 1974).

4. Politics and Administration

Developing countries, perhaps even less than so-called 'developed countries', appear to see a distinction between 'politics' and 'administration'. Administration, in developing countries, in Africa, Asia and Latin America is rarely 'value-free' at the levels of actual policy implementation. In most cases, the hope is for an incorrupt, neutral, impartial, professional, non-partisan bureaucracy. Indeed it is hard to see how development can take place without these qualities. Corruption (sometimes drug-related), nepotism and regional contacts are prevalent in some states. All too often it is a question of who you know rather than what you know. Clearly, corruption and nepotism are inefficient and wasteful. It is probably true of governments everywhere that an efficient ship is a happy ship, most particularly at the level of actual implementation.

Implementation of Policy: Some Continuing Issues

The future of serious investigations into policy questions will very probably have to take implementation into account. To put it crudely, people ask 'what does it mean for me', or 'how does it work out in ways which I can understand?' Thus local government policies about libraries rarely reach the 'consumer' in such terms as 'how can I borrow the book I want to read?' Unemployment policies become reduced to questions such as 'where can I collect unemployment pay?'

In a socialist state, the policy which allocates resources may lose control and coordination of the process of allocation at the lower levels. Complaints are often heard of delays and inefficiencies, particularly in the worst instances of bureaucracy. In China, for example, more than a hundred stamps of approval are needed to authorize certain benefits. If one is missing, then no permission is forthcoming (*BBC Peking Report*: 28 March 1988). In all states, delay is '. . . a function of the number of decision points, the number of participants at each point, and the intensity of their preferences' (Pressman and Wildavsky, 1973: 118).

The growth of government agencies has made government and the implementation of government policy increasingly complicated. One writer speaks of 'third-party' government. This term, 'third-party' government signifies that government is in the West increasingly carried on by specialist organizations and bodies such as boards, district committees, corporations, and professional bodies. Each of these bodies is usually extra-departmental, which operates outside the structure of the government department as usually understood. At all levels, people use their discretion in different ways, and the result may be that people who notionally serve the public may not be responsible to the public, through government departments or due legislative body. There are many important political questions which have emerged — including such controversial and elusive matters as accountability, privatization, culture, discretion, grass-roots participation, bias, and questions of equality in the provision of resources. Implementation is a complex matter. We cannot easily abolish poverty, want, lack of opportunity, sexual or racial discrimination, merely by suggesting that we have policies to counteract these human problems. There is no guarantee that policies can ever succeed in achieving their objectives. Guesswork and 'fuzzy gambling', to use Dror's term are part of the problem and of the solution, given that in Dror's words 'All decisions face uncertainty and the important ones face ignorance.'

BIBLIOGRAPHY

Anderson, James, E. (1975), *Public Policy Making*, Nelson, London
Brown R.G.S. (1975), see Chapter 1.
Caiden, Gerald E. (1982), *Public Administration*, Palisades Publishers, California.
Chapman, Richard, A. (1963), *Decision Making*, Routledge, and Kegan Paul, London.
Collis, Maurice (1966), *Raffles*, Faber, London.
Dror, Yzekel (1971), *Design for Policy Sciences*, Elsevier, Amsterdam.
Dunsire, Andrew (1973), *Administration: The Word and the Science*, Martin Robertson, Oxford.

Fox, Charles J. (1987), *Biases in Public Policy Implementation, Evaluation*, Policy Studies Review, Vol. 7, No. 1.

Heussler, Robert (1963), *Yesterday's Rulers*, Oxford University Press, Oxford. See Chapter 9.

Hodgkinson, Christopher (1978), *Towards a Philosophy of Administration*, Basil Blackwell.

Kelly, David (1952), *The Ruling Few*, Hollis and Carter, London.

Laswell Harold D. & Kaplan, A. (1950), *Power and Society*, New Haven, Yale University Press.

Lindblom, C.E. (1968), *The Policy Making Process*, Prentice-Hall, New Jersey.

Mann, Dale (1976), *Policy Decision-making in Education*, Teachers College Press, New York.

Oakeshott, Michael (1967), *Rationalism in Politics*, Methuen, London.

O.E.C.D. Economic Studies (1985), *The Role of the Public Sector*, Brussels.

Parkinson, C. Northcote, *Parkinson's Law*, Pelican.

Passmore, Gloria, (1971), *Community Development in Rhodesia*, University of Rhodesia.

Pempel T. (1982), *Policy and Politics in Japan*, Temple University Press, Philadelphia.

Pressman J.L. and Wildavsky A., (1973), *Implementation*, Berkeley.

Roberts, Geoffrey K. (1971), *A Dictionary of Political Analysis*, Longman, London.

Schumacher, E. (1974), *Small is Beautiful*, Abacus, London.

Self. Peter (1971), *Administrative Theories and Politics*, Allen and Unwin, London.

Simon, Herbert A. (1946), *The Proverbs of Administration*, in Public Administration Review, (Winter 1946).

Smith, Brian (1976), *Policy Making in British Government*, London.

Storing, Herbert (ed.) (1962), *Essays on the Scientific Study of Politics*, Holt, Reinhart and Winston, Sussex.

Taira, Koji (1983), *Industrial Policy and Employment in Japan*, Current History, Vol. 82, No. 487, November 1983.

Weber, Max (1970), *Economy and Society*, Vol. 3, New York, Bedminster Press.

Wildavsky Aaron (1979), *Speaking Truth to Power: The Art and Craft of Policy Analysis*, Little Brown, Boston.

12
Policy-Making in the Developing World

Policy-making in developing states differs in a number of ways from that which is carried on in developed industrial states. Western liberal democracies in the ideal sense are supposed to make policies in the light of the expressed preferences of the electorate, using political parties as the chosen instrument of policy. Non-Western states often reject competitive party politics, seeing the need for a single national policy, and possibly also a national ideology. Several possible characteristics may thus be described.

THE 'TOTALITARIAN' TENDENCY

Most developing states use the organs of state government and party where appropriate to develop economic policies. Whereas in the West there is a tendency to separate politics and economics, in non-Western countries politics and economics are seen as one. The idea of using 'political' methods to advance economic objectives was first used by Stalin as he set out to modernize the Soviet economy. The Soviet Union was an underdeveloped state and may be seen as the first developing country as Stalin collectivized the peasantry and made plans for industry (stressing heavy industry). Stalin achieved many of his goals but at a terrible cost in terms of human suffering (Conquest, 1971: 11 and 1985).

Since the Stalin example many other states have, in the name of socialism, followed the lead of the Soviet Union. In Ghana the point was put in borrowed Biblical form by Nkrumah (1956) who announced: 'Seek ye first the political Kingdom and all else will be added unto you.' In numerous countries in Africa, Asia and Latin America, the state has been seen as the central instrument of policy. The private sector is weak and unable to provide much guidance, and in any case, is often controlled by international multi-corporations.

In South Africa the semi-totalitarian instruments of the apartheid state gave effect to a doctrine of race separation. Apartheid had its ideological and even religious, aspects, but essentially it could be seen as a form of economic control by one group over another. At its height the doctrine of Grand Apartheid allowed only 13 per cent of the land area to the country's black African population, some 75 per cent of the total (Tomlinson Report, 1955: 194–208). Whites enjoyed greater material benefits. The state's overall policy involved a network of scattered policies which involved a deliberate attempt to use political means to distribute economic benefits.

Other developing states have not easily avoided the temptation to use, and often abuse, their power to enforce policies and they have frequently been no less brutal than the old-style South African government. As far as international morality is concerned no one state has a particular monopoly on misbehaviour to its own people.

Some developing states, among which might be counted Duvalier's Haiti, Bokassa's Central African Republic and Amin's Uganda, have been legendary totalitarian dictatorships. There has been no development in these states but much political oppression in such cases, so the trade-off between politics and economics is not always balanced. The point was well put by R.N. Carew-Hunt, which although it refers to the Soviet Union, is nevertheless a point which could be made with regard to certain totalitarian states: 'In the West there has been a tendency to stress the *political* aspect of democracy rather than its *economic* aspect, and although at times this may have been carried too far, the fault is on the right side, seeing that a people which surrenders its political rights in return for promises of economic security will soon discover it has made a bad bargain, as it is helpless if the promises are not kept' (Carew Hunt, 1975: 9).

POLICIES IN THE CONTEXT OF POVERTY

Most African states make policies in the context of poverty. In 1982, of 34 countries with per capita incomes below US$400, 21 were African. Their freedom of action is necessarily circumscribed by massive real problems of overpopulation and economic deprivation. Thus it is difficult to make policies in respect of education, social welfare or indeed any development where there are huge areas of starvation and disease such Ethiopia and the Sudan. Policies which secure adequate food for the people often appear to be beyond the capacities of public administrators. Such concepts as 'democracy' may appear to be irrelevant where food supplies are an apparently higher priority (Lancaster, 1985: 145).

In other areas too, such as the Philippines, any government appears to be helpless in face of relentless poverty. Governmental mismanagement and even corruption may be the only 'policies' that governments like that controlled by former President Marcos can offer. However adept or dedicated a government may be, if it has to operate in conditions of relentless poverty then it is clearly extraordinarily difficult to operate (*OECD*, 1985: 259–60).

POLICIES IN THE CONTEXT OF ETHNIC DIVERSITY

Policies must, it must be assumed should apply in an even-handed way whatever the composition of the state. A plural society naturally makes this a difficult proposition. There are many states which have complicated ethnic diversity. These include the Lebanon, South Africa, Sri Lanka, Malaysia, and India. A compelling difficulty lies in the inequitable distribution of resources among groups in those states. In some states certain ethnic groups, appear to enjoy a preferential treatment. In Malaysia for example, Malays known as *bumiputras* are usually preferred, in respect of official policy-making, to Chinese. In Indonesia and Thailand, policies are made which are deliberately designed to exclude Chinese. In some states in South-East Asia, Chinese are not admitted to citizenship irrespective of how long they have been actually established in the country. Japan, too, is highly discriminatory at the official level.

Chinese, or more precisely overseas Chinese, are the recipients of particular policies which may act against them in education, the use of the Chinese language, or the practice of Chinese customs generally. When policies exist which deliberately act against *some* ethnic groups these policies are discriminatory in nature. In the USA policies which so discriminate are against the law, and attempts to provide separate but equal facilities for certain (black) groups in the field of education, for example, have long since been declared unconstitutional. Government departments and agencies now may follow procedures known as 'affirmative action', which means that positive action will be taken to provide for certain disadvantaged groups. The USA has been careful to adopt a public position in its policy-making to ensure that 'disadvantaged' groups do not suffer.

In those non-Western countries which are Islamic fundamentalist, then policies and practices of these countries are favourable to believers in Islam (Esposito, 1986: 53–81). A modern Western state by contrast aspires to be *secular*, that is it makes policies which reject any political religious or racial tests for its inhabitants. Policy-making is particularly difficult to devise in those states where there is fundamental diversity with groups demanding either additions to, or differences from, the services provided by an impartial state. In Britain, immigrant communities often demand to be given extra resources, for example in schools, to take account of their distinctive culture and identity.

Developing states are not characterized by a secular and impartial approach to their problems. The state may even link up with one group to the detriment of another. In Sri Lanka, the Tamil group in the north is perceived as a rebellious element in the fabric of the nation. But secular and impartial administration is a pre-requisite for good administration. Such administration is often conspicuous by its absence.

WESTERN IDEAS OF POLICY-MAKING IN THE DEVELOPING WORLD

Western policy-makers naturally reflect a Western view of the world. They may even be prejudiced, believing that North American or Western European

185

concepts and practices constitute a model for developing states. Such a view may be quite wrong. But Western scholars are not without their uses. Western scholars in the burgeoning area of policy studies seek to probe into certain policy practices, offering useful comment where appropriate. Western political scientists in general and policy scholars in particular have offered a useful focus to developing policy in countries. They have been interested in such matters as civil rights, peace, women's liberation, environmental protection, crime, pollution and a whole range of policies from agriculture to defence. Western policy-makers may differ from non-Western policy-makers in that the former approach policy in a manner which may seen 'mechanical' to non-Western people. Westerners often appear to be prepared to tinker with and perhaps alter certain policy problems as if they are 'social' engineers. Culture, however, intrudes. Social engineering is an idea which comes more easily to, say, North Americans than to, say, Thais.

Asian policy-makers continually come to terms with their own local psychology. There may be a certain fatalism in the society which has its roots in religion or in a mixture of religion and ideology. There is a clear difference in various questions of policy as seen from the perspective of New York or Paris compared with, say, Delhi or Djakarta. The Western policy-maker can, like a scientist, mix together economics, psychology, sociology, political science, mathematics and Western logic to arrive at a 'scientific' answer to complex social issues, such as pollution for example. The policy-maker from Asia and Africa may be faced with a set of constraints which inhibit his freedom of action. In the West there are often relatively few constraints which are not economic; in developing countries religion, for example, is a considerable force, particularly Islam.

CONSTRAINTS ON POLICY-MAKING IN NON-WESTERN STATES

1. Psychological and Cultural

The idea that policy studies can be conceived of as a process, with starts and stops, is essentially a Western view. Where religions flourish such as in India, an essential unity between all forms of life is perceived to be part of the understanding of the universe. The sacred cow mentality exerts an influence over policy-makers. In Indonesia, forms of magic also serve as a reminder of the presence of irrational forces. The Asian mind refuses to place things in watertight compartments. In the Western tradition there is an acceptance of formal opposites, and an oppositional logic (Barrett, 1958: 49). Oriental philosophies do not necessarily normally that opposites are necessarily exclusive. The idea of free will is also far less developed in Asia. In China, the largest population in the world, many forms of folk religion still exist. Chinese thinking stressed the presence of opposites, black and white, male and female, life and death — the yin and the yang. Geomancy is popular, the so-called belief in *fung-shui*, which is the need to strike a harmony between wind, water and the elements. Ancestor worship and Chinese traditional practices still form a part of the Chinese life-style.

The Chinese have for long discussed the concept of the 'mandate of heaven'. Where policy-makers succeed they have visibly taken over the mandate; where they fail, they have lost the mandate. Taiwan claims the mandate so does Beijing. In Hong Kong, the British have almost lost it. Extreme sensitivity to social values is required in all these circumstances. What is perceived as a mere matter of social engineering in many secular-minded Western states is often a serious threat, as with Islam. It does not seem appropriate for the policy-maker to disturb the deepest impulses in a society. If the cow is a sacred animal in the Hindu religion, for example, then policy-makers should proceed carefully in policy matters relating to animals. Western-type modernization, with its assumptions that the 'politics of men will give way to the administration of things', may not easily blend with fatalism. 'The political belief systems of the developing nations of Asia and Africa fit somewhere between those of traditional religion-based societies and governments and the secular functionalism and scientific managerial faith of developed societies' (Apter, 1965: 17).

2. Economic Constraints

Policy-makers everywhere in the world usually suffer from a common complaint, namely lack of adequate financial and physical resources to implement desired objectives. Western policy makers, aware of the economic factor in policy-making have offered a number of techniques which can be used to ensure the best use of limited resources. Value-for-money exercises have been developed and the analysis of costs and benefits has become an important aspect of modern. The OECD believes (1985) that irrespective of the national economic system, the way ahead is through 'private initiative and the spur of competition' (*OECD*, 1985: 30). This view is in sharp contrast with that once expressed by Nkrumah in Ghana: 'Seek ye first the political Kingdom and all else will be added unto you.' Many of the politicians in the developing world preferred 'politics' to 'economics'. However, economic constraints have operated in the large majority of new states. Economic growth is perhaps easier to discuss than to resolve.

In states where povety is endemic, and even worsening, where for example an average wage is less than US$1 per day, imported cost and benefit approaches may have dubious validity. In order to develop many Third World states, their governments have had to borrow large sums of money, political sovereignty notwithstanding the interest on the debts outstanding has itself placed an economous burden upon developing states in Latin America in particular, especially Mexico, Brazil and Argentina, amongst a number of others. Debt-servicing has become significant enough to absorb a huge proportion of income required for current needs and re-scheduling of such debts has become a necessity. Hence, in such conditions, the most important policy becomes a policy of finding enough resources from an already impoverished economy to pay off national debts.

3. Political Constraints

Policy-makers do not make policy anywhere in a vacuum. In Western states, cabinets and parliaments determine many matters and in most cases, party policy is the principal constraint upon all rulers, including both officials and politicians. The object of all party·activity is to capture the apparatus of the state. The policy-makers in the state apparatus may or may not be the policy-makers in the party. There is however a natural tendency for the party to try to turn the state apparatus to its own account. Parties initially begin with some view regarding the sort of society which it wishes to establish. It late translates these views into policy and uses the electoral process to legitimize its plans. It should be the other way round, or one might suppose, but in practice voters are not the independent noble creatures of democratic mythology.

In some new states as in some Western states, a political order sees its primary concern as a will to survive. It does not make many, if any, policies. The Philippines under President Marcos offers a very good example. The election of 1986 was fought under no particular political programme or stated list of proposed policies. Survival was the central issue, and Marcos lost. A government requires to have some notion of its policies.

If a government has no apparent or discernible policies then there remains little room for manoeuvre in the interplay of politics. There can be an intellectual bankruptcy of policies as well as a financial bankruptcy preventing the implementation of policies.

Policy-makers in the developing world do not necessarily act independently. They must be stimulated to make policies say in the fields of education or housing. Without such stimulation policies will not be generated. On the other hand, policies can be frustrated by politicians and by soldiers turned politicians. Policies can also be frustrated by priests (or mullahs) turned politicians. Policies on birth control can be devised or destroyed by politicians, but no administrator can legitimately be seen to initiate them. His task is seen as devising the ways and means to carry out policies, while involving himself in their initiation where his inclinations and talents so demand.

In those developing states in which the military hold the reins of power a neat equation may typically develop in decidedly non-democratic states (Clapham, 1984: 154). The generals make the policy, assisted by technocrats (say, for example, Western-educated economists). At the lower levels of society discipline is maintained by the secret police or by traditional rulers.

Westerners believe that Western forms of government offer guideline

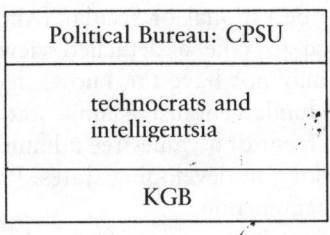

| generals, mullahs and allies |
| technocrats |
| secret police or traditional rulers |

In the Soviet Union, the situation before Gorbochev's reforms would look as follows:

| Political Bureau: CPSU |
| technocrats and intelligentsia |
| KGB |

standards which are unquestionably superior to anything devised in the non-Western world. Simplistic commentators speak of 'democracy' in the West as if it is somehow neatly exportable irrespective of conditions elsewhere. The ballot-box has been extolled as a world-wide panacea. In fact, elections are frequently an occasion for trouble. Flight Lieutenant Jerry Rawlings dismissed the ballot-box with contempt, saying that he refused to put any 'bits of paper in a box' for anyone. Policies too, are made in such ways as to reflect local, not external, needs. Authoritarian states in the developing world have no monopoly on secure policy-making.

POLICY-MAKING IN NON-DEMOCRATIC STATES

The formulation of public policy in nations of a non-democratic nature takes different forms and depends on whether the nations govern from the left or the right. Both have command style governments directed from the centre. One might imagine that authoritarian governments would find the process of policy taking a relatively simple matter. Given the command and centralized pattern of authority, one would have imagined that policies could be made without the normal arguments faced in parliamentary states.

In fact, policy makes in non-democratic states do not find problems disappear simply because they have excessive powers over policy denied to the policy-maker in liberal states. Whatever policy fields are covered and whether supported by an electorate or not — in family planning, education, the arts or nuclear energy, to take some examples — the ultimate test of policy-making is success or failure on the ground.

189

DEVELOPING STATES AND DECISION-MAKING

We have already considered (Chapter 10) various schools of thought regarding decision-making as these were first enunciated in the West. In particular we discussed the rational-deductive approach, the incremental approach and the mixed policy-process approach. In developing countries these three approaches may be less clear-cut than they are in Western democracies.

The rational-deductive approach appears at first to be inappropriate to a developing country. A former colony may have high expectations, it may be argued, but it also suffers a number of apparent disadvantages in the process. A poor country will not be rational or secular (Almond and Powell, 1966: 24–25). It cannot afford to take a detached view, weighing up possible alternative solutions. It may not have the knowledge, particularly statistical knowledge necessary. A fundamentalist Islamic state sees religion more imperative than the development of a value-free administration. Even a modern sense of time may be lacking in developing states. Procrastination may be at least partly, a cultural phenomenon.

In short, developing countries would prefer to plan and to be rational, but are frustrated when there is no guaranteed great leap forward. In part, Western academics and policy-makers may have to accept some of the blame when things go wrong. Developing states have even less control over their environment than do the developed. Population growth in Africa and the Middle East is of the order of 3 per cent. Despite everything done, between 1980 and the year 2000 population growth in developing countries will be of the order of one-and-a-half billion (*OECD Report*, R.M. Poats, 1985: 271).

A further problem is what Milne calls 'an illusion of innovation in policy-making' (Milne, 1972: 392). Innovation which is not completed is not really innovation. There is for example a tendency by policy-making, in some countries to begin projects because they are reluctant to complete those begun by their predecessors; Maddick 1963: 171; Milne, 1972: 392).

A related problem is that of imitation. Policy based on imitation is fruitless if it ignores local customs and culture. Some Asian states understandably exasperated by the colonial legacy merely threw out the baby of solid growth with the bathwater of former colonial sovereignty. Burma could be a good case in point. The practices and procedures of the old colonial powers were rejected merely because these were regarded as left overs from the colonial era. It was thought appropriate to imitate say Soviet or US models, but such models were not necessarily appropriate either.

A knowledge of say, budget practices in Texas, may not necessarily assist the administrator in Tanzania or Thailand. A developing state needs to know how to improve by degrees its per capita GNP rather than set up impossibly unrealistic and radical goals for itself. In 1978, China produced under Hua Guofeng, a plan which was so unrealistic that within a few months it had to be scrapped.

'Incrementalism', 'muddle through', 'successive limited comparisons', these all have a certain attraction for developing countries. If the local political culture is 'resistant to large sudden changes', then a step-by-step approach may well be apparently preferable to a strategy of 'great leaps'. Where resources are limited then developmental policies should reflect such limitations. A number of new policy alternatives emerge, such as those which encourage thinking of pilot projects or small-scale nucleus planning (Weidner, 1970b: 414, Waterston, 1965: 285–287).

Incrementalism has however several drawbacks when applied to developing states. Few deny that innovation is restricted by the incremental approach, even that incrementalism results from or leads to, conservatism (Dror, 1964: 154–155). The question really is one which asks how big an increment is being envisaged? Modernization in China, for example is seen as a matter of some concern by the policy-makers. Some parts of the modernization process are to be welcomed, but modernization cannot be tolerated where to be 'modern' is a threat to the established order, as was shown in June 1989.

A further drawback is that the incremental process encourages fragmentation of decision making. Many people may make local decisions incrementally; they do so because of the logic of incrementalism, but the system may not encourage local decision-making, and may not be equipped to accommodate it. Thus in Islamic states there is a central system of beliefs which cannot be disregarded on grounds of administrative convenience. Islam is a total way of life (Esposito, 1986: 54).

Developing countries are tempted to resort to policies which cannot be put into practice. There are a number of reasons for this which include the dogmatism of some developing countries ideologies, high local aspirations and internal feuding (Dror, 1968: 110). Where there is Utopianism as in so many new states, people are offered a vision, even if the rhetoric is out of step with the reality.

BIBLIOGRAPHY

Almond Gabriel and Bingham Powell (1966), *Comparative Politics: A Developmental Approach*, Little Brown, Boston.
Apter David (1965), *The Politics of Modernisation*, Chicago University Press, Illinois.
Barrett William (1958, 1961), *Irrational Man*, Heinemann, London.
Bell (1968).
Bryce James (Lord), *The American Commonwealth*, Macmillan, 1915, p. 456, London.
Carew-Hunt R.N. (1964), *The Theory and Practice of Communism*, Penguin.
Carr E.H. and Davies, R.W., *Foundations of a Planned Economy*, Volume One, Penguin, 1974, London.
Chan Heng Chee (1976), *The Dynamics of One Party Dominance*, Singapore University Press, Singapore.
Churchward L.G. (1968), *Contemporary Soviet Government*, Routledge & Kegan Paul, London.
Clapham, see Chapter One.

Clarkson Stephen (1979), *The Soviet Theory of Development*, Macmillan, London.
Conquest Robert (1971), *The Great Terror*, Pelican, London.
Conquest Robert (1985), *Inside Stalin's Secret Police: N.K.V.D. Politics, 1936–39*, Macmillan, London.
Dror Yzekel (1968), *Public Policy Making Re-examined*, San Francisco, Chandler.
Du Toit A. and Giliomee H. (1983), *Afrikaner Political Thought*, Volume One, Philip, Johannesburg.
Esposito John L., *Islam in the Politics of the Middle East*, Current History, Feb. 1986, Vol. 85, No. 508.
Harris Peter, 'Modernisation: The Word and the Deed', in *Modernisation in China*, H.K.U., 1979.
Hepple Alexander, *Verwoerd*, Pelican, London.
Hingley Ronald (1981), *Russian Writers and Soviet Society, 1917–1978*, Methuen, London.
Jennings Sir Ivor (1969), *Cabinet Government*, Cambridge University Press, Cambridge.
Lancaster Carol (1985), *Africa's Development Challenges*, Current History April 1985, Vol. 84, No. 501.
Lenin V.I., *What is to be Done?* Foreign Languages Publishing House Moscow, n.d. (1902).
Liang Heng and Judith Shapiro (1983), *Intellectual Freedom in China after Mao*, Fund for Free Expression, N.Y.
Maddick H. (1963), *Democracy, Decentralisation and Development*, Asia Publishing House, London.
Mary McAuley (1978), *Politics and the Soviet Union*, London, Penguin, p. 228.
Milne R.S. (1972), *Decision-Making in Developing Countries*, *Journal of Comparative Administration*, Vol. 3, No. 4, Feb. 1972.
Nove Alec and Nuti D.M. (editors), (1976), *Socialist Economics*, Penguin, London.
Organisation for European Cooperation and Development (O.E.C.D.).
Paton Alan (1962), *Hofmeyr*, Oxford University Press, p. 167.
Peng Guangxi (1976), *Why China Has No Inflation*, Foreign Languages Press, Beijing.
Rippon Simon (1984), *Nuclear Energy*, Heinemann, London.
Schapiro, L.B. (1972), *Totalitarianism*, Macmillan.
Skilling, Gordon and Griffiths F. (eds) (1971), *Interest Groups in Soviet Politics*, Princeton University Press, New Jersey.
Sixth Five Year Plan (1981–1985), Beijing.
Stewart Philip D., *Soviet Interest Groups and the Policy Process*, World Politics Vol. XXII, October 1969, No. 1, pp. 29–50.
Tomlinson F.R., Report of the *Commission for the Socio-Economic Development of the Bantu Areas within the Union of South Africa*, UG61/1955 Chapter 25.
Tower Press (Government of South Korea), *George Orwell's 1984 North Korea*, Seoul.
Truman Harry, *Precinct to President* (Ed. Morrow Interview).
Waterston A. (1965), *Development Planning: Lessons of Experience*. Baltimore, John Hopkins Press.
Weidner E.W. (ed) (1970), *Development Administration in Asia*, Durham, N.C., Duke University Press.
Wright (1985).
Xu Dixin (1982), *China's Search for Economic Growth*, New World Press, Beijing.
Xue Muqiao (1981), *China's Socialist Economy*, Foreign Languages Press, Beijing.

Conclusion

In the West, there is a sound and growing body of knowledge of public administration and public policy analysis. We may describe this as scientific, modern and secular. Such an approach to public policy and administration is, at its best, dynamic, and has produced many new ideas on the subject. Organizations in the West are not 'sacred' bodies apart perhaps from the Vatican. Since the end of World War II there has been much interest in organizational theory.

Much modern writing on public administration comes from the USA, where such subjects as policy studies are devoted to 'the study of the nature, causes, and effects of alternative public policies for dealing with specific social problems' (Nagel, 198: xvi). Public administration is of course a subject of considerable antiquity. Both Plato and Confucius can be said to be interested in the training of the public official, but rather more seeing the problem in terms of power and morality. Today's public administration and policy analysis are much more inclined towards problem solving. Today's public administration utilizes all relevant available knowledge to tackle such matters as environmental protection, poverty, women's rights, the motor-car and its impact on society, and, as far as it can, such matters as peace and war.

Solving problems is the Western response to the ills which beset modern society. Some problems such as drug-taking, or the debates and dilemmas associated with homosexuality, appear to be without solution. There is no magic by which complex social problems can be solved. The best that can be said is that modern social science clarifies these and other difficult issues and solves these matters where they can. This at least is an advance on the past. In Africa, peoples were introduced to the modern state only in this century (Perham, 1970: xiv).

Western public administration is imbued with the notion that causes and effects are examinable and hopefully soluble. There are tools to be used. These tools include budgetary analysis, cost-benefit analysis and operational research as well as such devices as 'think-tanks' and mathematical models. It must be remembered however that colonial administration was totally ignorant of these techniques, which in any case are the product of post-war developments in public administration. For the most part developing countries have been in existence for as long as advanced and developed public administration, especially in its quantitative aspects.

When Westerners came to administer non-Western states as colonizers they approached their charges with all the prejudices of which they were capable. French, Belgian, Spanish, Portuguese and British nationals exported some of their institutions. Some matters were insoluble even then. These included social and religious taboos. The Indian Mutiny was in some ways the result of a gigantic misunderstanding regarding the attitude of Muslims to unclean animals. Soldiers refused to touch the grease of pigs for example (Hibbert, 1980: 22). More particularly in the nineteenth century, British colonial administrators were chosen not for their knowledge of India, but for 'strength of character, readiness to accept responsibility, care for the people whom the administrator was serving, albeit autocratically —' (Macpherson in Heussler, 1963: x). The British social and class structure as well as educational, legal and sport were exported *via* the colonial service. For the most part, British administrators overseas tended to see colonies as public schools, as it were, complete with headmaster, prefects and schoolboys. Few 'theories', as opposed to institutions took hold, and the empire was run by instinct rather than by any pre-conceived principles. 'Our great virtue', one British colonial civil servant suggested, 'was not having an idea' (Hailey, 1939: 18).

In 1946 the British finally hit upon the idea of administrative training when they instituted the Devonshire Courses so called after the name of the committee recommending a measure of preparation for would-be administrators for Britain's colonies. These courses were no more than exposure to scattered knowledge on a number of subjects including economics, language, law and tropical health, government and authropology. This was an advance on training on the spot under serving District Officers (Administration), but it was often carried out in a defensive spirit given that colonies were under attack in the United Nations in the 1950's. In this respect, French colonial training was more comprehensive than was the British. French administrative cadets were made to understand their co-called civilizing mission (*mission civilisatrice*). French civilisation and culture was seen without qualification as a benefit to native populations. 'Everyone has two motherlands; France and his own' ('*chacun a deux patries; la France et la sienne*') (Heussler, 1963: 149—50).

Administration was seen as part of the imperialist impulse. Mostly it envisaged the metropolitan country as standing in a parent relationship to the dependency. The colony would receive institutions, customs and practices and in most cases Christianity (Protestant or Catholic) on such terms and conditions determined by the colonizing power. The exercise was regarded as *moral* rather than *scientific*. Imperialism implied some form of citizenship. British colonialism, on the other hand, perceived people as subjects rather than citizens (Robertson, 1984: 53). The essence of colonial administration generally suggested the missionary.

After independence, and from the mid-sixties, colonial administration gave way to local administration, or administration by new, often Western trained, administrators. In many cases there was little or no substantial change, because the administrative structures inherited from the colonial period — parliaments and law courts for example — were useful. But having removed the colonial administrative structure, new states were often constrained to act much more independently. Colonial customs and practices were discarded in many places in the emphoria of decolonization, such as parts of (if not the whole of) parliamentary government. Such changes as did take place were often restricted to capital cities. Administration in the localities always followed more traditional lines possibly at the village and regional level.

In the West the interest in how organizations work and how they should work has been intensified. We have explored the internal operations of 'bureaucracies' and have 'de-mystified' to some extent, the process of decision-making. Public administration has become more precise, technical and quantified and has even entered, via statistics the area of prediction. Ethical questions are not entirely ignored but are assessed, analyzed and evaluated in a matter-of-fact way. Government has been seen increasingly as a means to an end rather than an end in itself. All of these developments add up to an increasingly *secular* approach to administration. The conclusions reached are that much social progress can be made by a realistic appraisal of the role of government and of the careful scrutiny of policy programmes using this secular approach. Public administration may be seen as a form of Western technology. It would be unrealistic for this technology to be applicable in different cultures at all times and in all places. Yet independent or not, a 'secular' spirit in administration was a pre-requisite to a developing state.

Many of these developments have much to offer the student of public administration in new and developing states. There may be good reason for policy-makers in Africa and Asia to use such secular Western techniques as they may consider to be useful and constructive, as well as uncontaminated, by ideological bias. Socialist states, both Third World and in the Soviet sphere, however, are unlikely to test say the party's organizational efficiency. Whereas the departments of state in Western countries have, albeit reluctantly, opened their doors to scrutiny (perhaps through such means as the Freedom of Information Act in the USA), in some socialist countries such demystification has not taken place.

The Communist Party of the Soviet Union itself obviously decides its own rules, organization, size and scale of operations. Socialist parties elsewhere, and single-party states almost everywhere, have been inclined to resist close analysis. Single-party states logically are above scrutiny, and can be seen as quasi-mysterious organizations. Attempts to apply the canons of public administration to such states would meet with severe opposition. The secular spirit does not prevail. When in 1986 Gorbachev denounced the corruption and inefficiency of the CPSU he could do so from a position of authority. Had he chosen *not* to make his comments to the XXVIIth Party Congress, then he would have left the matter of organizational inefficiency unspoken. The single-party is defined as a good above question or suspicion, unless the party organization declares its own inadequacies. In 1990 communist parties in Eastern Europe come to accept power-sharing with other political groups.

Allied to the 'mystery' of the party organization is the language of analysis. Socialist states and some developing states reject any idea of a value-free analysis of their situation whether of party or state. The use of 'black-and-white' language may illustrate the point. Thus in speaking of India, a Soviet commentator declared that: 'everybody realises that foreign imperialism, though deprived of political power is directly responsible for all the hardships of the people (of India) and no one can hide this fact' (Clarkson, 1978: 250). Under these circumstances there is little opportunity for a meaningful exchange of views. Any attempt to analyse Third World organizations by Western scholars may be met with the argument that it is the product of bourgeois thinking, or that it is inappropriate for cultural or ideological reasons.

The West has *secular* tools for analysis, and an ideal-type, as it is called, derived from Weber, for assessing ideal administrative forms is among them. Weber's picture is of a network of officials characterised by legal rules, a paid administrative staff, the keeping of clear records, specialization by function and the impartiality of the office. This latter point suggests the authority of the office on merit principles, but not of that of the person (Weber, 1968: Vol. 3).

What Weber called 'bureaucracy' is a construct of how a network of officials might operate, though not of course suggesting *how* bureaucracy operates. Weber's ideal is 'secular'; the reality however especially in the developing world is often quite different. In China, for example, officials were traditionally autocratic if not corrupt. A common expression was 'all crows are black', which implies that officials are unpleasant and inefficient. If Weber's scientific network of officials could be realized then developing states would have the benefits of modern administration without its deficiencies. What these were have been set out by Weber as precision, speed, unambiguity, knowledge of the files, continuity discretion, unity, strict subordination, reduction of friction ... and costs (Weber, 1968, 1003–4).

One solution to the problem of exporting secular Western techniques in public administration might be to concentrate for the most part mainly on the export of Western techniques. It is possible to suggest that non-Western developing states have something to learn from Western management styles even if they have rather less to learn from the culture of the West. The tools of the West can be utilized, while disturbing the local culture as little as possible — a Chinese and Japanese solution to the problem.

Some techniques utilized by Western administration may apply virtually irrespective of cultural differences, although it must be stressed that techniques too can have strong cultural implications. These techniques would appear to be measuring costs and benefits, output budgeting, management by objectives and operational research, with emphasis on quantitative methods. We may suggest that all public administration enterprises have five common but distinct forms of activity or application, and it could be argued that these could apply irrespective of culture. These relate to public sector expenditure, employment, decision-making, communication and level of expertise.

PUBLIC SECTOR EXPENDITURE

All governments tax, although in some states like the People's Republic of China, taxation is low. Public financial institutions and policies should therefore be at the heart of the study of public administration anywhere. Even modern capitalist states spend huge sums of money on the public sector including social services. How the money which is to be spent is raised is of course another question, but not one so central to the concern of students of public administration. However, taxation has to be collected and both developed and developing states need to discover techniques in budgetary matters as in all others. Administrative convenience to put it no higher than that is a factor in the collection of taxes. In Africa a flat sum poll tax has been the traditional method of collecting taxes. It is the simplest form of direct tax to collect and there is something to be said for its continued use, although it may be objected to on other grounds. In many developing states, there is some considerable difficulty in the problem of taxation collecting as well as of the whole question of public expenditure. The difference between Western and non-Western developing states is essentially one of scale in this respect.

PUBLIC SECTOR EMPLOYMENT

Governments both central and local are large-scale employers of all possible types of labour, from medical doctors and scientists to armies of unskilled labourers. The public sector in many countries is often far larger than the private sector. Many professionals such as teachers and nurses depend almost entirely upon government for employment (OECD, 1985). Sometimes this situation gives rise to serious problems as in China where 30,000,000 to 50,000,000 people are regarded as surplus to needs (*Xinhua*, June 21, 1988).

An important question relates to proportion of minority groups, including ethnic groups in important public sector posts. This is a universally complex problem in all places from Northern Ireland to South Africa and India amongst many others. In India, for example, Muslims comprise about 12 per cent of the population, but they occupy only 4 per cent of government posts. At higher levels of the civil service there are only 142 Muslims out of a total of 7,000 officials; out of 441 high court judges (1984 figures) there were only 15 (*FEER*, 20 March 1986: 34). Complaints are heard in all societies about employment opportunities with government, but one constant is the debate about the correct level of public sector employment. In most developing states public sector employment is particularly important, because there are few alternatives to access to a higher standard of living. The share of general government in total employment in a number of countries exceeds 30 per cent (e.g., Sweden, Denmark) but in Japan it is below 7 per cent. In the poorest countries, government is the most important source of employment

197

for groups which might otherwise be largely disadvantaged as with Malaysia's *bumiputras* (Malays).

PUBLIC SECTOR DECISION-MAKING

Public administration everywhere is a matter of making decisions. Whether one is speaking of the simple village decision about water supply, where to place dams or bridges or rough access roads, it is part of the process of public administration. These are decisions which may be just as complex and just as significant in the lives of simple agricultural communities as are huge decisions of say, international aircraft design to Europeans. One of the ways in which public sector decision-making has been studied is through the concept of community development at the village level, but through modern decision-making theory at sophisticated Western central government level (Passmore, 1972, Maddick, 1970, Braybrooke and Lindblom 1971). Most government is the outcome of 'an amalgam of countless individual decisions' (Spiers, 1975: 143).

PUBLIC SECTOR COMMUNICATION

Governments everywhere collect, store and disseminate information. Governments can release or control information, and in so doing alone can offer a description of how the society works. Sometimes information is deliberately falsified as it was in China during the Cultural Revolution (when the State Statistical Bureau was instructed to produce only favourable statistics). Governments have, as we suggested in Chapter I, become heavily involved in the business of information and communication, and will presumably in the future continue to become involved in the most sophisticated forms of communications technology. The computer has become a tool which makes instant communication possible, but in poor countries, computers are still often rareties. Information is necessary however even in the poorest countries which are only partly literate. Government is everywhere a matter of communication, preferably two-way communication. In a developing country like Thailand for example, as well as in Western developed states, we see examples of the information society whose care is modern communications technology (Virulrak, 1985: 13). Information and communications are at the heart of government.

THE EXPERTISE OF THE PUBLIC SECTOR

The public sector is asked more and more to take a lead in new and often largely unexplored fields. People in the public sector clearly need to produce answers to complex problems, such as the usage of two or more languages in a multi-lingual society. In the private sector, the dominance of one language could be the *unstated* policy, while in the public sector there must be an appearance of consistency. Governments have to try to be open and fair. If governments fail to give a lead in ethics, its expertise must also suffer. Expertise is often highly technical, calling upon architects, forensic scientists, computer analysts and engineers. The more developed the economy the more developed the tools for interpreting it. Developed states have made many advances in the direction of modern technology. Some of these techniques may be still in the process of being worked out. Others have been developed for decades. An example would be that of operational research (OR). A 'model' is constructed in mathematical terms. Problems are seen then not in isolation, but as part of a larger problem (Duckworth, 1967, and MacRae and Page, 1967: 47–50). OR is useful in as much as it comes into play only *after* value choices have been made....' Where indigenous values are treasured, as in developing states, then technical expertise can take over, provided people are assured that their particular spiritual ideals are protected, rather than diminished by the new science.

OR, first used in Britain to solve wartime military problems, has been used in highway safety, agriculture, and even birth control (Henry, 1975: 133–6). Today OR has become a most sophisticated technique (Ackoff and Sasieni, 1968). The sorts of management problems which are relevant to OR can be seen by reference to certain matters as follows:

1. What should be done with idle resources?
2. What is the best way to use resources in the public sector?
3. How can we serve large numbers most effectively?
4. How can we give priority to those most in need?
5. How can we find the shortest route between two points?
6. How can we replace defective parts quickly?
7. How can we make one decision-maker's decisions succeed over those produced by others?
8. How can we solve these justly and quickly, given the wide variety of political institutions in different states?

In colonial times the classical District Commissioner would face these problems almost daily in his travels around his district. He would perhaps approach them intuitively, making decisions as it were by role of thumb. Colonial theories were political in that 'law and order' were perceived to be the sole object of the system. It was never intended that colonies should develop complex economic policies. Colonies had fiscal needs, that is they used taxation to finance local needs. Usually in Africa for example, a poll tax (or personal tax) was used for this purpose (Due, 1963: 61–62). Colonies therefore had fiscal but not economic (i.e., developmental) policies. Indeed, metropolitan or mother countries themselves were not 'Keynesian' before the end of World War II. Developing countries, which are mainly former colonies, have had to consider very carefully what public administration devices they wished to borrow from the West.

Western techniques which have a relevant application in developing contexts include budget making and planning, but even these may not always be wholly applicable. However budgetary and mathematical devices are as 'neutral' as possible. They include such devices as 'planning — programming — budgeting' systems, devised in the United States in the sixties. Instead of itemising budget requests, for example, PPB classifies expenditures by the government into programmes (Bourn, Open University, 1974: 72–89). 'Zero-base' budgeting asks for requests for extra financial support to be looked at in a new way. Instead of asking to 'add-on' the cost of new projects to the already existing budget, the case for new projects as well as old-existing projects should be argued from the beginning. People should perhaps be asked to assess the value of their organization from first principles. Administrators often take the previous authorizations as not requiring justification. This applies universally in developed and developing countries.

A continual theme in public administration is 'value for money' (expressed in military terms as 'more bang per buck'). However, sometimes the logic of rational budget-making has been undermined by political, cultural or ideological factors. For example, central government aid to minority groups may not all find its way where it is most needed. Ethnic sub-groups in developing areas may not see benefits. For example, it is difficult to quantify the value of the Chinese language to Chinese in South-East Asia. Nevertheless, new ways of looking at allocation of resources in the public sector will continue to concern public administrators.

Public administration everywhere is concerned with institutions and structures of government. However, public administration is also concerned with solving problems, a considerable number of which are common to most cultures and civilisations. Public administration concerns itself almost universally with questions of spending, (if not raising), public money, employing people, making decisions in public, collecting and disseminating information about itself and other bodies and with encouraging guidance and expertise in a vast range of public matters.

Some countries perform these tasks well and some perform them badly or even not at all. The student of public sector ethics will judge whether standards are acceptable, or that a moral and accountable administration has been achieved. Often leaders fail to offer a good example, and rank and file may respond. At a high level, and dramatically, 'people power' may reject authority as was the case in the Philippines and Haiti in 1986. Moral imperatives are always important in developing areas as they are in developed Western states. The difference is that developed Western states may behave in a secular manner. Social justice may be seen to be a matter of distribution or redistribution of resources in the West, but it is at least a secular matter. In part, Weber's picture of the 'bureaucracy' is still a useful reminder of the contrast between two administrative styles, namely between one version of

Western and one version of developing. Weber saw bureaucracy whose vital characteristic is that of efficiency. 'It creates uniformity and predictability in large-scale societies because the acts of thousands of officials are all oriented to identical norms' (Lachman, 1970: 114). But most importantly: 'Modern loyalty is devoted to impersonal and functional purposes', which equates to our notion of secular Western administration.' While it is easy to show how 'bureaucracy' fails to live up to its ideals and even to represent it as unable to improve its behaviour by learning from its errors as Crozier put it. Since Weber's time many have been attracted to new ideas. For example we read in the writings of Dror a rich contribution to the literature, developing such concepts as reality and problem preception, grand policy and critical choice, transincrementalism, complexity, fuzzy betting, learning, policy, architecture, tragic choice and meta-policy' (Dror in Nagel, 1982: 3–10).

Developing states may well structure their government and public admin-istration upon different assumptions, taking religion, ideology race or culture as given facts before concerning themselves with more abstract forms of public administration or policy analysis. After all, women in Africa carry heavy loads on their heads, Chinese 'doctors' practice acupuncture and Arabs pray several times a day. None of these things is amenable to any simple administrative theory.

BIBLIOGRAPHY

Ackoff R.L. and Sasieni M.W. (1968), *Fundamentals of Operations Research*, John Wiley, Sussex.

Braybrooke D. and Lindblom C.E. (1971), *Strategy for Decision*, Free Press, Glencoe Publishing Co. (affliated to Macmillan) Encino, California.

Bourn J. (ed.) (1974), *Approaches to the Study of Public Administration*, Open University.

Clarkson Stephen (1978), *The Soviet Theory of Development, India and the Third World in Marxist-Leninist Scholarship*, MacMillan, London.

Dror, see Chapter Eight.

Duckworth, W.E. (1967), *A Guide to Operational Research*, Methuen, London.

Due John (1963), *Taxation and Economic Development in Tropical Africa*, MIT Press, 1963, Mass.

Hailey Lord (1939), *An African Survey*, Oxford University Press, Oxford.

Henry Nicholas, see Chapter Six.

Heussler, see Chapter Nine.

Hibbert Christopher (1980), *The Indian Mutiny*, Penguin, London.

L.M. Lachman (1970), *The Legacy of Max Weber*, Heinemann, London.

MacRae Stuart and Page Stuart (1967), *Tools for Administrators*, Arnold, London.

Maddick, see Chapter 12.

Nagel Stuart ed. (1985), *An Encyclopedia of Policy Studies*, University of Illinois-Urbana, Illinois.

Passmore, see Chapter 4.

Perham Marjorie (1970), *Colonial Sequence, 1949–1969. A Chronological Com-mentary Upon British Colonial Policy in Africa*.

Robertson David, see Chapter Four.

Spiers Maurice (1975), *Techniques and Public Administration*, Fontana, London.
Virulak Surapore (1985), *Modern Communication Technology*, Nonthaburi, Thailand.
Weber Max (1968), see Chapter One.

Index